Sybex's Quick Tour of

The Desktop is where your applications, folders, and shortcuts are located. You can choose between the classic Windows Desktop, which is familiar from previous versions of Windows, or you can use the new Active Desktop, which brings the Web directly to you.

My Computer lets you browse the contents of your computer, open folders, open documents, and run your favorite applications.

My Documents is a desktop folder you can use to store documents, graphics, and other files that you want to access quickly.

Internet Explorer starts up the Internet Explorer Web browser.

Network Neighborhood opens a viewer that presents system information about your computer's place in a network.

Recycle Bin makes it easy to delete and undelete files and folders.

The Microsoft Network opens a connection to Microsoft's online service.

My Briefcase lets you synchronize files between two computers.

Online Services allows you to access one of the popular commercial service providers, such as AOL.

Outlook Express opens the Outlook Express e-mail program.

The **Start button** pops up the Start menu, from which you can run almost all of your applications.

The **Quick Launch toolbar** provides an easy way to start frequently used applications.

The **Taskbar** displays a button for every program running on your computer.

The **Channel bar** lets you open your favorite Web site without first opening your Web browser.

Every **Window** has a **Minimize**, **Maximize** (alternating with **Restore**), and **Close** button.

The **Standard toolbar** provides fast access to common functions.

The **Address toolbar** shows the location of the page currently displayed in the main window; this may be an Internet address or a file or folder stored on your hard disk.

The **Links toolbar** lets you access different parts of Microsoft's Web site.

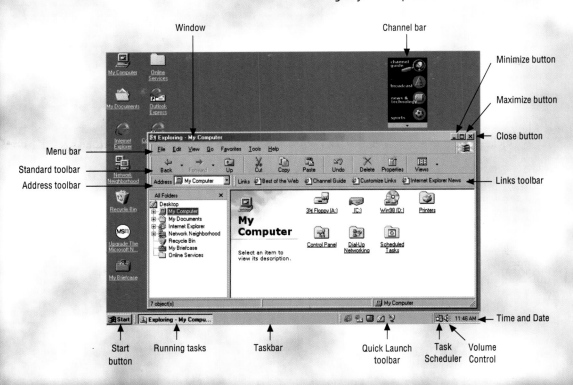

Windows 98 and Internet Explorer bring the Internet right onto your Desktop. There are Internet access points available in every folder, and you can add Web content to your Desktop and folders to customize the way your system looks and feels.

CONFIGURING WITH THE CONNECTION WIZARD

Use the Connection Wizard to find an Internet Service Provider (ISP) and open a new account, or to configure an existing account. Plug your modem into the phone jack and choose Start ➢ Programs ➢ Internet Explorer ➢ Connection Wizard, then follow the instructions on the screen.

USING INTERNET EXPLORER

Once you have established an Internet account, click the Internet Explorer icon on the Desktop and start your explorations; you can also start Internet Explorer from the Quick Launch toolbar.

TUNING IN TO CHANNELS

The Channel bar on the Desktop lets you access the Channel Guide quickly and easily. You can use it to subscribe to the Web channels that you want to view or place on your Desktop. The channel content is updated by the content provider on a regular basis; all you have to do is sit back and watch.

BROWSING FROM EVERYWHERE

You will find Go and Favorites menus in all the windows, including Explorer, My Computer, My Briefcase, the Control Panel, the Printers folder; even the Recycle Bin has them.

Go	
Back	Alt+Left Arrow
Forward	Alt+Right Arrow
Up One Level	
Home Page	
Search the Web	
Channel Guide	
Mail	
News	
My Computer	
Address Book	
Internet Call	

You can also use the Address toolbar or the Links toolbar, available in all these windows and on the Taskbar, to access Web sites on the Internet. The Auto Complete

feature automatically completes a Web address that you have previously visited as you start to type the address into the Address toolbar.

Favorites	
Add to Favorites...	
Organize Favorites...	
Manage Subscriptions...	
Update All Subscriptions	
Channels	▶
Links	▶
Software Updates	▶

You can even access certain technical support Web sites from within the Windows 98 Help system.

WEB-RELATED APPLICATIONS

But it doesn't stop there; in addition to the Internet Explorer browser, Windows 98 also contains several other important Web-related applications, including:

Address Book Identifies the computers and individuals to which you may send and receive files and e-mail.

FrontPage Express A quick-and-easy Web-page editor you can use to create or customize your own Web pages.

NetMeeting A conferencing application which allows people working in different locations to collaborate simultaneously on the same project.

NetShow Player A viewer that displays streamed audio, video, and illustrated audio files downloaded from a Web site without waiting for long downloads.

Outlook Express An application used to send and receive e-mail and read and post messages to Internet news groups.

Personal Web Server Provides a Windows 98-based Web server you can use to set up a Web site on your local network or intranet, or to develop and test your Internet content before uploading it to your Internet Service Provider (ISP).

Web Publishing Wizard Manages the process of posting new Web content to a Web site.

Sybex, Inc.
1151 Marina Village Parkway
Alameda, CA 94501
SYBEX® *Tel: 510.523.8233*

Sybex's Quick Tour of Windows 98

Every application running on your computer and every open folder gets its own button on the Taskbar. The Taskbar may also show other icons from time to time, indicating that an e-mail message is waiting or that you are printing a document.

You can switch from one task to another by clicking its button on the Taskbar, but when you have a lot of applications running, the Taskbar can get pretty crowded. You can make it bigger by simply dragging the top edge of the Taskbar upward.

MOVING THE TASKBAR

You don't have to have the Taskbar at the bottom of the screen. If you'd prefer, you can have it at the top of the screen, on the left side, or on the right side. Just click a blank part of the Taskbar (not on one of the buttons), and drag the Taskbar to the new location.

TASK SWITCHING WITH ALT+TAB

Another quick way to switch from one running task to another is to hold down the Alt key on the keyboard and then press the Tab key once. A dialog box that contains an icon for each application running on your system will open. Each time you press the Tab key, a different icon is highlighted. This indicates the application that will run when you finally release the Alt key.

The name of each application or folder is displayed at the bottom of this dialog box.

ADDING A TOOLBAR

Windows 98 includes a default set of toolbars that you can add to your Taskbar.

Address Allows you to open an Internet address without first opening Internet Explorer.

Links Contains a set of Internet addresses, which users can add, remove, or re-arrange.

Desktop Adds a toolbar containing all your Desktop icons to the Taskbar. Because this toolbar is longer than the screen is wide, you can use the small arrows to see the other icons.

Quick Launch Adds buttons for commonly used applications.

To add one of these toolbars, right-click a blank part of the Taskbar, choose Toolbars from the pop-up menu, and then select a toolbar by name.

CREATING YOUR OWN TOOLBAR

To create a new toolbar, right-click an empty area on the Taskbar, and select Toolbars ➤ New Toolbar. Type the path to the folder (or the Internet address) that you want to appear as the toolbar and click OK.

Drag the new toolbar to the Desktop, and then position and size it accordingly.

USING THE QUICK LAUNCH TOOLBAR

The Quick Launch toolbar, located on the Taskbar, provides shortcuts to several often-used Windows features.

 Opens Internet Explorer.

 Opens Outlook Express.

 Opens the TV Viewer.

 Brings the Desktop back to the front.

 Views selected Web channels.

START MENU

Click the Start button to do almost anything on your computer, from running an application to configuring your printer.

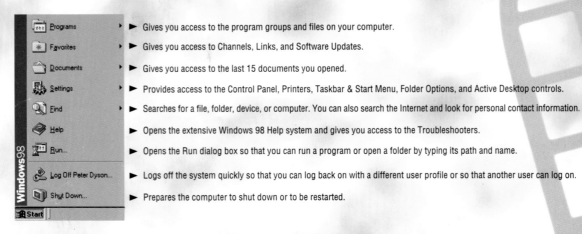

Programs ▶	► Gives you access to the program groups and files on your computer.
Favorites ▶	► Gives you access to Channels, Links, and Software Updates.
Documents ▶	► Gives you access to the last 15 documents you opened.
Settings ▶	► Provides access to the Control Panel, Printers, Taskbar & Start Menu, Folder Options, and Active Desktop controls.
Find ▶	► Searches for a file, folder, device, or computer. You can also search the Internet and look for personal contact information.
Help	► Opens the extensive Windows 98 Help system and gives you access to the Troubleshooters.
Run...	► Opens the Run dialog box so that you can run a program or open a folder by typing its path and name.
Log Off Peter Dyson...	► Logs off the system quickly so that you can log back on with a different user profile or so that another user can log on.
Shut Down...	► Prepares the computer to shut down or to be restarted.

RUNNING A PROGRAM

To start an application, click Start ➢ Programs, choose a program folder to open the next menu (if required), and then click the name of the program you want to run.

ADDING AN APPLICATION TO THE START MENU

The quickest way to add a program to the top of the Start menu is to open the folder that contains the program, and then drag the program's icon onto the Start button.

FINDING THINGS QUICKLY

Windows 98 adds several powerful items to the Find menu, which in

addition to finding files and folders, now includes options for finding a computer, information on the Internet, or information about people.

To locate a file, click Start ➢ Find ➢ Files or Folders. Type the name (or part of the name) into the Named field, enter any text you think the

file might contain into the Containing text field, and click Find Now. A window opens displaying the files that match as Windows finds them.

To locate a computer, click Start ➢ Find ➢ Computer, enter the name of the computer into the Named field, and click Find Now. To track down information on the Internet, use Start ➢ Find ➢ On the Internet. This option connects you to a single Web site giving you access to some of the most powerful and popular search engines on the Internet, including Infoseek, AOL NetFind, Lycos, Excite, and Yahoo. To find information such as a person's e-mail address, click

Start ➢ Find ➢ People. In the Look In list, select the name of the directory service you want to use, type in the information on the person you are looking for (usually just the first name followed by the last name), and click Find Now.

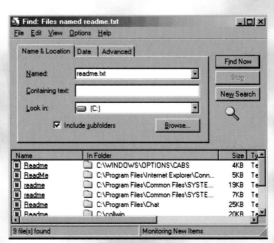

WINDOWS 98

No experience required.

WINDOWS® 98

No experience required.™

Sharon Crawford

SYBEX®

San Francisco • Paris • Düsseldorf • Soest

Associate Publisher: Gary Masters
Contracts and Licensing Manager: Kristine Plachy
Acquisitions & Developmental Editor: Sherry Bonelli
Editor: Anamary Ehlen
Project Editor: Brenda Frink
Technical Editor: Maryann Brown
Book Designers: Patrick Dintino, Catalin Dulfu
Electronic Publishing Specialist: Cynthia Johnsen
Production Coordinator: Charles Mathews
Production Assistants: Beth Moynihan, Rebecca Rider
Indexer: Ted Laux
Cover Designer: Design Site
Cover Illustrator/Photographer: Design Site

Screen reproductions produced with Collage Complete.

Collage Complete is a trademark of Inner Media Inc.

SYBEX is a registered trademark of SYBEX Inc.

No experience required. is a trademark of SYBEX Inc.

TRADEMARKS: SYBEX has attempted throughout this book to
distinguish proprietary trademarks from descriptive terms by
following the capitalization style used by the manufacturer.

Netscape Communications, the Netscape Communications logo,
Netscape, and Netscape Navigator are trademarks of Netscape
Communications Corporation.
Netscape Communications Corporation has not authorized,
sponsored, endorsed, or approved this publication and is
not responsible for its content. Netscape and the Netscape
Communications Corporate Logos are trademarks and trade
names of Netscape Communications Corporation. All other
product names and/or logos are trademarks of their respective
owners.

The author and publisher have made their best efforts to prepare
this book, and the content is based upon final release software
whenever possible. Portions of the manuscript may be based
upon pre-release versions supplied by software manufacturer(s).
The author and the publisher make no representation or warran-
ties of any kind with regard to the completeness or accuracy of
the contents herein and accept no liability of any kind including
but not limited to performance, merchantability, fitness for any
particular purpose, or any losses or damages of any kind caused
or alleged to be caused directly or indirectly from this book.

Photographs and illustrations used in this book have been downloaded from publicly accessible file archives and are used in this
book for news reportage purposes only to demonstrate the variety
of graphics resources available via electronic access. Text and
images available over the Internet may be subject to copyright and
other rights owned by third parties. Online availability of text and
images does not imply that they may be reused without the permission of rights holders, although the Copyright Act does permit
certain unauthorized reuse as fair use under 17 U.S.C. Section 107.

MSNBC is not a sponsor of and does not endorse Sybex
Publishing or the upcoming computer trade books about
Microsoft Windows 98 Operating System to be published
by Sybex Publishing.

Screen Shots of MSNBC used by permission from MSNBC.

Copyright ©1998 SYBEX Inc., 1151 Marina Village Parkway,
Alameda, CA 94501. World rights reserved. No part of this
publication may be stored in a retrieval system, transmitted, or
reproduced in any way, including but not limited to photocopy,
photograph, magnetic or other record, without the prior agreement and written permission of the publisher.

Library of Congress Card Number: 98-84015
ISBN: 0-7821-2128-4

Manufactured in the United States of America

10 9 8 7 6 5 4 3 2 1

For Jan Aragon Denno, partner in duck rescue,
wonderful friend.

Acknowledgements

My heartfelt thanks to my editor, Anamary Ehlen, for her consistent support and collaborative attitude. Every correction was an improvement and every suggestion was offered in a spirit of partnership. It was a pleasure at every stage.

Secondly, I owe a debt of gratitude to technical editor Maryann Brown who—despite an association that goes back *years*—cut me absolutely no slack on the question of technical accuracy. She picked every nit and verified every grand pronouncement to make the book as free from errors as humanly possible. Needless to say, any errors that remain are due strictly to my pigheadedness (or to Microsoft's last-minute programming changes).

I'm also very grateful to Dean Denno, who grew noticeably grayer in the process of testing Windows 98, extracting all its mysteries and staying reasonably good humored throughout.

A virtual bouquet to David Rogelberg, an agent who far transcends that mundane description.

Once again, thanks to Dianne King and Dr. Rudolph S. Langer, who had just enough faith.

Contents at a Glance

Table of Contents

Introduction

In August 1995, Windows 95 emerged on the scene and rapidly became the leading operating system on the desktops of home and corporate users in North America (and made big strides in the rest of the world as well). Many millions of DOS and Windows 3.1 users converted to Windows 95 because it was, in fact, revolutionary. The interface and features were dramatically altered and considerably easier to use. Internally, it was special too—more stable and reliable.

Now comes Windows 98 which, while quite different from Windows 95, is more *evolutionary* than revolutionary. So if you've used Windows 95, you'll see a lot that's familiar in Windows 98—starting with the basic look. But there are many changes in Windows 98 that range from the subtle (say good-bye to the double-click) to the surprising (a whole package of new Internet tools).

Why This Book?

As you've no doubt noticed, the bookstores have plenty of Windows 98 titles. These books include everything from thousand-page tomes (that presumably include details so esoteric only Bill Gates could love 'em) to things with names like *Learn Windows 98 While You Sleep*. Some of these books assume you aspire to become an expert's expert, no matter how much pain is involved. Others are written in a condescending style that in the past was reserved for the town twit. If neither of these approaches appeal to you, keep reading.

This book is different. It's meant for the person who has already used a PC but is a novice in the particular area of Windows 98. You will not be talked down to. The assumption is that you're new to Windows 98—not that you just fell off the turnip truck.

So there's no chapter telling you what a mouse is—but there *are* 23 essential skills designed to get you to proficiency in the shortest possible time (and the very first skill tells you what's *different* about the mouse in Windows 98).

How to Use the Book

As you can see from the Table of Contents, this book covers a wide range of Windows 98 topics. Some you will have more interest in than others, so I've divided the book into separate and discrete skills. The first few skills will introduce you to the interface and the basic concepts built into Windows 98. After that, each skill can be read independently without a lot of cross-referencing.

Use the book as a Windows 98 directory, if you wish. Get what you need and put the book aside. When the day comes that you need to learn about remote access or building your own network, just turn to the relevant skill and get goir right away.

Elements in This Book

At the beginning of each skill, you'll see a list of the topics covered. And at the end of a skill, you'll see a list of the intended results. Here and there you'll see certain elements designed to draw your attention:

 NOTE   Notes are pulled out of the text to make a specific point. They may highlight some point of information that might escape notice in a normal paragraph. Notes can also be specific advice and pointers to other resources.

 TIP   Tips are time and labor savers. They're not-so-obvious shortcuts or approaches that have been discovered over time. They're *always* worth reading.

 WARNING   Warnings fall into the category of you-can't-be-too-careful. Although Windows 98 is extraordinarily forgiving of errors, it's always easier to *stay* out of trouble than to *get* out of trouble. So you'll see a few of these icons, but less than in books about previous versions of Windows.

DISCUSSIONS IN BOXES

Occasionally you'll see text set off in a box like this indicating a "side issue" or technical point of interest that may not directly relate to the topic at hand.

In case you care, these boxes are called *sidebars*, although they're never at the side. The term probably arose in magazine publishing when sidebars were set off to the left or right of a page instead of smack in the middle as these are. (This paragraph is a perfect example of the "side issue" nature of sidebars.)

Moving Onward

I hope you enjoy your introduction to Windows 98 and find this book useful. I'd appreciate feedback on any errors or omissions you discover. Just drop a note to me at:

`Win98NoExp@scribes.com`

And, of course, if you like the book, it would be an act of mercy to let me know about that, too.

SKILL 1

GETTING YOUR BEARINGS

- Choosing a look
- Mousing 101
- Using the Taskbar
- Getting help

Every version of Windows to date has been more configurable than the last, and Windows 98 is even more adjustable to suit your needs. You'll probably want to experiment with different ways of using Windows 98 to find a combination that suits you best. In this skill, you'll learn the basic navigational tools you need to start your exploration of Windows 98.

In the basic look and feel of the desktop, there are lots of choices. Some of your choices may be influenced by whether you're working on a stand-alone machine, a network, or a network with an intranet. On the other hand, you can choose your look solely by what appeals to you most.

Clicking Your Mouse

It may sound trivial at first, but a big improvement in Windows 98 is the ability to get rid of the mouse double-click. The standard mouse setup—click once to select, double-click to open—is still an option. That is, when you move your mouse pointer to an icon, you must click on the icon once to select it. After it's selected, you then specify an action to be performed. One action is to open the object the icon represents by double-clicking the mouse button.

In Windows 98, you can adopt a mouse behavior that mimics how the mouse functions on a Web page. In this mode, simply pointing at an object selects it, and a single-click of the mouse button opens the object. After using this method for a while, I think you'll agree that this is how mice should have always behaved. For one thing, as on a Web page, the pointer changes shape as it passes over an object that can be opened.

The "Web mouse" option is available in either the Web view or Custom View, described in the next sections.

Throughout the rest of the book, I assume that you're using the new point to select, click once to open option. If you stick to the traditional click once to select, double-click to open, you'll have to mentally translate the instructions.

Selecting a View

A major addition to Windows 98 is the ability to seamlessly integrate the look of your desktop with that of the Internet. Similarly, if you're working on a corporate intranet, you can use Internet Explorer as an interface for browsing not only the intranet but your own computer as well. Skill 3 has more on how to get and use the Internet Explorer look for your desktop.

In this skill, we'll be configuring the default desktop—the one that appears when Windows 98 is first installed. For this desktop, you can choose from three styles:

- The Web view, in which your computer looks and acts like a page from the World Wide Web

- The Classic style, which makes your desktop work just like the Windows 95 desktop

- A Custom view which you configure. The Custom view allows you to select the features you want from the other two views.

To reach the settings for the desktop views, open any folder on the desktop (My Computer is a good choice) and select Folder Options from the View menu. This selection will open the dialog box shown in Figure 1.1.

Web View

Selecting Web Style in the Windows Desktop Update area (see Figure 1.1) has several implications. First of all, your mouse will have the "point to select, click to open" function that is characteristic of pages on the World Wide Web. Clicking the right mouse button will open a menu of choices (see below) that apply to the object you're pointing to at the time, as it does in *all* the available styles.

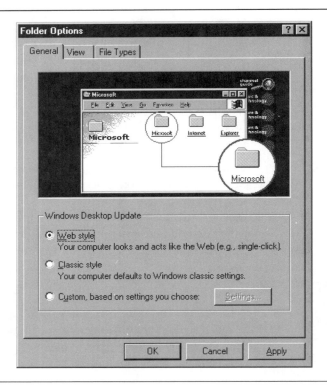

FIGURE 1.1: The General tab of the Folder Options dialog box, where you can set the desktop view

In addition, each folder will have a Web-like look. Figure 1.2 shows the Online Services folder that's automatically installed on your desktop. As you move your mouse pointer from icon to icon, the text at the left of the window changes, describing each item. The amount of information is fairly skimpy—no more than you'd get by right-clicking on the object and selecting Properties—but it does have the advantage of not requiring that extra click.

Skill 1

FIGURE 1.2: A folder in Web style

Icons and filenames are all underlined in the Web style of indicating a *hyperlink*. On the Web, as in Web view, a hyperlink is an active object that you can click on to connect to some related object. When you point to such an object, the mouse pointer turns into a cartoon hand.

The Web view works best when the folder's view is set to Large Icons. It doesn't work nearly so well when you choose View ➤ Details, as Figure 1.3 demonstrates. In this view, much of the information is pushed off to the right, and you either have to scroll over or open the window to full size.

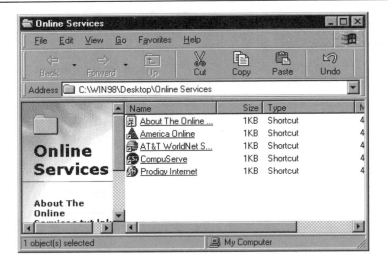

FIGURE 1.3: The Details view in Web style

If you spend a lot of time on an intranet and/or the Internet and you feel most comfortable having a consistent interface, the Web view may work very well for you.

Classic View

If you're familiar with the look of Windows 95, then you know what the Classic view is. Choose Classic Style and your desktop will have the look and feel of Windows 95. In other words, you'll click once on a file or folder or icon to select it. Opening a file, folder, or icon will require a double-click of the left mouse button.

Your windows (see Figure 1.4) will look very much like those in Windows 95. (There are some changes in the toolbar, which we'll get to later in this skill.)

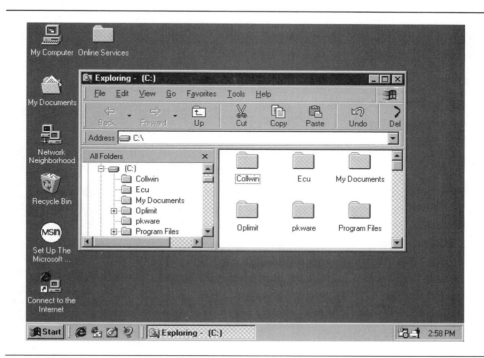

FIGURE 1.4: In Classic view, the desktop looks and acts like a Windows 95 desktop.

Classic style also means that each folder opens in its own individual window. If you customarily access files or folders that are several folders deep, you can end up with a lot of open folders on your desktop a lot of the time.

If you're used to Windows 95 and want to keep changes to a minimum, you can select this option. However, it's no easier to learn the new features using the "Classic" style and in the end, it deprives you of some of the neatest features in Windows 98. Fortunately, you have more choices than just the Web view and the Windows 95 view.

Your View

The Custom choice presented in the Folder Options dialog box allows the selection of just the features you want from Web view and Classic view. No need to just take what they dish out—make your own choices.

First click the Custom button, then Settings. In the Custom Settings dialog box (see Figure 1.5), you can choose a mixture of Web Style and Classic options.

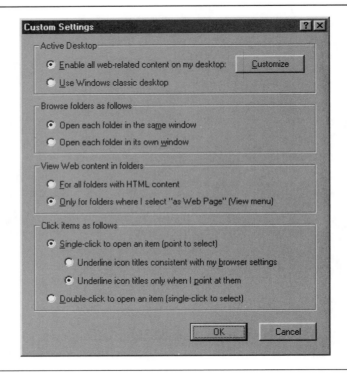

FIGURE 1.5: Selecting some options for your desktop

Understanding Custom Settings

On the Custom Settings page, you can mix and match features that are new to Windows 98 with earlier Windows 95 options.

Active Desktop   Choose whether you want the Web-style look or the so-called Windows classic desktop. If you choose to *Enable all web-related content*, you can then use the Customize button to configure desktop properties. (See Skill 2 for information on how display properties work.)

Browse Folders As Follows   This is a pretty simple choice. You can have everything you open create a new window or have every folder open in the same window. Multiple windows are OK if you have a large monitor and don't mind the layered look. In general, though, you're probably better off having each folder open in the same window.

View Web Content in Folders   Again, this is part of the Web look. If you choose *For all folders with HTML content*, the folders will display as Web pages, and you can modify their fonts, colors, and so forth using View ➢ Customize This Folder. If you choose *Only for folders where I select "as Web Page,"* then all your folders will have a traditional look. You'll be able to modify a particular folder by selecting View ➢ As Web Page from that folder's menu bar.

Click Items As Follows   Here's where you choose your mouse's role. You can single-click with icons underlined all the time, or single-click with icons underlined only when you point to them. (This is purely a matter of aesthetics—there's no functional difference between the two.) Or you can use the traditional Windows single-click to select and double-click to open.

All these potential ways of configuring options are not there just to confuse you—though they may well do that. They're offered so that you can set things up to suit yourself. So expect to spend at least a little time experimenting to find out what you really like.

Right Mouse, Left Mouse

The left button on your mouse is used to select items and to open them (in the case of folders and files) or start them up (in the case of programs). Move the mouse pointer to an icon or other object, and the color changes to indicate that the item is selected. Click once and the object will be moved to action—what the action is, of course, depends on the nature of the object.

The right mouse button is used just about *everywhere*. You can place the pointer almost anyplace, press the right mouse button, and something will happen. Usually, you'll see a pop-up menu like one of these:

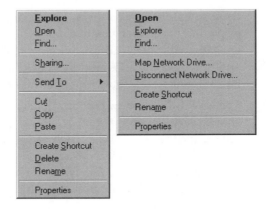

The contents of the pop-up menu will vary depending on whether you're pointing at a file, a folder, a Windows 98 element, or an icon representing hardware of some type.

To open a menu, click only once on the menu title. Slide the mouse pointer to the item you want to select and (only then) click one more time.

Holding the mouse button down as you move the pointer is limited to those times when you want to actually drag and drop an object. However, there's different behavior depending on whether you're using the left or right mouse button.

Click and Drag Object With	Destination	Result
Left mouse button	Within a drive	Object is moved
Left mouse button	Across drives	Object is copied
Right mouse button	Anywhere	Menu allowing choice between moving the object, copying the object, or creating a shortcut

As you can see from this table, the right mouse button is by far the easiest to use. The left mouse button requires you to remember where the object is relative

Skill 1

to your hard drive(s). If you get in the habit of using the right mouse button, you can be saved from that silliness.

Throughout this book, a click refers to pressing the left mouse button, and right-click means pressing the right button. (Unless you're using a left-handed mouse, in which case everything is reversed!)

Working with the Taskbar

The Taskbar is at the bottom of your screen—though you can move it to the top or either side of the screen by clicking and dragging it to the new location. The Taskbar is the jumping-off point for almost everything you do in Windows 98. It's a handy repository for your open programs and can be set up to help you conveniently use programs you need most often, connect to an Internet (or intranet) address, and track what's going on in your system.

To save desktop space, you can set the Taskbar to hide. It'll reappear when you move the pointer over the hidden Taskbar. To hide the Taskbar, follow these steps:

1. Point to an empty spot on the Taskbar and click the right mouse button once. A pop-up menu will appear.

2. Select Properties from the menu. This will open the Taskbar Properties dialog box.

3. Place a checkmark in the box next to Auto Hide. Click OK.

Or for another variation, set the Taskbar to be always visible, even when you have a program running full screen. Follow the above steps except put a checkmark next to Always on Top.

At the very left of the Taskbar is the Start button—more about that a little later. At the right side is an area called the System Tray. Here you'll find graphical representations of various background operations. For example, if you're running Task Scheduler (described in Skill 16), you'll see an icon like this:

Or on your laptop computer, you may see an icon indicating the presence of a PC Card modem or a power management program.

Point to a System Tray icon and a flyover box will open, telling you what the icon represents. Right-click on an icon to open a pop-up menu with options.

Adjust PC Card Properties
Disable PC Card Tray Icon

Toolbars on the Taskbar

I am happy to nominate the "toolbars" on the Taskbar as the most confusing nomenclature in Windows 98. They're actually a nice addition to Windows 98, and you're bound to find them useful once you get past the fact that *toolbars* are also those collections of icons at the top of most windows. The toolbars on the Taskbar are configurable, and you can use as many or as few as you wish, though using several can crowd the Taskbar unbearably.

To display a particular toolbar, right-click on a blank spot in the Taskbar and select Toolbars from the pop-up menu. A list of available toolbar names appears. Click on the toolbar name to select it. Toolbars with checkmarks are already displaying. To remove a toolbar, click on the name to remove the checkmark.

Quick Launch Toolbar

By default, one of the toolbars—the Quick Launch toolbar—is already installed.

The icons represent Internet Explorer, Outlook Express, Desktop, and Channels. Just point to each icon to open a descriptive flyover box.

The Desktop icon is particularly handy. If you have a bunch of open windows and need to get at an icon or something on your desktop, just click the Desktop icon, and everything open is minimized to the Taskbar. This is very useful if you have some dialog boxes open that won't normally minimize. Windows 98 forces them to the Taskbar—out of the way—until you click on the minimized icon again.

A program on the Quick Launch toolbar can be started with a single click—no need to open the Start menu or go to the desktop. To add a program to the Quick Launch toolbar, just drag the program's icon to the toolbar and drop it. You can remove programs from the Quick Launch toolbar the same way—just click on the icon and drag it to the desktop. These icons are, in fact, shortcuts, and you can read all about their properties in Skill 4.

 NOTE   Get a grounding in Internet Explorer in Skills 5 and 6, Outlook Express in Skill 9, and Channels in Skill 11.

Address Toolbar

Select this toolbar and an address text box will display on your Taskbar.

You can type in local intranet addresses here or Internet addresses for a quick connection. You can even enter local addresses to quickly open a folder on your hard drive. Click the arrow to the side of the text box to open a list of past addresses you've entered.

Links Toolbar

Select this toolbar to display the links that are shown at the top of your Internet Explorer window. Like the Address toolbar, this is another way to make quick connections—in this case, to the sites represented by the links.

 NOTE   Links are properly a part of Internet Explorer, so check Skill 5 for information on how to make and use links.

Desktop Toolbar

It's true that you can always get at your desktop by clicking the Desktop icon in the Quick Launch toolbar, but you can also make a toolbar where every icon on your desktop is represented.

The Desktop toolbar looks like this:

As you can see, the usefulness of this toolbar is somewhat limited because each button is so large. However, if you click and drag the upper edge of the Taskbar itself to make it wider, you can at least get five or six buttons to display. You can also click on the arrows at either end of the Desktop toolbar to bring more icons into view.

Custom Toolbar

To make your own toolbar, select New Toolbar from the pop-up menu. A dialog box will open like the one shown in Figure 1.6. Select a folder or type in another address.

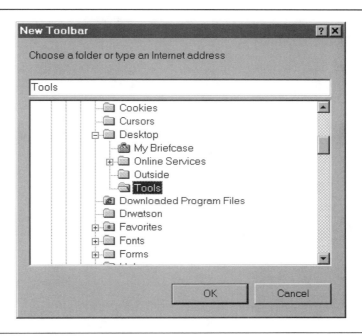

FIGURE 1.6: Select a folder to be displayed as a toolbar.

In Figure 1.6, I selected a folder called Tools. The resulting toolbar is shown in Figure 1.7.

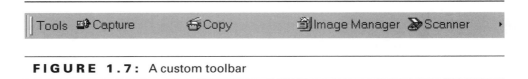

FIGURE 1.7: A custom toolbar

The toolbar will have the name of the folder you selected and will appear in the pop-up menu. To delete a custom toolbar, open the menu. A checkmark next to the name of a toolbar indicates that it's active.

Select the custom toolbar you want to delete. Selecting it will delete it. The default toolbars remain available on the toolbar menu whether selected or not. A custom toolbar will evaporate when deselected, so you'll have to recreate the custom toolbar if you want to use it again.

The Start Button

For a clear signal of where to begin, there's the Start button in the lower-left corner of your screen.

Click once on the Start button to open a menu of choices. These choices will sometimes vary depending on how your computer was configured by the manufacturer. But here are the basic choices that will appear on virtually every machine.

Programs

Slide your pointer to the Programs entry and a cascading menu will open, showing all the programs currently installed. It's a pretty big list on most computers. In Skill 10 you'll learn how to install and run programs as well as how to add to (and subtract from) this menu.

Also on this menu is the Windows Explorer (see Skill 3), one of several ways you can navigate around your hard drives and your network. However, if you're an aficionado of the Web view, you may prefer to navigate using Internet Explorer even for local tasks. See Skill 5 for an introduction to Internet Explorer as an exploration tool.

> **NOTE**   The Programs menu includes an MS-DOS prompt, which you can use to run command line scripts, or DOS commands. The use of this prompt is covered in Skill 22.

Favorites

The cascading menu off Favorites is a list of Internet or intranet addresses that you've added to your Internet Explorer Favorites list. To add to or subtract from this list, see Skill 5.

Documents

The Documents menu lists the files you've recently worked on. Highlight any one and you'll open the file. To clear the Documents menu—remove everything—right-click on the Taskbar and select Properties from the pop-up menu. Click on the Start Menu Programs tab (see Figure 1.8), then just click the Clear button.

But what if you want to remove some of the files in the Documents menu and leave others? That's a little more complicated but definitely doable. Just follow these steps:

1. Right-click the Start button and select Explore. This will open the Windows Explorer.

2. In the left pane, click on the plus sign next to your Windows folder to open the subfolders.

3. Click once on the folder named Recent. The contents of the Documents menu will display in the right pane of Windows Explorer. You can delete any of the files that you choose.

When you return to the Documents list on the Start menu, the deleted files will no longer be listed.

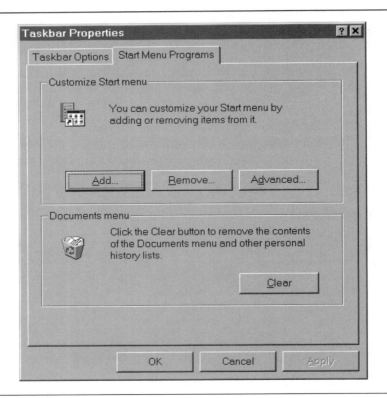

FIGURE 1.8: Clearing the Documents menu

  NOTE   Deleting files from the Documents menu does *not* delete the files from your
hard disk.

Settings

This entry on the Start menu leads to several choices.

Try out any you're interested in and if you need more information, you can find it in the following locations:

Control Panel   The individual icons in the Control Panel refer to just about all the basic functions in Windows 98. For information on dealing with any of them, check the relevant skill. For example, everything to do with the Multimedia icon is covered in Skill 21. Date & Time settings and other configuration options are in Skill 15.

Printers   This opens up settings for your printers.

Taskbar & Start Menu   Another way to set Taskbar options and to add and remove items from the Start menu

Folder Options   And still another way to set folder options (as described earlier in this skill)

Active Desktop   A quick way to turn the Active Desktop on and off

Windows Update   An Internet connection to operating system upgrades and fixes. See Skill 16 for information on how to use this feature.

If you're not sure what skill might contain the information you're looking for, check the index for the item's name (either the icon name or menu name).

Getting Help

To access the Help system in Windows 98, you can select Help from the Start menu. However, the best way is to just press the F1 key. Why is the F1 key better? Because if you're looking for generic help, it will open the main Help screen (the same screen you get by selecting Start ➤ Help). However, if you're actively using a specific portion of Windows 98, pressing F1 will open *context-sensitive* help.

Here's an example: If you're looking at the Imaging applet, trying to figure out what's going on, pressing F1 will open the Help screen shown in Figure 1.9. It takes you to Help topics specifically for Imaging.

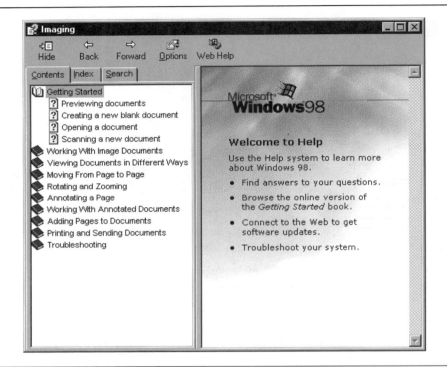

FIGURE 1.9: Help for the Imaging applet

If you were to select Help from the Start menu in the same circumstance, an all-purpose Windows 98 Help screen would open (see Figure 1.10).

Both types of Help screens work in the same way, but the content will differ.

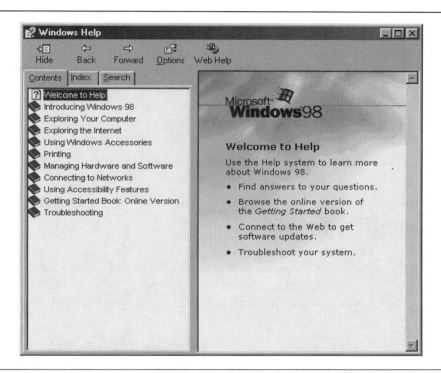

FIGURE 1.10: The all-purpose Help screen

Using Help

The Help system is quite easy to use—especially if you already know what kind of help you need. If you're having difficulty putting your problem into words, it may take longer, but eventually you should be able to find what you're looking for.

There are three approaches to Help, defined by the three tabs on the Windows Help dialog box. You can use any or all of these avenues, depending on what you seek.

Contents   If you have a general idea of what you want to know and need to narrow it down, select this tab. Click on a general topic to open subtopics.

Index   When you pretty much know what you want, click this tab. Type in the first letters of the subject, and the highlight will move to that topic. Click the Display button to open the Help file for that topic.

Search   If you know exactly what you're searching for, use this tab. Type in the keyword, and then click List Topics.

On-the-Spot Help

Then there are those occasions when you're looking at a dialog box full of settings—most of which you don't understand. Place your pointer on the text and click the right mouse button. If you see a "What's This?" box like the one shown here, you can click on it and get a window of explanation.

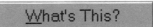

In some dialog boxes, there's a button with a question mark on the title bar. Click on this button and then point to the area you're perplexed about and click the mouse button. A window of explanation will open, if one's available.

Are You Experienced?

Now you can...

- ☑ Select the basic look of your desktop
- ☑ Choose one click or two
- ☑ Manipulate the Taskbar
- ☑ Make toolbars for the Taskbar
- ☑ Use the Help system

SKILL 2

SETTING THE LOOK AND FEEL

- Choosing a desktop theme
- Setting wallpaper and screen savers
- Setting colors and fonts
- Changing and arranging icons
- Using accessibility options

Most people who frequently use a computer get rather possessive about it. They want everything set up *just so.* You probably do, too. Windows 98 offers so many configuration options that given enough time, you could definitely design your machine to be unlike any of the other millions of Windows computers in the world. But even if you don't want to invest a lot of time in desktop design, you will probably still want a desktop that's easy on your eyes and easy to use.

In this skill, we'll talk about the many ways you can affect how your computer looks. We'll start with *desktop themes*, which are entire packages of thematically connected wallpaper, colors, and icons. In case you don't want the whole package, later in this skill we'll cover how to make more limited configuration changes.

Choosing a Desktop Theme

Included with Windows 98 is a whole package of *desktop themes*. Each theme includes wallpaper, special icons and pointers, unique sounds, and a screen saver—all related to a single motif. Some of the 17 themes are Mystery, Travel, Sports, and Science.

To view the available themes, click Start ➤ Settings ➤ Control Panel and click the Desktop Themes icon. Figure 2.1 shows the theme called Leonardo da Vinci. Use the Theme pull-down list to view the available themes.

You can use any one of these themes by selecting it and then clicking OK. Or if you want to preview it first, click Apply to see how everything will look (without closing the dialog box). If you decide you like what you see, click OK. If not, click Cancel.

 NOTE   Desktop Themes are not installed by default. If you don't have a Desktop Themes icon in the Control Panel, click the Add/Remove Programs icon, then the Windows Setup tab. Select Desktop Themes, click OK, and follow the instructions.

FIGURE 2.1: Leonardo da Vinci, one of the available desktop theme packages

Customizing a Theme

Of course, you may not want the whole desktop themes package as it stands. You may like a particular theme but hate the fonts used or find the sounds annoying. Fortunately, you can get rid of elements you don't like. In the Settings area (see Figure 2.1), remove the checkmarks from elements you don't want included.

In Figure 2.2, I've removed the Leonardo theme's wallpaper. Everything else remains the same.

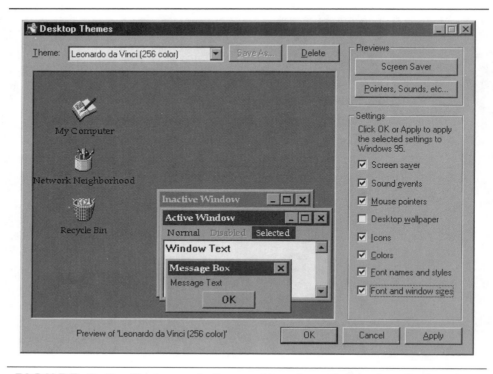

FIGURE 2.2: The Leonardo theme without its wallpaper, but all other elements intact

Rather than have to guess whether the sounds and pointers that come with a theme are acceptable, you can check them out by clicking the Pointers, Sounds button in the Previews area. The dialog box that opens (see Figure 2.3) lets you check out the pointers, sounds, and icons (visuals) that come with a theme. Highlight the element's name, and you'll be able to see it in the Preview box. For sounds, click on the right-pointing arrowhead to play the selected sound.

TIP   Some of the desktop themes require what's called "High Color" settings. If your display adapter can't render more than 256 colors, you may not get satisfactory results with the High Color themes. However, it does no harm to try. For more on your display adapter settings, see Skill 21.

FIGURE 2.3: Use this dialog box to preview all the gadgets and gizmos that come with a theme.

Selecting Wallpaper

Wallpaper is actually the background for your desktop. How a desktop setting got to be called *wallpaper* is anyone's guess, but the term has been around as long as the graphical interface. Anyway, Windows 98 comes with a supply of wallpaper—mostly boring. The real fun of wallpaper is in providing your own pictures of your kids or your dog or that beach in Tahiti you're determined to visit one day.

To set up wallpaper, follow these steps:

1. Right-click on a blank spot on the desktop to open the pop-up menu.

2. Select Properties from the menu. This will open the dialog box shown in Figure 2.4. Select the Background tab if it's not already showing.

3. Click on any of the choices in the Wallpaper list, and the selection will pre-view in the screen at the top.

4. Experiment with Center, Tile, or Stretch in the Display pull-down list box to find the effect you like.

5. Click OK when you're done.

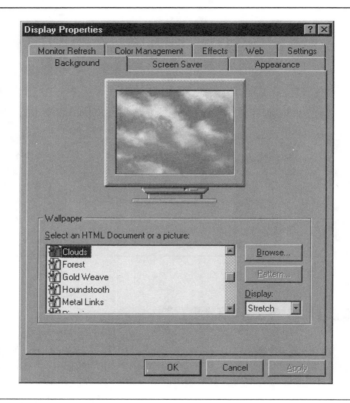

FIGURE 2.4: Selecting desktop wallpaper

NOTE Most of the wallpaper designs look very different depending on whether you're showing them as centered, tiled, or stretched. The more complicated the design, the more distracting it can be when shown full screen. But everyone's taste is different, so experiment to see what you like.

Supplying Your Own Wallpaper

Almost any graphic file format can be used as wallpaper, though Windows bitmaps are the most common. By default, the only pictures shown in the Wallpaper list are bitmaps that are also in the main Windows folder on your hard drive. To use another picture, you'll need to tell Windows 98 about it.

Here's how to use your own graphic as wallpaper:

1. Right-click on a blank spot on the desktop to open the pop-up menu.

2. Select Properties from the menu. This will open the dialog box shown in Figure 2.4. Select the Background tab if it's not already showing.

3. Click the Browse button. Locate the file you want to use.

4. Click Open.

5. If you like the way the file looks in preview, click OK.

 TIP   Sometimes a picture selected this way won't "stick" after a reboot. If that happens, just move the picture file into the main Windows directory on your hard drive. Select it again using the above steps, and it should be permanently on the desktop—at least until you decide to change it.

You can use almost any graphics file as wallpaper—look for files with extensions such as .bmp, .gif, .jpg, .tif, or .pcx. However, you're not limited to conventional graphics files. You can also use any HTML page (look for files with the extension .htm). You can make wallpaper out of any Web page as well. See Skill 7 for instructions.

Choosing Screen Savers

Add screen savers to the list of computer misnomers. At one time—long ago—it could be argued that the constant motion of a screen saver protected your monitor screen from "burn-in." That is, the permanent etching of your screen by whatever picture was left on the screen too long.

Burn-in hasn't been a problem for many years, yet screen savers continue to be popular. One reason is that they are the equivalent of covering your work when you leave your desk. The other is that they're just plain entertaining!

Skill 2

To select one of the screen savers that come with Windows 98, follow these steps:

1. Right-click on a blank area of the desktop and select Properties from the pop-up menu.

2. In the Display Properties dialog box, click the Screen Saver tab, as shown in Figure 2.5.

3. Select a screen saver from the drop-down list box.

4. To see the one you've selected in full-screen, click Preview. Move the mouse when you want to return to the dialog box.

5. Click the Settings button to see what's configurable. This will vary depending on the screen saver chosen.

6. Click OK to close the dialog box when you're done.

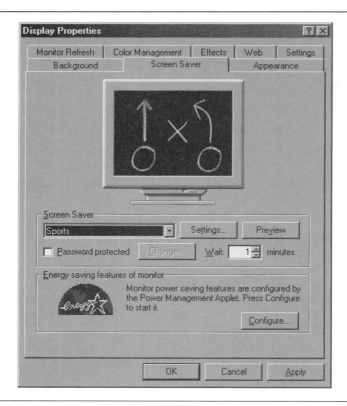

FIGURE 2.5: The dialog box for selecting a screen saver

Adding a Password to the Screen Saver

In general, you can just move the mouse or press any key on the keyboard to clear the screen saver. If you're the least bit paranoid about leaving your computer unguarded while you go down the hall to cadge some jellybeans, you can add a password to the screen saver. Then when the mouse is moved or a key is pressed, a dialog box asks for the password, and the screen saver won't clear until the correct password is entered.

To add a password to the screen saver you select, put a checkmark in the Password Protected box on the Screen Saver page (shown in Figure 2.5). Click the Change button and type the password in twice, then click OK.

If you want to stop using the password, clear the checkmark in the Password Protected box. When you want to start using it again, return the checkmark. The password you've entered will stay the same until you change it.

TIP   Even though this password is not case sensitive, make no assumptions about other passwords. In general, passwords are *always* case sensitive, so you need to remember whether you used upper or lower case, or a mixture of the two.

It's important to understand that the screen saver password represents only the most minimal level of security. A determined intruder can just reboot your computer and bypass the screen saver password entirely.

TIP   Adding an overall Windows password will prevent the simple "reboot to access" intrusion. See Skill 15, "Configuring the System."

Setting Windows Colors and Fonts

You can also easily set the colors and fonts for the windows on your desktop. Right-click on a blank spot on the desktop and select Properties from the pop-up menu. Click the Appearance tab in the Display Properties dialog box (see Figure 2.6).

There are a world of changes that can be made here. Experiment to find what suits you best. I'll explain some of the possibilities in the following sections.

Desktop Schemes

What, you may ask, is the difference between desktop *schemes* and desktop *themes*? Well, desktop themes, as described earlier, include sounds, special pointers, custom icons, and so forth. A desktop scheme is really just a *color* scheme with some changeable elements such as font size and selection. In the Display Properties dialog box that you just opened, select one from the Scheme drop-down list, and it'll display in the preview box (as shown in Figure 2.6).

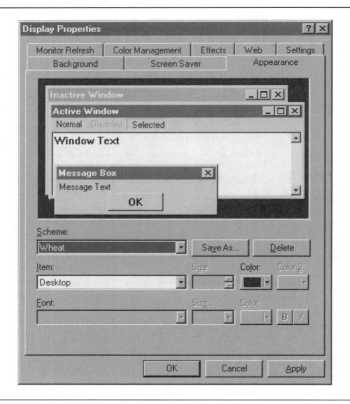

FIGURE 2.6:   Previewing a desktop color scheme

Modifying a Color Scheme

Perhaps you like a particular color scheme except for one or two colors. To change those elements, follow these steps:

Skill 2

1.   With the scheme you just selected still visible in the preview box, click the element you want to change—the color of the desktop, the window title bar, or whatever. The name of the element will appear in the Item list (see Figure 2.7). What can be changed about the element will show to the right of the Item list. (Anything grayed out can't be changed in the selected color scheme.)

2.   Click on the up and down arrows in the Size box to change the dimensions of the element. Click the Color button (or buttons) to select different colors.

3.   If the element you're changing has modifiable text, you can change the typeface, its size, color, and whether it's bold or italic.

4.   When you're done customizing the desktop scheme, click the Save As button to save the scheme under a name you choose. It'll be added to the Scheme drop-down list so you can change schemes later and return to the customized one when you wish.

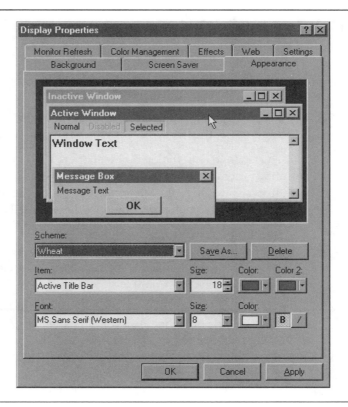

FIGURE 2.7: When you click on an element in the preview window, the name of the element appears in the Item list.

NOTE Many of the default color schemes are varieties of high-contrast displays that are particularly useful for people with vision impairments. There's more on how to make Windows 98 easier to see under "Setting Accessibility Options" later in this skill.

Managing Icons

When you start out with Windows 98, you'll notice certain icons on the desktop known as *system icons*. My Computer, the Recycle Bin, My Documents, and Network Neighborhood are all examples of system icons. You can substitute new icons, modify the existing ones, and change their positions relative to one another.

Changing System Icons

To change a system icon, follow these steps:

1. Right-click on a blank spot on the desktop and select Properties from the pop-up menu.

2. In the Display Properties dialog box, click the Effects tab. At the top of the page, select the icon you want to change, then click the Change Icon button.

3. The Change Icon dialog box will open. If you don't like the choices shown there, the two largest collections of icons can be located by clicking the Browse button. In the System folder inside the main Windows folder, look for shell32.dll or cool.dll (you may have already been shown the latter).

4. Select the icon you want and click OK.

To return to the original icon, you need only to select the icon on the Effects page and then click the Default Icon button.

TIP For instructions on changing shortcut icons, see Skill 4, "Managing Files and Folders."

Adjusting the Icon Arrangement

By default, the icons on your desktop are organized into orderly rows and columns. If you want to be able to drag icons hither and yon and have them stay where you put them, right-click on the desktop and select Arrange Icons ➢ Auto Arrange. This will remove the checkmark from Auto Arrange and thus turn the automatic ordering off.

Now you can click and drag icons to any location on the desktop, and they'll stay where you drop them. To have your newly arranged icons snap to a grid (without returning to Auto Arrange), right-click on the desktop and select Line Up Icon from the pop-up menu.

Changing the Icon Spacing

In general, the Auto Arrange function produces a good alignment of icons—of the columns and rows variety. But in some cases, your icons may appear to be too close together—particularly if some of the icons have long titles.

To adjust the amount of space between icons, follow these steps:

1. Right-click on a blank spot on the desktop and select Properties from the pop-up menu.

2. In the Display Properties dialog box, click the Appearance tab. In the Item drop-down list, select Icon Spacing (Horizontal) or Icon Spacing (Vertical).

3. Adjust the number down or up (43 is the default setting). Click the Apply button to test the new setting.

4. Click OK when you're finished.

Auto Arrange must be *On* for the Apply button to show the results of any proposed change.

Changing the Size of Icons

To change the size of desktop icons without changing any other element, follow these steps:

1. Right-click on the desktop and select Properties from the pop-up menu.

2. In the Display Properties dialog box, click the Appearance tab. Select Icon from the Item drop-down list.

3. Change the number in the Size box to something larger or smaller than the default size of 32 pixels.

4. Click Apply to check what the new size will look like. Click OK when you're finished.

Bear in mind that if you make the icons very much smaller than the default, the resultant spacing may be too tight—even if the horizontal and vertical icon spacing settings haven't been changed. So if you want smaller icons, you'll probably need to change the spacing settings as well.

Setting Accessibility Options

Like Windows 95, Windows 98 comes with many options to make the operating system more usable if you have a vision, hearing, or mobility impairment. However, many of the options are useful for their own sake, so everyone may want to take a look at them.

To set the accessibility options click the Start button and select Settings ➤ Control Panel. In the Control Panel, click the Accessibility Options icon. Five pages of settings are available in Accessibility Properties (see Figure 2.8).

The following sections describe the options on each page.

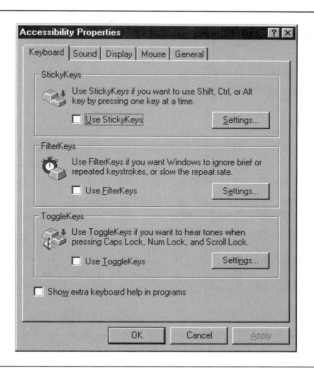

FIGURE 2.8: The accessibility options cover five pages.

Helping Your Fingers Do the Walking

Some of the keyboard functions necessary to run Windows require considerable dexterity. The StickyKeys option lets you do key combinations (like Ctrl+Alt+Del) one key at a time. FilterKeys can change the way Windows recognizes repeat keystrokes to help if you tend to hold keys down for too long. ToggleKeys will sound a tone when CapsLock, NumLock, or Scroll is pressed.

TIP The Toggle Keys option on the Keyboard page is of great help if you often hit the CapsLock key inadvertently and end up with text looking like: cALL mR. jAMES iN sT vINCENT. With ToggleKeys on, you'll hear a quiet but distinct warning beep when CapsLock is switched on.

For all three keyboard options, you can click a Settings key to specify just how each option will work. Each has a shortcut so you can turn the option on and off from the keyboard without having to open the Control Panel again.

For additional keyboard help, check the box for *Show extra keyboard help in programs*. Any programs that offer cues for keyboard use will now display them.

Getting Visual Cues

If the sounds that Windows 98 produces to notify you of events are of no use to you, you can substitute visual cues for the sounds by activating SoundSentry. Click the Sound tab in Accessibility Properties and click the box for ShowSounds. Programs that care capable of displaying captions in place of speech or other sounds will do so.

TIP If the accessibility options aren't installed, you can add them by selecting Start ➤ Settings ➤ Control Panel ➤ Add/Remove Programs.

Improving Visibility

Click the Display tab to choose a color scheme that will enhance the visibility on the desktop. Select *Use High Contrast* and click the Settings button. High Contrast is available in white on black, black on white, or Custom. (See Figure 2.9.) The Custom color schemes are the same as those described earlier in this skill under "Desktop Schemes."

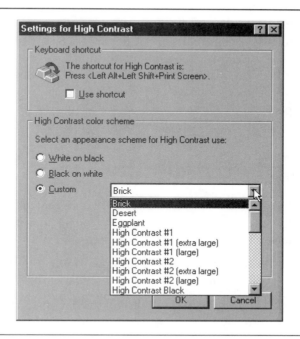

FIGURE 2.9: Choosing from the available High Contrast schemes

Avoiding the Mouse

Click the Mouse tab and select MouseKeys to use the keyboard to move the pointer around the screen. With this option selected, the keys of the numeric keypad will control the pointer. Click Settings to configure MouseKeys so that the pointer moves at the speed you want.

General Accessibility

The General tab includes some additional settings. Automatic reset, if checked, will turn the accessibility features off after a set time. Clear this box if you want the accessibility options to remain on continuously.

The Notification section allows for two types of messages. Check the first, *Give warning message when turning a feature on*, if you want a visual reminder that a feature is being activated. Click the second, *Make a sound when turning a feature on or off*, if you want an audio notification.

If a device other than a keyboard and mouse is attached to the computer, click the Support SerialKey Devices box and click the Settings button. Supply the serial port and baud rate for the device being attached. You might need to reboot the computer for the device to be recognized.

Advanced Accessibility

In addition to the Accessibility Options that are installed by default, Windows 98 includes additional Accessibility Tools that can add visibility to the desktop. To install these tools, follow these steps:

1. Open Add/Remove Programs in the Control Panel. Click the Windows Setup tab.

2. Highlight Accessibility in the list of components and click the Details button.

3. Put a check mark next to Accessibility Tools and click OK twice. You'll need to supply your Windows 98 CD-ROM so that the files can be installed.

To set these options for visibility, you'll need to start the Accessibility Wizard. Here's how:

1. Click the Start button and select Programs ➢ Accessories ➢ Accessibility ➢ Accessibility Wizard.

2. In the first dialog box, you're asked to select the smallest size text that you can read. As you can see in Figure 2.10, I chose large type but not the largest. Click the Next button to continue.

FIGURE 2.10: Select a text size you find readable.

On the next page (in much-too-small type) are the following options:

Change the font size   This option increases the size of the typeface in the menus and title bars of windows. (See "Setting Windows Colors and Fonts," earlier in this skill, for a more controllable way of enlarging the same fonts.)

Switch to a smaller screen resolution   This option will make everything on the screen larger at the cost of leaving less room on the desktop.

Use Microsoft Magnifier   This option creates a window at the top of the screen in which the elements you're using are magnified.

Not all the options may be available because of the limitations of your particular hardware.

3. Make the choices you want and click Next.

The changes will be made immediately and you can accept them or undo them and start over. If you choose the largest type in the first dialog box, the Magnifier will be turned on.

More about Magnifier

You can also access the Microsoft Magnifier by clicking the Start button and selecting Programs ➢ Accessories ➢ Accessibility ➢ Microsoft Magnifier.

A magnifying window will open at the top of your screen like the one shown in Figure 2.11. In the Microsoft Magnifier dialog box, select the magnification level you want and the actions you want to show in the window, then click OK.

FIGURE 2.11: Looking at the Magnifier

In addition to being helpful to those of us with limited vision, the Magnifier is also great for graphics work when you need to select something on screen with great precision.

Are You Experienced?

Now you can...

- ☑ Choose a desktop theme
- ☑ Select desktop wallpaper
- ☑ Modify a color scheme
- ☑ Change and arrange desktop icons
- ☑ Use accessibility options

SKILL 3

USING THE DESKTOP ELEMENTS

- Using Windows Explorer
- Mapping and sharing network drives
- Copying and formatting floppy disks
- Using Send To
- Making shortcuts
- Using the Recycle Bin

In this skill, we'll cover more of the desktop elements, including Windows Explorer and the Recycle Bin. You'll also learn how to use important features such as shortcuts and the Send To menu.

Using Windows Explorer

Windows Explorer offers the easiest way of viewing folders, files, and other resources located on your machine (see Figure 3.1). The default Explorer is a two-pane window. When you click on an item in the left window pane, the right pane displays the contents. You can choose different viewing options from the View menu.

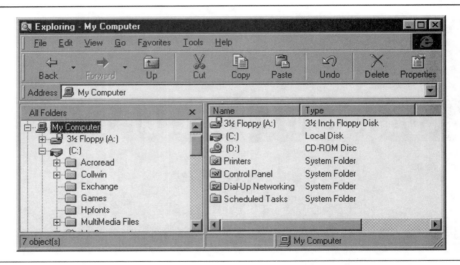

FIGURE 3.1: Windows Explorer at its most informative: the Details view

 TIP   More than one window of Windows Explorer can be opened at a time. In fact, that's often the easiest way to move files from one place to another.

The Explorer is always available from the Start menu. Click on the Start button, slide the pointer to Programs, then to Windows Explorer, and click.

If you use Windows Explorer a lot, as most people do, you may want to put a shortcut to the Windows Explorer on your desktop. Here's a quick way:

1. Begin as you normally would open Windows Explorer: Click Start and slide the mouse pointer to Programs, then Windows Explorer. Don't click just yet.

2. Using the right mouse button, drag the Windows Explorer shortcut icon out onto your desktop.

3. When you release the right mouse button, a pop-up menu appears. Choose Copy Here or Create Shortcut Here. (Since it's a shortcut you're dragging, the results are the same.)

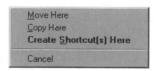

Inside Windows Explorer, folders are organized in a fashion that doesn't look all that different from Windows 3.1 or DOS except the top level folder/directory is called Desktop and the filenames look peculiar.

NOTE   Note the plus and minus signs next to folders. A plus sign means there's at least one more layer of folders that you can see if you click on the plus icon. Click on the minus sign and the lower level will collapse into the upper level.

Viewing Extensions

You'll probably notice first that most files shown in Windows Explorer's right pane are missing their extensions. The thinking behind this is that these files are registered (in other words, the system knows what they are and where they came from) and can be activated by merely clicking on them—so why would you need to know the extension?

In a perfect world, of course, you wouldn't. But the Explorer screen shown in Figure 3.2 demonstrates how confusion can arise.

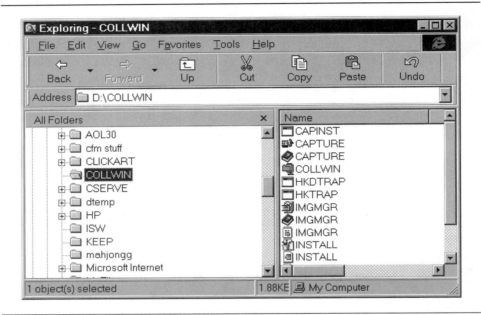

FIGURE 3.2: In some cases, the lack of extensions can prove confusing—as when there is more than one file with the same name.

There are two files named CAPTURE, two called INSTALL and *three* named IMGMGR. If you know what the icons mean or expand the window to show the file types, you can figure out which file does what. But if you prefer to see file extensions, here's how to do it:

1. Click the Start button, select Programs ➤ Windows Explorer, and click to Open Windows Explorer.

2. Click the View menu and select Folder Options.

3. In the dialog box that opens, click the View tab, then click the box next to *Hide file extensions for known file types* to remove the checkmark. Click OK when you're done.

TIP   If you really want to see everything, look under Hidden Files and select Show All Files, so even hidden and system files will show in Windows Explorer.

Of course, many, if not most, of the programs you'll be using will be started using the Start menu or from the desktop itself, so the file extensions are less important as time goes on.

Using Another Computer's Files

If your computer is connected to others in a local area network (LAN), the Network Neighborhood icon will appear on your desktop and in the left window of the Windows Explorer. You can see a list of computers on your network when you click Network Neighborhood in the left window of Windows Explorer (or when you click the Network Neighborhood icon on the desktop). To see the contents of other computers' hard drives, the drives have to be *shared*. There are two steps to this. First, the network itself has to be set up for file and printer sharing.

NOTE   The basics of setting up sharing over a network are discussed in Skill 14.

Once this has been done, you can choose to share some or all of your files with others on the network and they can, in turn, share with you.

Sharing a Drive or Folder

How do you give others access to drives or folders on your computer? Once the network has been set up for file sharing, as described in Skill 14, just follow these steps:

1. Click the Start button, select Programs ➤ Windows Explorer, and click to open Windows Explorer. Find the drive or folder you want to share.

2. Right-click on the drive or folder and choose Sharing from the pop-up menu.

3. On the Sharing page of the Properties sheet, select Shared As, as shown in Figure 3.3.

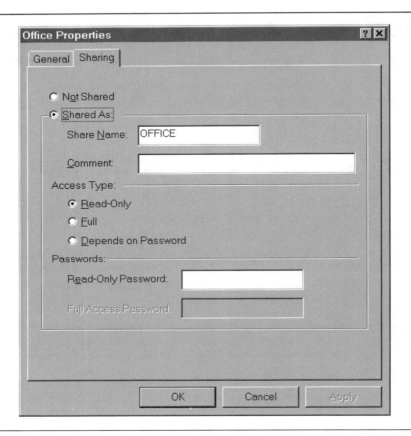

FIGURE 3.3: Sharing a drive with other users on your network

4. Accept the default Share Name or change it to something that others will understand. Share names are limited to 12 characters, but the shorter the better.

5. Indicate what type of access you want others to have, and enter a password if you want to limit access. Remember that if you grant full access, others will be able to change the files on your computer.

6. Click OK to accept the revised Properties sheet.

The drive or folder you have chosen to share will now appear under the name of your computer when others on your network open their Network Neighborhood. If you specified a password, they will need to know it to gain access.

TIP   If you don't want others to be able to make changes to your drive or folder, choose the Read-Only access type on the Sharing page of the Properties sheet. Read Only also means that others will be unable to *add* any new files to the shared drive or folder. Use passwords for only the most sensitive files.

Mapping a Drive

If you find yourself often going through Network Neighborhood or Explorer to get to a particular drive, you may want to *map* it. You can make any shared drive or folder on another computer appear just as if it were a drive on *your* computer. A mapped drive will show up in Windows Explorer as another hard drive. For example, if you have a C: drive plus a CD-ROM drive that uses the letter D:, you can map a shared network drive as letter E:.

 TIP   A mapped drive is even better than a shortcut in one important respect: If you're using older programs, they're not going to recognize things like Network Neighborhood, and they will flat out refuse to open or save files to anywhere other than your own computer. Map a drive, and the program will cooperate because now the drive on the other computer will appear (to the program at least) to be on your computer.

Here's how it's done:

1. Click Network Neighborhood in Windows Explorer or the Network Neighborhood icon on the desktop, and find the folder or drive you want to show as one of your local drives.

2. Right-click on the object and select Map Network Drive from the pop-up menu. This will open the dialog box shown in Figure 3.4.

FIGURE 3.4: Mapping the Office folder to be Drive E:

3. Click OK when you're done. Open Explorer or My Computer and look. Figure 3.5 shows how the folder being mapped in Figure 3.4 ended up looking in Windows Explorer.

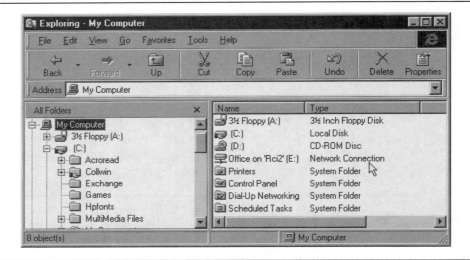

FIGURE 3.5: After being mapped, the folder on the other computer is listed as a drive among your own—and you can use it just as if it *were* your own.

 NOTE The Reconnect at Logon box should be shown if you want the connection to the mapped drive to be made every time you start your computer. If the computer where the mapped drive resides is turned *off* when you log on, you'll get an error message.

Disconnecting from Mapped Drives or Folders

To get rid of a mapped drive or folder, you can highlight it and right-click. Select Disconnect from the pop-up menu.

When you disconnect a mapped drive, you're just removing it from the list of drives shown on your computer. It has no other effect on the drive. You can always go back and remap it if you need to.

Exploring Floppy Disks

Click the floppy drive icon in the Explorer's left window to see the contents of the diskette currently in the drive. Windows Explorer also provides the graphical interface for the care and maintenance of floppy disks. If you yearn for DOS, you can also open a DOS window to copy, format, and label a floppy disk.

Making Exact Copies

To make an exact copy of your floppy disk, put the disk in the drive and open Windows Explorer. Right-click on the icon for the floppy drive and select Copy Disk to open the dialog box shown in Figure 3.6. It doesn't say so, but these selections must be the same type of disk. For most people, that means the same drive (unless you have two identical diskette drives or two Zip drives).

> **TIP**
>
> If you do much work with floppies, you may want to put a shortcut to the drive on your desktop. Just drag the floppy drive icon from the left window of the Explorer to your desktop.

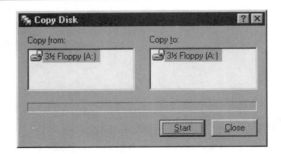

FIGURE 3.6: Windows 98's direct route to copying a floppy disk

Formatting Floppies

Here's how to format a floppy disk:

1. Put the floppy disk you want to format into your A: or B: drive as appropriate.

2. Click the Start button and select Programs ➤ Windows Explorer.

3. In the left pane of the Explorer window, right-click once on the floppy drive icon. Do not open the floppy drive. A pop-up menu will appear.

4. Select Format from the menu.

5. Select the Format Type and Other options you want from the dialog box that appears:

> **Quick** A quick format changes the names of any files on the disk so that they "disappear" as far as the operating system is concerned. This format is very fast (hence the name), but it doesn't check to make sure that the floppy disk is undamaged. It also doesn't work on new, unformatted disks.

> **Full** A full format is necessary for new floppies and desirable for old ones because it checks for errors and defects on the disk. It's a lot slower, though.

Copy system files only   This copies system files to a disk that's already formatted without removing any of the files already present. This allows you to turn any floppy into a bootable floppy—providing there's room available on the floppy disk for the system files.

Label   This will let you provide a label for the floppy.

Display summary when finished   This option is on by default. When the formatting is complete, it opens a sheet showing the details of the formatted disk. Clear the box if you don't want to be bothered with this information.

Copy system files   Check this if you want system files copied to the disk to make the disk bootable.

6. When you're finished selecting options, click the Start button.

> **TIP**   If Windows Explorer (or any open window) is showing the contents of the floppy disk, Windows 98 concludes that the floppy disk is in use and therefore can't be formatted. If you get that message, click on your C: drive icon in the Explorer or close the desktop window showing the contents of the floppy. Then right-click once on the floppy icon and select Format from the pop-up menu.

Using the Send To Option

When you're working in the Explorer (or any other folder for that matter) and you click on an object with the right mouse button, the menu that opens includes an option called Send To. When you first start using Windows 98, the system will put your floppy drive and other removable media such as a Zip drive on the Send To submenu automatically.

This is pretty handy, as you might guess. But it can be even handier. You can add any application or device you choose. So you can select a file and send it to your word processor or your printer.

The Long

As an example, here's how to add the Notepad applet to the Send To menu:

1. Click the Start button and select Programs ➤ Windows Explorer.

2. Click on your Windows directory, then right-click the file Notepad. Select Create Shortcut from the pop-up menu. The shortcut will appear in Explorer.

3. Right-click on the shortcut you've just made and select Cut from the menu.

4. Scroll to the SendTo folder (it's a subfolder under the main Windows folder).

5. Right-click on the SendTo folder and select Paste.

And the Short of It

If you want to be able to add stuff to the Send To menu without going through all the previous steps every time, just do the following once:

1. Click the Start button, select Programs ➤ Windows Explorer, and then click on the Windows folder.

2. Right-click on the SendTo folder and drag it to the desktop. Release the mouse button and select Create Shortcut Here from the pop-up menu.

3. Go back to the Explorer and open the SendTo folder under Windows.

4. Drag and drop the shortcut you just made to the SendTo folder.

Now when you highlight an object and open the Send To menu (the right mouse button menu), there's a shortcut to Send To as an option on the menu. Select that option, and the item you've selected will be instantly added to the Send To menu.

When the menu gets too crowded, open the SendTo folder in the Explorer and delete any extra clutter.

 TIP   For a quicker way to find the SendTo folder, click once on the Start button and select Run. In the Open box, type in **Sendto** (all one word) and press Enter. The SendTo folder will open on your desktop.

Taking Shortcuts

Shortcuts are convenient ways to get at all the things on your computer or network: documents, applications, folders, printers, and so on. They're most likely to be placed on your desktop, on the Start menu, or in the SendTo folder. In this section, I'll cover all the ways to make and modify a shortcut and how to place the shortcuts you want in the places you want them to be.

The small arrow in the lower-left corner of the icon identifies a shortcut.

The arrow is an important bit of information because you'll want to know (particularly before a deletion) whether something is a shortcut or a real object. You can delete shortcuts at will. You're not deleting anything that you can't recreate in a second or two. But if you delete an actual program or other file, you'll have to rummage around in the Recycle Bin to retrieve it. (And if it's been a while before you notice it's missing, the Recycle Bin may have been emptied in the meantime, and the object will be gone.)

 NOTE   Configuring and using the Recycle Bin is covered later in this skill.

Here's an example. I have a folder on my hard drive called *Games*. On my desktop, I have a shortcut to that folder:

If I delete the shortcut folder on my desktop, the folder on the hard drive remains untouched. If I delete the folder on the hard drive, the shortcut on the desktop is still there, but there's nothing for it to point to. And if I were to click on the shortcut, I'd get a dialog box like the one shown in Figure 3.7.

FIGURE 3.7: If you delete or move the original object, you'll see this when you click on the shortcut.

You'll find the Create Shortcut option in a lot of places, including:

- On objects' pop-up menus (See Figure 3.8)

- From various drop-down menus

- On the desktop pop-up menu as New ➢ Shortcut

Shortcuts are an excellent tool for configuring your desktop to suit you. You can make shortcuts to folders, to programs, and to individual files. Arrange them any way you want on the desktop, inside other folders, or on menus.

FIGURE 3.8: Create Shortcut is an option on most of the menus that pop up when you click the right mouse button.

NOTE   Until Windows 95, the term *shortcut* always referred to a keyboard shortcut—in other words, a combination of keys that would produce some action on screen. But now we have shortcuts meaning pointers. In this book, *shortcut* will always mean a pointer and *keyboard shortcut* will be used to indicate a key combination.

How to Make a Shortcut

Shortcuts are pointers to objects. So you need to either find the object you want to point to or be able to tell the system where the original object is located. The easiest way to make a shortcut to a program is to right-click on the Start button and select Explore. The contents of your Start menu, including the Programs folder, will be in the right pane of the window that opens. Click your way down through the tree until you find the program you want.

You can also open Windows Explorer and similarly find the program. Windows Explorer (or My Computer) is where you'll need to look to find drives, printers, or folders when you want to make shortcuts to them. Windows Explorer (or My Computer) will also be needed for a DOS program or any other program that doesn't manage to install itself off the Start menu.

With the Original in View

To make a shortcut when you have the original object in view inside Windows Explorer or My Computer, follow these steps:

1. Point to the object and right-click on it once.

2. Holding the button down, drag the object to the desktop.

3. When you release the mouse button, you'll see a menu like the one below.

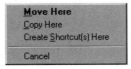

4.   Select Create Shortcut(s) here.

Here's a shortcut to the Windows Explorer. This shortcut, when clicked, will open the Windows Explorer program.

 TIP   If you use the method of right-clicking on the Start button described above, you'll be using a shortcut to make another shortcut, without having to go back to the original object. Just right-click on the shortcut and select Make Shortcut from the menu that opens.

Cut and Paste a Shortcut

Another way to make a shortcut is to right-click on the program or file and select Create Shortcut from the pop-up menu. A shortcut to the object you clicked on will appear in the same folder. You can then move the shortcut by right-clicking on it and selecting Cut from the pop-up menu. Then right-click where you want the shortcut to be and choose Paste. (Or you can drag it from the folder and drop it in a new location.)

To Objects You Don't See

If the original object isn't handy or you don't want to go find it, you can still create a shortcut as follows:

1.   Right-click on the desktop and select New ➢ Shortcut.

2.   In the dialog box that opens, type in the location and name of the original object. If you don't know the path (and who ever does?), click the Browse button.

3. Using the Browse window, mouse around until you find the file or object you want to link to. You may have to change the Files of Type item in the Browse window to read All Files. Highlight the file with the mouse (the name will appear in the File Name box) and click Open.

4. The Command line box will now contain the name and location of the object. Click on Next and accept or change the name for the shortcut.

5. Click on Finish, and the shortcut appears on your desktop.

Renaming a Shortcut

When you create a shortcut, the system always gives it a name that starts with "Shortcut to" and then names the object the shortcut is pointing to. To rename the shortcut, you can right-click on the icon and select Rename from the menu that opens.

Type in the name you want. Click on a blank spot on the desktop when you're through.

 TIP
If you happen to be using the click once to select, double-click to open option described in Skill 1, you can also rename a shortcut (or most other icons for that matter) by clicking once on the name, waiting a second or two, and clicking again. That'll highlight the name and you can edit it as you wish.

Choosing a Name

When you rename a shortcut, take full advantage of long filenames to give it a name that's meaningful to you. No need to get carried away, but you might as well call a folder "March Budget Reports" rather than "MARBUDGT," as you might have previously. Certain characters aren't allowed in shortcut names:

/ \ < > | : " ? *

but you ought to be able to live without those few.

 TIP
On some systems, particularly multiplatform networks, you may be stuck with using the old 8.3 naming convention. Of course, any files you don't need to share can still have long names.

Putting Shortcuts Where You Want Them

Obviously, the point of shortcuts is to save time and energy. Merely placing a bunch of shortcuts on your desktop may help you or it may not. So here are several other ways shortcuts can be useful.

Putting a Start Menu Item on the Desktop

As you've seen, when you click on the Start menu and follow the Programs arrow, you get a hierarchical display of all the programs installed on your system. All those menu items are just representations of shortcuts. To find them and put the ones you want on your Desktop, you'll need to (if you'll pardon the expression) go Exploring.

1. Click the Start button and highlight the item you want.

2. If it's not on the first menu, you may have to go down another level by clicking one of the folders.

3. Right-click the shortcut you want and drag it to the desktop, selecting Create Shortcut Here from the menu that opens when you release the mouse button.

Adding a Program to the Start Menu

You undoubtedly have some programs that you'd like to get at without having to go through the menus or without searching around the desktop. To add a program to the top of the Start menu, just click on a shortcut, drag it to the Start button, and drop it on top. Then when you click the Start button, the program will be instantly available (as shown in Figure 3.9).

FIGURE 3.9: For instant access to your favorite programs, add them to the top of your Start menu.

You can remove programs from the Start menu be reversing the process. Right-click on the item and drag it to the desktop, choosing Move Here from the pop-up menu.

You can also clear programs from the Start menu by selecting Start ➢ Settings ➢ Taskbar & Start Menu. Click the Start Menu Programs and then the Remove button. Highlight the program you want to remove and then click the Remove button.

As you can see in Figure 3.10, you can also use this page to add programs to the Start menu, though it requires more steps than a simple drag and drop.

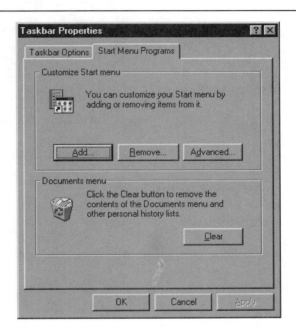

FIGURE 3.10: Use the Taskbar Properties page to add and remove programs from the Start menu.

TIP

Items you've added to the Start menu can be rearranged into whatever order you prefer. Click on an item and drag it up or down the list, then drop it at the new location.

Shortcut Settings

Every shortcut has a Properties sheet that you can access by right-clicking on the shortcut icon and selecting Properties from the pop-up menu. For shortcuts to Windows objects (as opposed to DOS programs), the more useful tab is the one labeled Shortcut (shown in Figure 3.11).

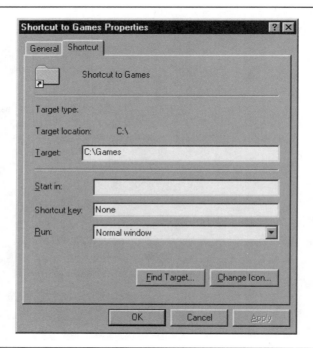

FIGURE 3.11: A shortcut's Properties sheet

Finding the Target

On the Shortcut tab, click the Find Target button to find out just where the shortcut is pointing. When you click this button, a window opens into the folder containing the application or file the shortcut is for.

Changing a Shortcut's Icon

Shortcuts to programs will display the icon associated with that program. However, shortcuts to folders and documents are pretty dull. In any case, you can change the icon for a shortcut by following these steps:

1. Right-click the icon and select Properties from the pop-up menu.

2. Select the Shortcut tab and click the Change Icon button.

3. Select an icon from the default shell32.dll file (see Figure 3.12), or click the Browse button to look in other files.

4. Click OK twice, and the new icon will be displayed.

Many icons are available from icon libraries that are distributed as shareware. Icons are often included in executable files, so if you have a shortcut to an application (a file with an .exe extension), you can pick from those icons as well by browsing the application file.

FIGURE 3.12:   The shell32.dll file has many icons to choose from.

Adding a Shortcut Key

If you're fond of opening certain applications with key strokes, you can still do so in Windows 98—with some limitations. To set up a key combination to open a shortcut to a program or folder, follow these steps:

1. Right-click the shortcut and select Properties.

2. On the Shortcut page, click in the Shortcut Key field.

3. Type in a letter, and Windows will add Ctrl+Alt. (So if you enter a W, the keyboard combination will be Ctrl+Alt+W.)

4. Click OK when you're finished.

To remove a keyboard shortcut, you need to click in the Shortcut Key field and press the Backspace or Delete key until the entry is cleared.

It's best to limit keyboard shortcuts to just a few programs or folders, because these shortcuts have precedence in Windows. So if you define a keyboard combination that's also used in a program, that program loses the ability to use its original key combination.

Shortcuts to Other Places

Shortcuts quickly become a normal way of accessing files and programs on your own computer, but they're a much more powerful tool than you'd suspect at first.

DOS Programs

Shortcuts to DOS programs are made in the same way as other shortcuts. Find the program file in the Windows Explorer, and do a right-mouse drag to the desktop.

Disk Drives

Right-click on a disk drive in the Windows Explorer or My Computer, and drag it to the desktop to create a shortcut to the contents of a drive. When you click on the shortcut, you'll see its contents almost instantly—it's much quicker than opening the entire Explorer.

Other Computers

You can put a shortcut to another computer—or part of it—on the desktop. It can be a computer you're connected to on a network or even a computer you connect to using Dial-Up Networking. Just use Network Neighborhood to find the computer (or part of it or even a single file), right-click on it, and drag it to your desktop (or another folder) and create a shortcut there.

Using the Recycle Bin

In the bad old days of computing, it was far too easy to accidentally delete a file from your system—and there was no going back. There were, of course, tools you could buy like the Norton Utilities. Norton included a program that could retrieve deleted files—providing you acted quickly enough. And DOS itself, starting with version 5, included a program to undelete files. The weakness of both approaches was if you didn't undelete right away, your file could easily be overwritten by another file, and then there was *no way* to recover.

The Recycle Bin, introduced in Windows 95, will retain all your deleted files for as long as you want, and you can adjust the amount of security from "just a little" to "all I can get" to match your own personal comfort level.

What It Is

The Recycle Bin is a reserved space on your hard drive. When you delete a file or drag it to the Recycle Bin icon,

the file is actually moved to that reserved space. If you have more than one hard drive, each drive has its own reserved space. There's an icon that represents the Recycle Bin on each drive—though the contents displayed when you click on any icon will be the same as the Recycle Bin on any other drive. If you want a deleted file back, you can click the Recycle Bin icon to open it and retrieve any file.

The Recycle Bin functions as a first-in, first-out system. That is, when the bin is full, the oldest files are the first ones deleted to make room for the newest ones. As configurable as the rest of Windows 98 is, the Recycle Bin cannot be:

- deleted

- renamed

- removed from the desktop

though there are a number of settings you can change to make the Recycle Bin suitable for your use.

NOTE   See "Adjusting the Recycle Bin Settings" later in this skill for information on how to determine the amount of disk space used by the Recycle Bin as well as other settings.

Sending Files to the Recycle Bin

By default, Windows 98 is set up to deposit all deleted files into the Recycle Bin. When you right-click on a file and select delete, or highlight a file and press the Delete key, you'll be asked to confirm if you want to send the file to the Recycle Bin. After you click Yes, that's where the file is moved to. Deleted shortcuts are also sent to the Recycle Bin.

TIP   If you delete an empty folder, it's not sent to the Recycle Bin, but you can recover it by immediately selecting Undo Delete from the Recycle Bin's Edit menu. If the folder came from the desktop, just right-click on a blank spot on the desktop and select Undo Delete from the pop-up menu.

Sending a Floppy Disk's Files to the Recycle Bin

Normally, files that you delete from a floppy drive are *not* sent to the Recycle Bin. They're just deleted. However, if that strikes you as just a little too impetuous, there's an easy way to make sure that the files on your floppy do go to the Recycle Bin.

1. Click the Start button and select Programs ➢ Windows Explorer.

2. Use the scroll bar for the left pane to move up so you can see the entry for your floppy drive.

3. Click (with the left mouse button) on the floppy drive icon. In the right pane, select the file(s) you want to delete but still want in the Recycle Bin.

4. Right-click on the file(s) and select Cut from the pop-up menu. Right-click on the desktop and select Paste.

5. Highlight the file on the desktop. (If there's more than one, hold down the Shift key while you click each one in turn.) Right-click on a highlighted file and select Delete. You'll be prompted to confirm that you want to send the file(s) to the Recycle Bin.

There's no more direct way to do this function because the Recycle Bin stubbornly refuses to accept any files that are sent directly from a floppy.

TIP You can also use this method when you're deleting files from any external drive (such as a Zip drive), and you want the security of having the files safely stashed in the Recycle Bin for a while.

Bypassing the Recycle Bin

If you've got a file that you know for sure you want to delete and that you don't want taking up space in the Recycle Bin, just hold down the Shift key when you select Delete. But be sure that's what you want to do, because there's no way in Windows 98 to recover a deleted file that's bypassed the Recycle Bin.

NOTE If you have the Norton Utilities for Windows, you can use their Unerase program to recover deleted files that are not in the Recycle Bin—again, you must do this very quickly before another file overwrites the one you want to recover.

Files That Won't Go Willingly

Some older programs (not written specifically for Windows 95 or later) allow you to delete files from within the program. Files deleted this way will not be sent to the Recycle Bin. Similarly, files you delete at the DOS prompt will also disappear into never-never land rather than into the Recycle Bin.

Therefore, you should make all your deletions through the Windows Explorer or My Computer or on the desktop. If Windows 98 knows about the deletion, the file will automatically go to the Recycle Bin.

Recovering a Deleted File

Retrieving a file from the Recycle Bin is remarkably easy. Just click on the Recycle Bin icon. The Recycle Bin window can be set up in any of the choices on the View menu. The Large Icons view (see Figure 3.13) is useful because it lets you identify which programs made which files.

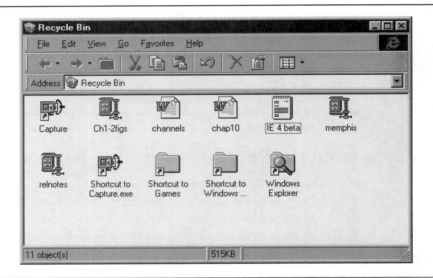

FIGURE 3.13: In the Large Icons view, you can quickly identify files that were made by a particular program.

The Details view (see Figure 3.14) is the best view if you're looking for a file recently deleted. Just click on the Date Deleted bar to arrange the files in date order. A second click will reverse the order. Similarly, if you know the name of the file, a click on the Name bar will list the files in alphabetical order.

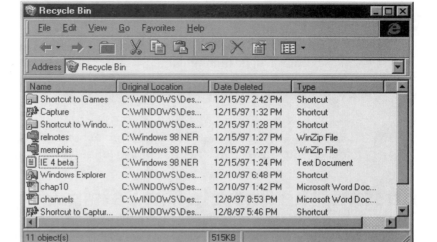

FIGURE 3.14: The Details view is useful to search by date or name.

To retrieve a single file, click on it with either the left or right button and drag it to a folder or the desktop. If you just want to send it back to its original location, right-click on the filename and select Restore from the pop-up menu.

More Than One File

To recover more than one file at a time, hold down the Ctrl key while selecting the filenames. Then right-click on one of the highlighted names and select Restore from the pop-up menu. Or use cut and paste to send the whole bunch to a different location. And of course, you can click (either right or left button) and drag the files to your desktop or another open folder.

To retrieve a number of files all in a series, click on the first one and then hold down the Shift key while selecting the last one in the series.

Let's say you deleted a whole folder and the only thing all the items in the folder have in common is that all were deleted at the same time. Here's how to recover them:

1. Open the Recycle Bin by clicking the icon.

2. Select Details from the View menu.

3. Click the Date Deleted bar. Use the scroll bar to move through the list until you find the group of files you want to retrieve.

4. Click on the first one's name, then, while holding down the Shift key, click on the name of the last one you want. All the files from the first to the last selection will be highlighted.

5. Right-click on one of the highlighted files and select Recover from the pop-up menu.

All the files will be returned to their original home, and although the original folder was not listed in the Recycle Bin, the files will be in their original folder.

Adjusting the Recycle Bin Settings

You can adjust the amount of space the Recycle Bin claims and change other settings that affect how the Recycle Bin works. Mostly you have to decide just how much safety you want and are comfortable with.

How Much Space?

Right-click on the Recycle Bin icon and select Properties from the pop-up menu. The Recycle Bin's Properties sheet will open, as shown in Figure 3.15.

As you can see, you can set the amount of space reserved for the Recycle Bin for each hard disk drive individually, or make a global setting. By default, 10 percent of each drive is set aside for the Recycle Bin. On a large drive, that's a lot of megabytes, so you may want to reduce the size a bit.

Click the radio button for *Configure drives independently* and then click each drive tab in turn. Click the sliding arrow and move it to the right or left until the space reserved is to your liking.

 NOTE   There's also a field below the slider, showing the percentage of the drive that is reserved. If your drives are different sizes, you might want to make things easier for yourself by just reserving the same percentage on each drive.

Remember that the Recycle Bin is first-in, first-out, so if you make the reserved space very small, deleted files may pass into oblivion faster than you wish.

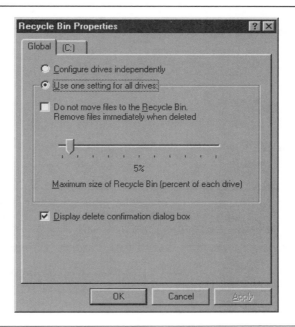

FIGURE 3.15: The Recycle Bin's Properties sheet

Getting Rid of Confirmations

On the Global tab of the Recycle Bin Properties sheet, a checkbox controls the confirmation notice that opens every time you delete a file or folder.

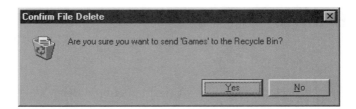

If you like the comfort of being consulted about every deletion, leave the checkmark in the box. If you clear the checkmark, files you choose to delete will move to the Recycle Bin without any further notice.

Doing Away with the Recycle Bin

You can't exactly do away with the Recycle Bin completely. As mentioned before, you can't delete it or remove it from the desktop. However, you can check this box:

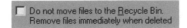

on the Recycle Bin Properties page. If you have the Recycle Bin space configured separately for each drive, you can pick which drives to apply this to.

 **WARNING** Bypassing the Recycle Bin is generally a very bad idea unless you have another program for undeleting files. Files that are deleted and not sent to the Recycle Bin are gone beyond recall.

Even if you do have a program that will rescue files deleted in error, it's still not a good idea to bypass the Recycle Bin completely. Most such programs are dependent on you getting to the deleted file before it is overwritten by something else. And that can easily happen in Windows 98, where there's usually something going on behind the scenes.

 TIP If you begrudge large portions of your hard drive, make the reserved space on the hard drive very small—maybe 5 or 10MB. Check the box on the Properties sheet to disable the confirmation requests. Then the Recycle Bin will be quite unobtrusive, but you'll still have some margin for safety.

Emptying the Recycle Bin

To get rid of everything in the Recycle Bin, right-click on the Recycle Bin icon and select Empty Recycle Bin. There's also an option to Delete Recycle Bin under the File menu.

To remove just *some* of the items in the Recycle Bin, highlight the filenames, right-click on one of them, and select Delete from the pop-up menu. You'll be asked to confirm the deletion (assuming you have the confirmation option turned on), and when you say Yes, the files will be deleted permanently.

Are You Experienced?

Now you can...

- ☑ Use Windows Explorer
- ☑ View file extensions
- ☑ Share your drives and folders
- ☑ Map a network drive
- ☑ Copy and format floppy disks
- ☑ Use the Send To menu
- ☑ Make and use shortcuts
- ☑ Use and configure the Recycle Bin

Skill 3

SKILL 4

MANAGING FILES AND FOLDERS

- Selecting files and folders
- Making new files and folders
- Setting folder views
- Registering file types
- Moving, copying, and deleting files and folders
- Using long filenames
- Undoing a mistake

In this skill we'll continue some of the discussion from Skill 3, with an emphasis on the basics of making and manipulating files and folders, and getting them organized in ways that are useful to you.

Selecting Files and Folders

A single file or folder is selected by moving the pointer to the icon. As soon as the object is in range, you'll see that it's highlighted. You can then click once with the right mouse button, and a menu will open with possible actions.

Selecting Everything

To select a bunch of files or folders, open the window showing the objects in question and then click Edit ➤ Select All. Everything in the window will be highlighted. Right-click on one of the highlighted icons (see Figure 4.1) and choose the action you want from the pop-up menu.

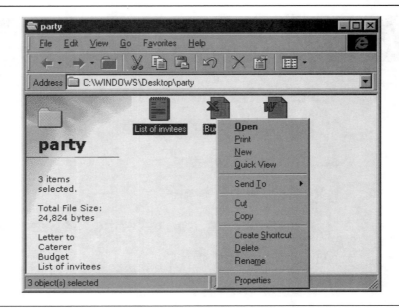

FIGURE 4.1: All the files are selected, and the right mouse menu lets you choose what you want to do with them.

Selecting Some but Not All

There are lots of ways to select some of the objects in a window. The easiest way often depends on how you have the files and folders displayed.

If you have large icons displayed, you might want to simply lasso the items in question. Right-click on an area near the first item and, holding the mouse button down, draw a box around the icons you want to select. When you're finished drawing the box, the icons will be highlighted and the pop-up menu will appear, giving you a choice of actions. Figure 4.2 shows icons selected in just this way. You can also draw the box using the left mouse button.

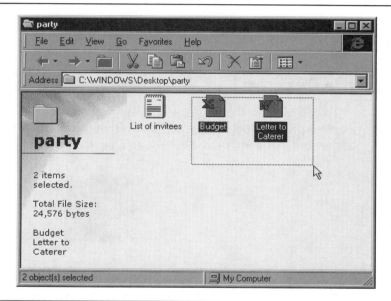

FIGURE 4.2: Icons captured by lassoing

If you have the icons displayed as a list or in the Details view, it's easiest to select them using the Ctrl key. In other words, hold down the Ctrl key while pointing to each item in turn.

If you want all the files in a series, highlight the first one, then hold down the Shift key and move the pointer to the last one. All the objects in between and including the two files will be selected.

TIP   If you're accustomed to using the single click to highlight an object, the "point to select" approach will take some practice—particularly when selecting a series of objects. Just remember to detour your pointer around items you don't want to select, and you'll be fine.

Making a New Folder

Folders, introduced with Windows 95, are the equivalent of DOS and Windows 3.1 directories. There are differences in that folders can contain shortcuts, can themselves be shortcuts to *real* folders in other locations, and can be placed right on the desktop.

On the Desktop

To create a new folder on the desktop, right-click on the desktop in some unoccupied space and select New ➤ Folder from the menu. A folder will appear with the cursor already placed for you to type in a name.

This folder is actually located on your hard drive in the Desktop folder inside the Windows folder. Figure 4.3 shows this new folder as it appears in the Details view of Windows Explorer.

TIP   If you can't see the Desktop folder, then it's set to be hidden. To reveal it, select View ➤ Folder Options ➤ View from the Windows Explorer (or other window) menu. In the dialog box that appears, under Hidden Files, click the radio button next to Show All Files.

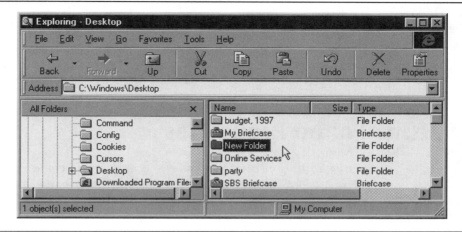

FIGURE 4.3: The new folder on the desktop can also be seen when you open Windows Explorer.

Inside Another Folder

To make a folder inside another folder (for example, in Windows Explorer), follow these steps:

1. Click the Start button and select Programs ➤ Windows Explorer.

2. Use the scroll bars to locate the folder where you want to place the new folder.

3. Expand the existing folder by clicking on it.

4. Move your pointer to a blank spot in the right pane and right-click once.

5. Select New ➤ Folder from the menu, without clicking on anything.

6. Type in the name for the new folder.

You can do this with a folder on the desktop. Just open the folder where you want to place the new folder and right-click once in a blank spot inside the open window.

TIP   Make a folder in the wrong place? Just right-click on the errant folder and select Delete. You'll be asked to confirm that you want to send the folder to the Recycle Bin. Click Yes and the folder's gone. Or read "Moving and Copying Files and Folders" later in this skill to move the folder to a better location.

Setting Folder Properties

Since everything else has Properties sheets, it should come as no surprise that folders do, too. Right-click on a folder and select Properties from the pop-up menu. You'll see a window like the one shown in Figure 4.4.

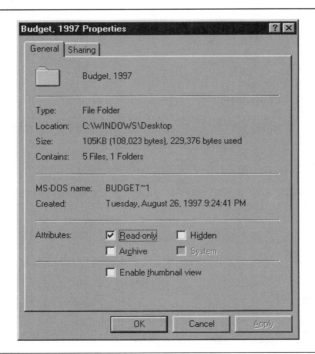

FIGURE 4.4: The Properties sheet of a folder

General Page

The General page provides information about the folder, including its size and the number of files and other folders to be found inside. As with Properties sheets for individual files, you'll find checkboxes for setting attributes:

Read-only   Set this attribute so that the folder cannot be written to. This is not a security measure, but it makes it harder to accidentally change something. A determined person can easily figure out how to change this attribute.

Archive   A check in this box means that all the files in the folder have been backed up by a program that sets the archive bit. If the box is filled, it means that some of the files are backed up but others are not.

Hidden   Folders and files that are hidden will disappear from the Windows 98 interface unless you specifically choose to display them. They'll still work as usual, but just won't be visible in the Windows Explorer or other programs.

System   System files are necessary to the operation of Windows 98. You don't want to delete them. In any case, a whole folder cannot be designated as System, so this box is always grayed out when you're looking at a folder.

TIP   To change a file or folder from hidden to visible, go to View ➤ Folder Options ➤ View on a window's toolbar and select Show All Files. Then find the file you want to change and open its Properties page so you can change the Hidden attribute.

Sharing Page

You can share your folder with others on the network by clicking the Sharing tab of the folder's Properties sheet. Here you can give other users read-only or read-write access. You can require a password from other users. You can also allow sharing at the drive level or the individual file level. If you set drive C: as shared on the network, you can't *un*share anything on drive C:. Everything will be accessible. Similarly, if you share a folder, all files in that folder will be shared.

TIP   If there's no Sharing tab on the Properties sheet, you'll need to click Start ➤ Settings ➤ Control Panel and click the Network icon. Activate File and Printer Sharing on the Configuration page. This will make the Sharing tab visible.

Viewing Folder Contents

Windows 98 adds a whole new layer of ways to look at folders in addition to the usual views of Large Icons, Small Icons, List, and Details. Depending on your needs, you may find more than one type of view helpful. There are also specific ways of changing and retaining views that will also be discussed in this section.

Folders as Web Pages

One of the options on the View menu of any folder is As Web Page. This option is a toggle: A click changes its state from on to off or vice versa. When you view a folder as a Web page, a hypertext template controls its appearance. The default template uses roughly the left one-third of the folder window to display the folder name and a variety of useful information.

When you select an object in the folder, information about the object appears in the left pane of the folder window. The type of information depends on the object. For a document file, it may include such properties as the author's name in addition to the file date and time, as in Figure 4.5.

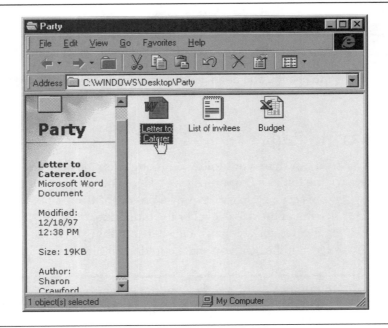

FIGURE 4.5: Select a document file in Web view, and information about it is displayed on the left side of the window.

For disk drives, the information includes space used and space available, along with a pie graph, as shown in Figure 4.6. For system folders and other objects, a general description indicates the object's function.

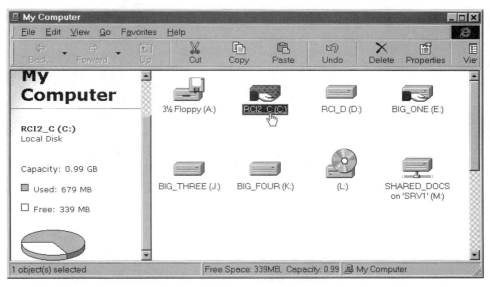

FIGURE 4.6: In Web view, you can easily see the total space, space used, and space available of your disk drives.

Customizing Folders

Also on the View menu is an option called Customize This Folder. Choosing it starts a Wizard of the same name, which offers three choices:

Create or Edit an HTML Document   This controls the appearance of the folder when View ➤ As Web Page is selected. This sounds good, but beware: As the next Wizard dialog explains, this really involves working with a hypertext template, not a simple HTML document. If you don't have a hypertext template editor installed, the template will be opened in Notepad.

Choose a Background Picture   Any picture in BMP, JPG, or GIF format can serve as a background for the folder view.

Remove Customization   Choose this to return to a plain background. This also returns you to the default template for the Web view if you have selected View ➤ As Web Page.

Selecting Options

Every folder has a Folder Options selection on the View menu. When you select
Folder Options, Windows 98 opens a dialog box much like the one shown in
Figure 4.7. The settings you make here are global, unlike the View menu settings
just described. In other words, you can't change the options for just one folder.
Any changes you make here take effect throughout your whole system.

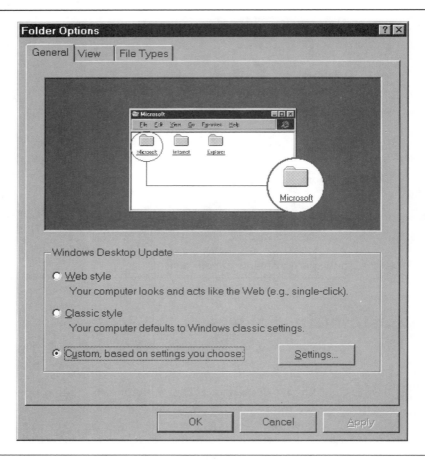

FIGURE 4.7: The Folder Options dialog box lets you set global properties
for all your folders.

Folder Options—The General Page

This is where you get to set the basic look and behavior of your folders. You can choose the Web style, in which:

- The folders you browse will all open in the same window, rather than a new window for each folder.

- All folders have a default Web view, which you can customize if you like.

- The names and icons of files and subfolders look and behave like hypertext links: They are underlined, they are selected when you point at them, and they open with a single click.

The Classic style will give you a Windows 95 look and feel:

- Each folder opens in a new window.

- Folders are given a Web page view only if you choose As Web Page on the View menu.

- Click to select an item and double-click to open it.

If you prefer some combination of these options (such as classic Windows looks with single-click file opening), choose Custom and click the Settings button to set your individual preferences.

The View Tab

The View tab includes settings for how files will display in folders. The two buttons in the Folder Views box allow you to give all folders the same view. Like Current Folder sets all folders to the same view as the folder you are currently working in; Reset All Folders sets them all back to the Windows 98 default view. In either case, changes take place the next time you open a folder.

There is also an Advanced Settings list where you can toggle a variety of folder properties. Here are the choices you can make:

Remember each folder's view settings This option insures that a given folder always opens with the view (Large Icons, Small Icons, List, or Details) to which you last set it. If you uncheck this, the same view setting will be applied to all folders you open in that window.

Display the full path in title bar   Ordinarily the title bar of a folder will show only the folder's title. Sometimes, of course, you may want to see just where on your hard drive a folder resides, or maybe you just miss the DOS command line. In that case, select this option, and the full path will be displayed on the title bar of each folder.

Hide file extensions for known file types   By default, this option is selected. It means that you won't see the file extensions for files that Windows 98 already knows how to use. So don't be dismayed to see that your filenames look peculiar without their familiar tails—like .exe or .doc—because any file without an extension can just be clicked to open. With this option selected, the only files with extensions will be those that have no associated application. (See "Registering File Types" later in this skill for information on how to tell Windows 98 about an unrecognized file.)

Show Map Network Drive button in toolbar   This adds the button for mapping network drives to every toolbar.

Show file attributes in Detail View   If you always want to see individual file attributes (whether a file is backed up or a system file, for example), check this box.

Show pop-up description for folder and desktop items   This controls the descriptive boxes that open when you move your pointer over icons such as My Computer. Remove the checkmark when you've seen enough of them.

Allow all uppercase names   Want folders with NAMES ALL IN CAPITAL LETTERS? Check this box, and you got 'em.

Hidden files   Choose one of these options:

> **Do not show hidden or system files**   Reduces clutter by not showing files with either the Hidden or System attributes. This will help make sure you do not accidentally rename or otherwise tamper with system files.

> **Do not show hidden files**   Reduces clutter and increases the security of your system a bit by not showing files whose Hidden attributes have been set.

> **Show all files**   All files will be listed, regardless of attributes.

Hide icons when desktop is viewed as Web page   With this option, you can hide your desktop icons for a better view of background Active Desktop displays. This setting—only the Taskbar and HTML items are visible on the desktop—is helpful if you're working in an intranet setting where virtually every task is done through Web pages.

Smooth edges of screen fonts   This will improve the appearance of large fonts but may slow your computer.

Show window contents while dragging   This option should be disabled if you notice an annoying jerkiness when you drag a window, or if it takes a long time to drag a window.

Thumbnail View

Most text files you create can be given descriptive names—look in a folder and you can instantly tell the difference between *Marketing Budget-Q1 1998* and *My Trip to Papeete.* But graphics files can be considerably more mysterious. If the software that makes the graphics supports it, you can choose to have the graphics displayed in the form of thumbnail versions. For example, Figure 4.8 shows a folder of scanned images in Large Icons view. Not a lot of information here. You may have to open several files to find the one you want.

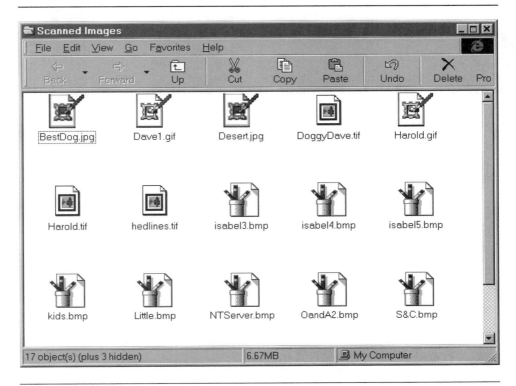

FIGURE 4.8: Looking at graphics files in a folder

Change to Thumbnail view (see Figure 4.9), and you at least have hope for picking the right one to open.

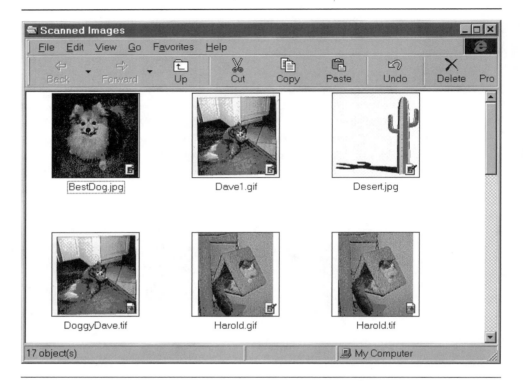

FIGURE 4.9: The same graphics files in Thumbnail view

The thumbnail option isn't available by default, so you have to set it for each folder where you want to use it.

1. Find the folder using Windows Explorer or My Computer.

2. Right-click the folder and select Properties from the pop-up menu.

3. At the bottom of the General page, put a checkmark in the box next to Enable Thumbnail View. Click OK.

4. Now open the folder and select View ➢ Thumbnails.

Depending on your computer's speed, it may take a few seconds for the thumbnail views to start showing up. Some files can't appear as thumbnails, but most graphic files can.

Making a New File

For most programs, you'll probably make new files as you always have: by opening the application and selecting New from the File menu. However, a number of applications do place themselves on a New File menu, and you can make new files from there.

On the Desktop

To create a new file on the desktop, right-click on the desktop in some unoccupied space, and select New and then the file type from the pop-up menu. A file icon will appear with the cursor already placed for you to type in a name.

Skill 4

This file is located on your hard drive in the Desktop folder inside the Windows folder. Figure 4.10 shows this new file as it appears in Windows Explorer.

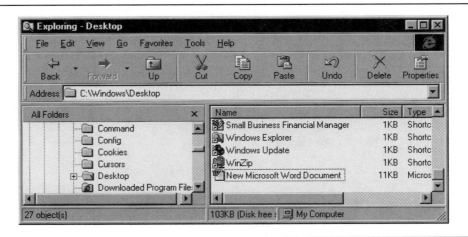

FIGURE 4.10: The new file on the desktop can also be seen in Windows Explorer.

TIP   If you can't see the Desktop folder, it's because Do Not Show Hidden Files is checked under View ➤ Folder Options ➤ View. Check Show All Files instead, and the Desktop folder will appear.

Inside Another Folder

To make a file inside another folder (for example, in Windows Explorer), open the folder that'll be the outside folder. Right-click on a blank spot and select New from the pop-up menu. In the dialog box that appears, select the type of file from the list and type in the name for the new file.

TIP   Make a file in the wrong place? Just right-click on the errant file and select Delete. You'll be asked to confirm that you want to send the file to the Recycle Bin. Or read "Moving and Copying Files and Folders" later in this skill to move the file to a better location.

File Properties

As a rule, most Properties sheets for files are a single page like the one shown in Figure 4.11. It will include some information about the file's location, size, and creation date. There will also be boxes for setting and removing attributes as described previously under "Setting Folder Properties."

A few programs include other pages on the Properties sheets for files. For example, Word for Windows file Properties sheets have additional pages, including a page of statistics about the file and another page of summary information about the file. As more programs are written specifically for 32-bit Windows (95 and 98), this trend toward including ever more data on the Properties sheets is likely to continue.

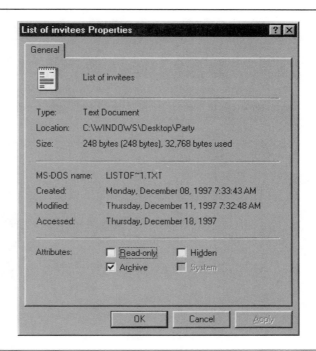

FIGURE 4.11: A file's Properties sheet

Registering File Types

When you click a file to open it—either in Windows Explorer or My Computer or another folder—Windows 98 checks to find what application (program) made the file. Files can't be opened except by an application. Ordinarily, when you install a program, Windows 98 *registers* the file types associated with the program. For example, files with the extension .doc are Word files, files with the extension .wpd are WordPerfect files, and files with the extension .pdf are Acrobat files.

Skill 4

In general, this system works pretty well. However, there are some annoying programs that, when you install them, change your file types without asking. You may try to open, let's say, a graphics file, and find that it doesn't open in the program you expected. To get back to the program you want, you'll need to change how the file type is registered.

To make changes in how files are registered, select Folder Options from the View menu in any window. Click the File Types tab in the Folder Options dialog box to see a listing of all the file types that are registered with Windows 98 on your machine. If you highlight a file type, you'll see details as shown in Figure 4.12. This includes the extensions used for the file type and the name of the program that works with the files.

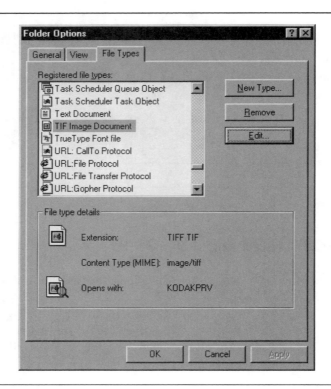

FIGURE 4.12: This list shows the file types that are registered with Windows 98.

In Figure 4.12, you can see that Windows 98 has decided that all TIF graphics files should be opened in the Kodak Imaging applet, but you want to use the Paint program instead. Here's how to make the change:

1. After highlighting the file type you want to change, on the File Types tab, click Edit. In the window that opens, look for the Actions window and highlight *open* (see Figure 4.13).

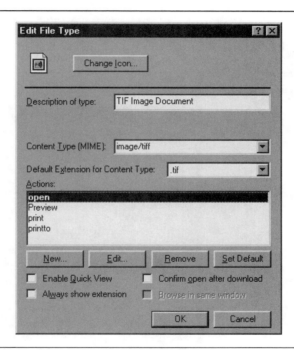

FIGURE 4.13: Editing a file type

2. Click Edit. Enter the path for the application used to open TIF files. Browse to find the application, if necessary (see Figure 4.14).

3. Click OK when you're finished.

Now when you return to the File Types page, you can see that TIF files will now open with Paint (see Figure 4.15).

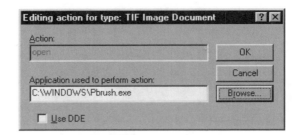

FIGURE 4.14: Changing the application registered to open TIF files to the Paint applet

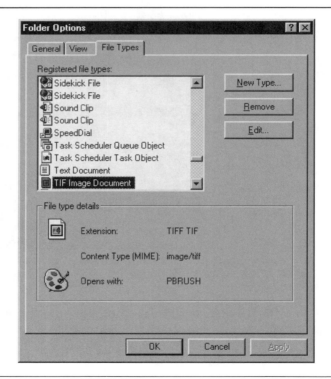

FIGURE 4.15: Now when you click a TIF file, the Paint applet will be used to open it.

As you can see from Figure 4.13, you can also change the icon associated with a file type and change other actions for the file type as well.

Moving and Copying Files and Folders

There are at least three different methods for moving and copying files or folders. You can adopt one method and use it all the time, or you can pick and choose from the various methods, depending on the circumstances.

Move or Copy Using Right Drag and Drop

This is my personal favorite because it requires a minimum of thought:

1. Locate the file or folder using Windows Explorer or My Computer.

2. Right-click on the file or folder.

3. Hold the button down and drag the object to its new location.

4. Release the mouse button and choose Move or Copy from the pop-up menu.

For the shortest distance between two points, you may want to open a second window of Windows Explorer so you can drag and drop directly. Or you can move or copy the object to the desktop, and then open the destination folder or drive and drag the object a second time.

Move or Copy Using Left Drag and Drop

This method requires a bit more mental attention because when you use the left mouse button to drag and drop, the result is a move only if the source and destination are on the same drive letter. If they are on different drives, the result will be a copy.

Follow these steps:

1. Locate the file or folder using Windows Explorer or My Computer.

2. Left-click on the file or folder.

3. Hold the button down and drag the object to its new location.

4. Release the mouse button and choose Move or Copy from the pop-up menu.

If you see a black plus sign in the transparent icon as you drag, a copy will be made when you release the left mouse button.

Notes for
Francine.txt   Notes for
                      Francine.txt

If you're dragging a *program* file (one with the extension .exe, .com, or .bat), Windows 98 will create a shortcut to the original file at the destination. You can tell that a shortcut is being made because a shortcut arrow will appear in the transparent icon that you're dragging.

MSHEARTS.EXE

In both cases, you can force a move to happen by pressing and holding the Shift key before you release the left mouse button.

 TIP   If you decide while dragging to cancel the move or copy, just hit the Escape key before you release the mouse button. This stops the drag but leaves the files or folders highlighted.

Move or Copy Using Cut/Copy and Paste

Using the right mouse button menu to move or copy files and folders is very efficient because you don't need both the source and destination available at the same time.

To move or copy a file, follow these steps:

1. Locate the file or folder you want to move or copy, using My Computer or Windows Explorer.

2. Right-click on the object and select Cut (to move) or Copy from the pop-up menu.

3. Find the destination folder and open it.

4. Right-click on a blank spot inside the folder and select Paste from the pop-up menu.

> **TIP** There are a few objects, such as disk icons, that you can't move or copy. If you try to, you'll get a message informing you of this fact and asking if you want a shortcut instead.

Deleting Files and Folders

The easiest way to delete a file or folder is to click on it once with the right mouse button and select Delete from the pop-up menu. Or you can highlight the object with the left mouse button and then press the Delete key on your keyboard.

Another method is to drag and drop the object onto the Recycle Bin icon. A plus of this method is that you won't be asked to confirm that you want to delete the file.

In any of the above methods, the Recycle Bin protects the user from over-hasty deletions. The data is not instantly deleted—it can be retrieved from the Recycle Bin if you later decide you want it back. There's much more on the Recycle Bin in Skill 3.

> **TIP** To delete a file or folder without sending it to the Recycle Bin, press the Shift key while you select Delete from the pop-up menu or while pressing the Delete key.

Using Long Filenames

Introduced with Windows 95, the ability to use long filenames is a very useful feature—in fact, it's hard to imagine how we got along without it. File and folder names can be as long as 250 characters. However, you don't want to get carried away because the full path, including folder and subfolder names, can't exceed 258 characters.

Filenames can include spaces as well as characters like the comma, semicolon, equals sign (=), and square brackets ([ ]). The following characters are still not allowed in either file or folder names:

\ / * < > : ? " |

File and folder names can also have both upper and lowercase letters, and the system will preserve them. However, this is for display purposes. When you type in the name, you don't have to remember whether you capitalized some part of it or not. Windows 98 will find it as long as the spelling is correct.

TIP   If you want to have folders or files with all uppercase names, you'll need to specify that by opening any folder and selecting View ➤ Folder Options ➤ View and then *Allow all uppercase names.*

Long Filenames in DOS

The DOS commands that come with Windows 98 also know how to handle long filenames. Figure 4.16 shows some files and shortcuts as they appear in an open window in Windows 98.

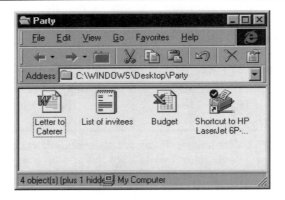

FIGURE 4.16   Contents of the Party folder

Figure 4.17 shows those same items in a DOS window.

As you can see, the long filenames are preserved on the right, while shortened versions appear on the left. As a rule, DOS will make the short filename by taking the first six letters of the long filename and appending a tilde (~) and a number. So if you have a series of files called Chapter 1, Chapter 2, and Chapter 3, they'll show up in a DOS window as Chapte~1, Chapte~2, and so forth.

 **WARNING**   Numbers added to make short filenames are used in the order that the files are created. So if you create Chapter 3 first, it will be named Chapte~1, not Chapte~3 as you might expect.

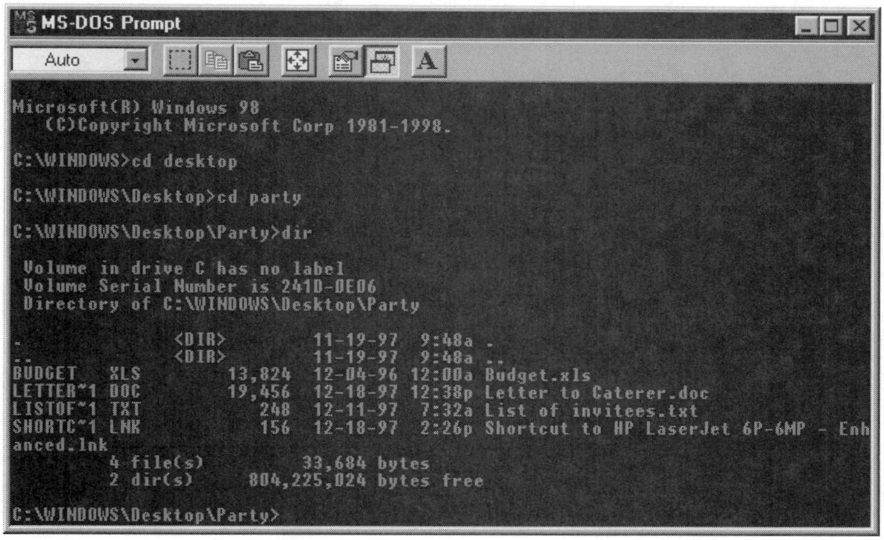

FIGURE 4.17: The same objects displayed in a DOS window

Limitations of Long Filenames

Unless you're running all 32-bit Windows programs (and few of us are), the long filenames will be truncated when you view them from inside the program. For example, if you've made a file in WordPad called Magdalena's Party Invitation and then want to open it in Word for Windows 2.0 (which predates Windows 95 and Windows 98), you'll see the filename has changed to Magdal~1.

After you modify and save the file, though, and return to WordPad, the long name will still be intact.

Similarly, if you copy some files to a diskette and take those files to a computer running DOS or Windows 3.1, you can edit the files on the floppy disk and, when you return to the Windows 98 machine, the long filenames will be intact. However, if you copy those files to the other machine's hard drive and edit them, later copying them back to the floppy, when you return to your Windows 98 machine, the long names will be replaced by short names.

Renaming Files and Folders

To rename a file or folder, right-click on the name and select Rename from the menu. If you're using the click once to select, click twice to open mouse setting, you can also click on the name twice (with about a second between each click), and the name will be highlighted so you can type in a new one.

Unfortunately, there's no provision for renaming a group of files. However, you can still find File Manager (winfile.exe) in the main Windows folder and use it to rename files in a single batch.

The Undo Command

When you move, copy, or rename something, the command to undo that action gets added to a stack maintained by Windows 98. The stack is built up as you move, copy, and rename. The most recent action is on top.

To undo an action, you can click the Undo button on the window's toolbar or you can right-click on the desktop or in a free area of a folder. The Undo command will be on the pop-up menu.

The unwieldy thing about Undo is that it's a big and global stack. You can merrily undo dozens of commands, and you may not be able to see where the Undo is taking place and just what moves and copies and renames are being undone (particularly if you've been working in a variety of folders). So it's best to use Undo quickly and to do it in the folder where you performed the original action. That way you can see the results of Undo.

TIP   If you don't remember what you did last, and therefore don't know what Undo will undo, rest your mouse pointer on the button, and the pop-up help will tell you whether it was a move, copy, or rename. The pop-up menu on the desktop always remembers what the last action was.

Are You Experienced?

Now you can...

☑ **Select files and folders**

☑ **Create new folders and files**

☑ **Register file types**

☑ **Move, copy, and delete files and folders**

☑ **Assign long filenames**

☑ **Undo a wrong move**

SKILL 5

BROWSING THE LOCAL SCENE WITH INTERNET BROWSER

- Accessing Internet Explorer from the desktop
- Opening local files in Internet Explorer
- Reading files offline
- Editing pages in FrontPage Express

Programs and features you use to gather and distribute information on the Internet are now included as an integral part of Windows 98. In this skill, you'll learn how to use Internet Explorer to open and read files on your computer and your network, and how to edit local pages using FrontPage Express.

Accessing Internet Explorer from the Desktop

By the name of the program, you can tell that Internet Explorer is used to find information on the Internet. But Internet Explorer is not limited to just displaying this information; you can also use it to access files on your computer or network.

Internet Explorer shows files that are coded in Hypertext Markup Language (HTML). You can use Internet Explorer to display any HTML page, whether the page is on the World Wide Web, your C: drive, or your network.

 NOTE   You'll learn more about HTML codes in the section "Editing a Local File in FrontPage Express" near the end of this skill.

There are two ways to open Internet Explorer from the desktop. You can:

- Click the Launch Internet Explorer Browser button on the Taskbar.

- Click the Start button, point to Programs, point to Internet Explorer, and then click Internet Explorer.

Opening Files on Your PC

You don't have to actually connect to the Internet when you open Internet Explorer. If you see the Dial-Up Connection box when you open Internet Explorer, click Work Offline to indicate you don't want to connect to the Internet.

When you're offline, you can open any file on your computer or network.

> **NOTE**   In this case, the term *network* refers to the shared and mapped drives that are available to you. A network is not the same thing as an intranet. An *intranet* is your company's own internal web that uses the same communication protocols as the World Wide Web.

There are many ways to open files on your PC in Internet Explorer. In this skill, we'll use the Address bar to type in a filename, open the Explorer bar to revisit recent files, and customize the Links bar with pages you visit most often.

Using the Address Bar

To make opening files standard across all programs in Windows 98, the Address bar is included not only in Internet Explorer, but in Windows Explorer, My Computer, Control Panel, and almost every other screen you open in Windows. You can even add the Address bar to the Taskbar.

> **NOTE**   For information about adding the Address bar to the Taskbar, see Skill 1.

The Address bar works the same way whether you are using it in Internet Explorer or on another screen. On any Address bar, you can either enter a filename or click the down arrow and look for the file you want to open. This section focuses on using the Address bar in Internet Explorer.

When you type a filename or the address of a Web page on the Address bar, the file opens in the appropriate application. For example, if you type **C:\My Documents\Myfile.htm** on the Address bar, the local file on your C: drive opens in Internet Explorer (because the .htm extension on the filename indicates the file is an HTML file, and HTML files are displayed in Internet Explorer). If you open a .doc file, the file opens in Microsoft Word. If you type a Web address, such as `www.microsoft.com`, you are connected to the Internet and the Web page opens.

Figure 5.1 shows a local filename on the Address bar, with the file displayed in Internet Explorer.

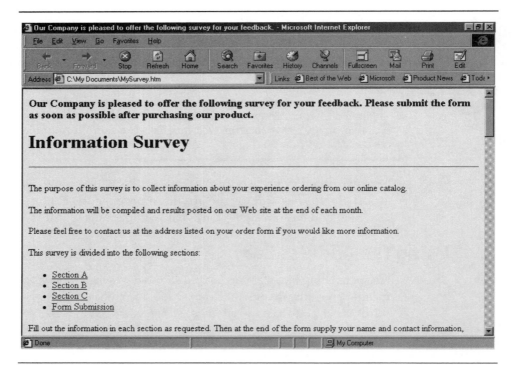

FIGURE 5.1: Local file displayed in Internet Explorer

Using the Explorer Bar

Whenever you open a file in Internet Explorer, the filename is stored in your History folder. The list of entries in your History folder is displayed on the Explorer bar, as shown in Figure 5.2.

To open the Explorer bar and view the files you've visited recently, click the History button on the toolbar.

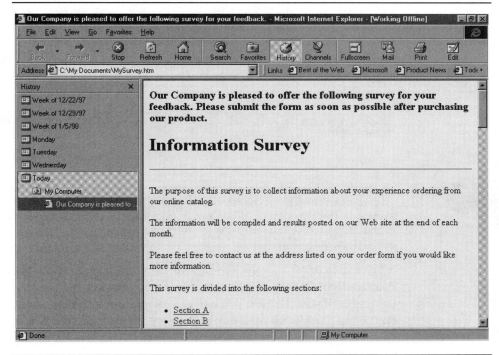

FIGURE 5.2: Viewing History entries on the Explorer bar

Skill 5

TIP   You can also reveal the history entries on the Explorer bar by selecting View ➢ Explorer Bar ➢ History.

To close the Explorer bar, click the Close button at the top of the Explorer bar, or click the History button on the toolbar.

Customizing the Links Bar

The Links bar, sometimes referred to as the Quick Links bar, is the section of the toolbar that holds the links you visit frequently. The Links bar is placed next to the Address bar, but if it's not convenient for you there, you can move it by dragging it to a different location on the toolbar.

Preselected links, like Best of the Web and Web Gallery, appear on the bar when you open Internet Explorer.

 TIP   If you can't see all of the headings on the Links bar, place the pointer on the bar next to the Links label. When the pointer changes to a two-headed arrow, drag the arrow to the left and right to resize the bar.

The Links bar is the place to store the links you want to see all the time on your toolbar. Be careful, however, not to overdo it. When the Links bar exceeds the width of your screen, you have to use the left and right arrows that appear on the bar to view all of the links. If you have a lot of links you refer to repeatedly, try saving some of them as Favorites. (Adding links to your Favorites list is covered in Skill 7.)

To add a link to the Links bar, use one of these methods:

- Access a page in Internet Explorer, and drag the icon from the Address bar to the Links bar, as shown in Figure 5.3. The shortcut arrow will appear, showing exactly where you can drop the icon.

- Locate the link you want to save within the body of the page, and drag the link to the Links bar.

FIGURE 5.3: Adding a link to the Links bar

To change the order in which the links appear, drag each link until you have them lined up in the sequence you want.

To delete a link from the Links bar, right-click the link and select Delete on the pop-up menu.

 TIP You can add the Links bar to the Taskbar. Right-click any blank spot on the Taskbar, point to Toolbars, and click Links.

Opening Files on Your Network

Having the Address bar on so many screens makes it easy to open files, no matter where the files are located. If you know the full name of the file, it doesn't matter whether the file is on your network, your computer, or even the Internet. You type the full filename on the Address bar, and the system finds the file and opens it for you.

If you don't know the full filename, there are a few more steps involved in opening the file. Suppose you want to open the Contract97.htm file that's on your network. Click the down arrow on the Address bar and select the network drive. If the network drive isn't on the list, just type in the address. The Windows Explorer window opens, and the folders and files contained on the drive are displayed. Select the Contract97.htm file, and it opens in Internet Explorer.

NOTE Remember, the file you select opens in the application associated with the file type.

You can use the same steps to locate a file and open it whether the file is on your network or on your computer.

Reading Web Pages Offline

While you're working offline, you can use your time in Internet Explorer to read files you've downloaded from the Web. Whenever you subscribe to a page, you'll be asked if you want to download information to read at your leisure.

 NOTE You'll learn how to subscribe to a site on your Favorites list in Skill 7, and how to subscribe to a channel in Skill 11.

Information downloaded from the sites you've subscribed to is stored in the Windows\Temporary Internet Files folder. You can read this information from your computer without connecting to the Internet. This is a good way to limit your connection time if your Internet service provider charges by the minute or hour.

 TIP Pages you've visited recently are also stored in the Temporary Internet Files folder.

To read a page offline:

1. Open Internet Explorer. If the Dial-Up Connection dialog box appears, click Work Offline.

2. Click the Favorites button on the toolbar. The Explorer Bar opens, and your Favorites list is displayed. You can read any of the pages you've subscribed to and marked for offline viewing.

3. On the Favorites list, click the page you want to read. The page is displayed in the viewing area on the screen, as shown in Figure 5.4.

If you see a message or dialog box prompting you to connect to the Internet, the page is not stored in your temporary folder, and you cannot read it offline.

 TIP   To view history pages offline, click the History button on the toolbar, and then click the page you want to see. History files are cleaned out by Disk Cleanup (see Skill 16) and according to the timeline you set up in the View ➢ Internet Options dialog box. You won't be able to view a history file offline if it has been deleted from the History folder.

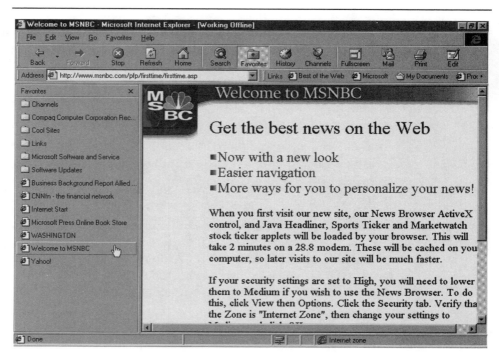

FIGURE 5.4: Viewing a page from the Favorites list offline: screen shot of MSNBC used by permission from MSNBC.

Editing a Local File in FrontPage Express

With FrontPage Express, editing a page coded in HTML is as easy as editing a text file on your computer. You don't need to know HTML to edit or create a page; you enter the text and graphics you want included on the page, and use the toolbars in FrontPage Express to format the page in HTML.

WHAT IS HYPERTEXT MARKUP LANGUAGE (HTML)?

Documents to be distributed on the World Wide Web, or on a company's intranet, are written using HTML codes. These codes define how the text will look (whether it's bold or italic, centered or indented, etc.), where graphics files are located and how they're placed, and where you'll go when you click a link on a page.

HTML codes are required for documents transmitted on the Web. If you're the type of person who likes to see behind the scenes or do it yourself, you can view the HTML codes in FrontPage Express and even edit the codes manually. If you'd rather concentrate on adding content and formatting a page, you can let FrontPage Express add the HTML codes for you.

Most files destined for the World Wide Web start as local files on your computer. After all, you don't want to post something for the world to see until you've reviewed it, proofed it, and tested it yourself.

A Web page is made up of different components, including:

Text   To relay narrative information

Tables   To convey statistical or survey data

Frames   To organize information on the page

Graphics   To add visual interest to the page and illustrate the text

Sound files   To augment the text and graphics

Animation or video files   To illustrate difficult concepts and bring the page to life

Web pages are not available to everyone on the World Wide Web until you publish them. During the development process, most people keep their HTML files stored on their local computer and revise them locally until the pages are ready to be posted on the Web.

To edit a Web page:

1. Open Internet Explorer. If the Dial-Up Connection dialog box appears, click Work Offline.

2. Enter the filename on the Address bar. The file is displayed in Internet Explorer.

 NOTE

Although FrontPage Express is a WYSIWYG program (which means what you see on the screen is the way it's supposed to look when it's published), it's a good idea to view your page in Internet Explorer to make sure the format is what you want. If you have access to other browsers besides Internet Explorer, test your page in the other browsers, too.

3. Select Page from the Edit menu. The FrontPage Express window opens and the page is displayed, as shown in Figure 5.5. You can add, change, and delete text, or use any of the commands on the menus and toolbars to change the appearance of the page. Comments or instructions that are used by the author of the page, and are not for publication on the Web, are visible in FrontPage Express.

 NOTE

If you have not used FrontPage Express before, you might get an error message when you click the Edit button. To resolve the error, you can follow the instructions in the dialog box that's displayed, or do this: Exit Internet Explorer, start FrontPage Express (click Start ➤ Programs ➤ Internet Explorer ➤ FrontPage Express) and then close it, and go back to Internet Explorer.

4. Select File ➤ Save to save your changes. Close the FrontPage Express window.

5. In Internet Explorer, click the Refresh button on the toolbar. Your changes will be displayed on the screen.

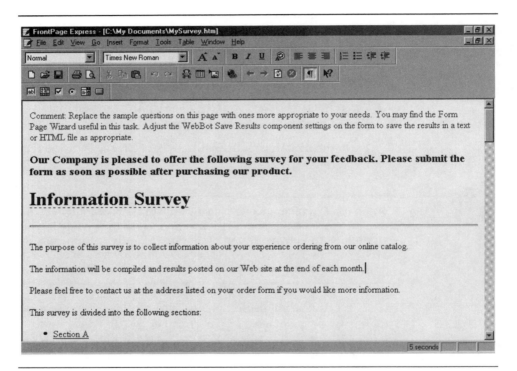

FIGURE 5.5: Editing a local file in FrontPage Express

To see the "raw" HTML codes used to create your page, select View ➤ HTML. The HTML codes are highlighted in color on the screen, as shown in Figure 5.6.

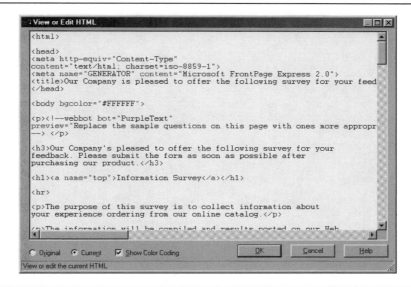

FIGURE 5.6: HTML codes are denoted by the < and > symbols and highlighted in color.

Are You Experienced?

Now you can...

- ☑ **Access Internet Explorer from the desktop**
- ☑ **Open local files in Internet Explorer using the Address bar and the Explorer bar**
- ☑ **Read information from the World Wide Web offline**
- ☑ **Edit an HTML page in FrontPage Express**

SKILL 6

CONNECTING TO THE INTERNET

- Selecting the type of service
- Connecting to an online service
- America Online
- CompuServe
- Prodigy Internet
- Microsoft Network
- AT&T WorldNet
- Connecting to an existing account
- Setting up a new Internet account

Here it is, almost the year 2000, and if you don't have a connection to the Internet, you may be feeling a bit left out. Or perhaps you've heard lots of stuff about the Internet and remain unimpressed. You're the skeptical type and wonder what's in it for you?

Actually, you can think of the Internet as one of those one-size-fits-all garments that, in fact, fit no one *perfectly*. However, with a nip here and a tuck there, you can usually get a decent fit.

Or, to try another analogy, you can think of the Internet as a very, very big college campus with many branches. There's plenty for everyone once you know how to find it. And like on a big campus, you can focus on serious study, goof off, or do some of both. It's all available. It's up to you to pick and choose.

In this skill, we'll cover the various ways to connect to the Internet and how choosing the "right" way for you can enhance your use of this vast resource. Then we'll go over the major online services that you can sign up with directly from Windows 98.

OBLIGATORY "WHAT IS THE INTERNET" SECTION

Nobody owns the Internet and nobody controls it. The Internet is in fact a loose connection of thousands of networks scattered all over the globe. The only thing all the networks have in common is the use of the same transmission language, known as TCP/IP. (Fortunately, you don't need to know anything about TCP/IP to use the Internet.)

The Internet started out as a government project in the 1960s called the ARPAnet (after the Advanced Research Projects Agency) which supervised it in the beginning. After more government and educational institutions got involved, it grew into an *internetwork*, sending information almost instantaneously from one computer to another. It was a method for scientists and academics to communicate quickly with each other. That's why it took a while for the news of the Internet to filter down to ordinary folk. Unless you worked or went to school at an Internet site, there was no reason for you to even know of its existence.

continued ▶

Since 1993 or thereabouts, the Internet has been a hot topic—with new people flocking to use it at a current rate of about a million new connections a month!

The backbone of the Internet is made up of very high-speed communications links owned by companies like AT&T and Sprint or, in some places, by governments. Connections to the backbone are made by Internet service providers (ISPs) who then sell access to individuals or companies.

Choosing a Service

In general, there are two basic ways to connect to the Internet. One is by way of an Internet service provider (ISP). ISPs are essentially a "pass-though" connection. Aside from basic technical support for the connection itself, an ISP just sets you up so you can use Internet mail, the World Wide Web, and perhaps some of the older basic Internet services such as ftp and gopher. If the ISP is local, you will have to make other arrangements to pick up your e-mail when you travel. If it's a national ISP, it may have phone numbers in locations where you travel.

 TIP   In my office, I have an ISDN connection to an ISP. When I travel, I have my mail forwarded to an AT&T WorldNet account that costs $4.95 per month for five hours of access. Because I use it just to pick up mail, I never use more than the five hours.

Another way of connecting is through an online service (such as America Online or CompuServe), which also provides a gateway for Internet mail and access to the World Wide Web. In addition, the service itself will have content such as forums for discussions, chat rooms, reference material (dictionaries, encyclopedias), news, weather, and other stuff. Generally, the online services have telephone numbers for access throughout the United States and Canada. Some also have international numbers so you can connect from Europe or Asia.

Skill 6

Internet Service Providers

Most cities and even many smaller towns have local companies that offer access to the Internet. If you can find a good one, it can be an excellent option.

You may find that a local company can give more personal attention to any problems you may face in setting up your service. And if you want help with a larger project such as setting up and maintaining a Web site for a home-based business, a good local service may be much better than a larger company.

Unfortunately, there are also some genuine duds among local Internet service providers—guys who think they're going to strike it rich on the Internet and set up an ISP in their basement with inadequate servers, few modems, and no clue at all.

Before you sign up with an ISP, ask friends and colleagues for their recommendations. Occasionally, local newspapers or computer-user magazines may provide reviews and comparisons.

 NOTE

Many local telephone companies and some cable TV companies are also getting into the Internet access business. Some phone companies offer packages that include an ISDN line and adapter, for faster access than you can get with any modem. The fastest home Internet access is via TV cable systems. It is currently available only in a few limited areas, but if you live in one of those areas, you should probably check into it.

You should expect an ISP to provide you with software and enough technical support to make you comfortable. Make sure the dial-up connection uses a *local* phone number, or your phone bill could end up higher than your Internet connection bill. And be prepared to switch companies if the one you try isn't up to the mark.

Online Services

Online services offer a variety of special features in addition to e-mail and Internet access. Each of the four major online services has its own history, strengths, and weaknesses. All of them have extensive networks of access phone numbers in the United States, and varying degrees and methods of access in other parts of the world.

America Online (the biggest) and the Microsoft Network (the newest) are attempting to make the online medium a whole new experience, using television as their inspiration. AOL also has very popular chat services. CompuServe (CSi) focuses on business users and computer professionals, with bigger libraries of downloadable files than any other service. It also offers extensive extra-cost services. Prodigy Internet is basically a national Internet service provider that includes some special features such as chat facilities and aggregates Web content for easier access.

 TIP
America Online and CompuServe include e-mail capability in their proprietary software. All the other online services will use Outlook Express for mail and newsgroups unless you install a third-party mail program. But why should you? Outlook Express is free with Windows 98, it's a terrific program, and you can read all about how it works in Skill 9.

All of the online services attempt to make the online experience easier for newcomers. That alone is reason enough for some new users to prefer them. In addition, all now use either Internet Explorer or Netscape Navigator (or both) for Internet access, so you are not limited to their specialized interfaces.

TIP
Whether you choose an online service or an Internet service provider, wait a week or two before sending your new e-mail address to absolutely *everyone* you know. And wait a month or two before getting your e-mail address printed on business cards or letterhead. Sometimes your first choice of service doesn't work out, and you may have to switch before finding a good fit.

The Online Services folder is shown in Figure 6.1. The About the Online Services file includes useful information and—most importantly—technical support phone numbers for each of the services, in case you have difficulty getting a service set up.

Skill 6

FIGURE 6.1: Online services sign-up central

The next sections describe the services that come with Windows 98, along with instructions for setting up a new account at each. You can also use the online services icons to reinstall software for a service with which you already have an account.

Remember that whenever you are online, your phone line will be in use, calling the access number you choose when you set up the online service's software. If this is not a local call, the toll charges from your phone company can run up very quickly. When signing up with any of these services, you will want to have your phone book handy to check your local dialing area.

Although all the services generally provide a free trial period, they require you to provide billing information, usually a credit card number or checking account information, when you sign up. It's up to you to cancel your account if you decide not to keep it. Otherwise, the charges will start appearing automatically after the free trial expires, whether or not you actually use the service.

America Online

America Online (AOL) is the biggest and in many respects the glitziest of the online services. It provides a supportive "home" community for people new to the online world. AOL's chat groups are well organized and generally civil, and have a consistent level of participation. AOL also features more online chats with celebrities than any other service.

AOL has an excellent collection of online periodicals, including *Rolling Stone* and @Times, which includes more of *The New York Times* than is available on the paper's Web site. AOL also develops original content such as Parent Soup and a series of regional guides. Many of these services are now also available on the Web, but the AOL version is often more complete.

Like the other online services, AOL handles members' e-mail to and from any Internet address. It also offers additional e-mail services that only work between AOL members. For example, you can call a message back before the addressee has read it, or send Instant Messages that pop up on the screens of friends who are currently online. Also, AOL allows several e-mail addresses per account; family members living apart can exchange e-mail while sharing a single AOL account. AOL software also provides "flash sessions," which allow the user to quickly upload finished e-mail and newsgroup messages, and download waiting e-mail and marked files. This minimizes time online, and allows you to automate the process and do something else while downloading.

AOL's selection of downloadable software, drivers, and other files is smaller than what CompuServe offers, but AOL makes it easier to find what you're looking for. The service's biggest drawback is also the one for which it has been in the news: not enough network capacity for its huge, and still growing, number of subscribers. That situation has improved since its worst period in late 1996 and early 1997, but still presents some difficulties.

To sign up for America Online, open the Online Services folder and click the AOL icon. Choose U.S., Canada, or UK service as shown in Figure 6.2. If your hardware is not up to snuff (Pentium or better), you get a warning that this version of AOL is not recommended. Contact AOL at the phone number listed in the About the Online Services text file in the Online Services folder to get AOL version 3 for Windows 3.1, which will run on 486 computers *and* Windows 98 (though slowly).

Skill 6

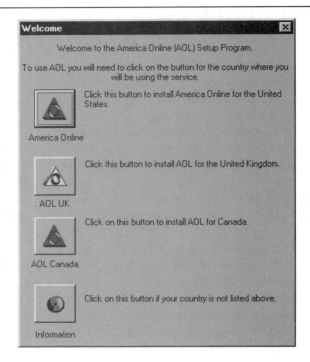

FIGURE 6.2: Choosing the service by country

Next comes the dialog box shown in Figure 6.3. Select the option that applies to you—it's the first one if you're not already a member of AOL, and the third one if you already have an AOL account and want to install it on this computer.

The next screens deal with the location of the software that's to be installed, the amount of disk space it'll require, and whether you want AOL to automatically launch when you first start up your computer. Then the installation begins. This takes only a couple of minutes.

When the You're Almost Finished! box (shown in Figure 6.4) opens, take advantage of the opportunity to print out AOL's quick reference guide. It's not very long, and it will give you valuable information about how to get around in AOL.

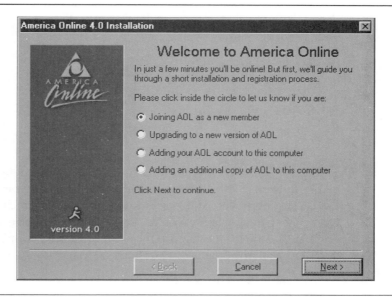

FIGURE 6.3: Getting started with AOL installation

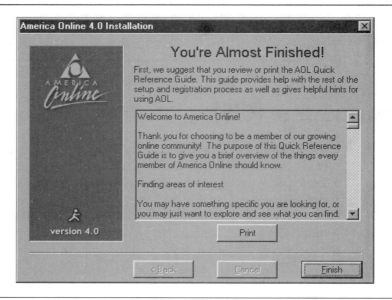

FIGURE 6.4: Click the Print button to print out a copy of the Quick Reference Guide.

Skill 6

After the installation is complete, you'll be asked if you want to sign on now. If you select No, an icon is placed on your desktop, and you can continue at any time by clicking it.

Click the new AOL icon to start the software. After detecting your modem (or LAN connection), it will first connect to a toll-free number and download a list of local access numbers. AOL has lots of local numbers, including quite a few that will work with new 56K modems. Try to find both a primary and a secondary number that are local calls; you may want to have your phone book handy if you don't know all the details of your local calling area.

 NOTE   The down side of AOL is that it's my number one account for *spam*. And what is spam (besides a famous food-like pork product)? Spam is unsolicited, unwanted, junk e-mail. It's a curse to many people online, and while I usually get very little of it on other services, my AOL account is awash in spam. It's not that AOL encourages spam or hasn't tried to deter it. On the contrary, AOL has sued spamsters and banned others—but they still haven't managed to stop it. Or, as far as I can tell, to have even slowed the tide. If you start receiving junk mail on AOL, use the keyword JUNK MAIL for info on combating it.

CompuServe (CIS)

CompuServe, also known as CIS (for CompuServe Interactive Services), is the oldest of the major online services. Although it was recently bought out by America Online, the new owners have promised to continue to operate it as a separate service.

Besides e-mail and Internet access, CIS offers hundreds of well-attended forums where discussions often involve novices as well as those experienced in the subject matter. From computers to law to women in aviation, the range is great. The software also makes it easier to follow a particular discussion thread than with other online services or Internet newsgroups. The software also includes a filing cabinet where you can stash e-mail and forum messages under subject headings you create.

CIS was the first online home of many computer and software companies, and still has the widest array of downloadable software and driver files. Many companies continue to sponsor support forums on CIS even as they also set up Web pages for the same purpose.

CompuServe's greatest strength is in business services. It has such resources as the Newspaper Archives, which is much more extensive than anything available in one place on the Web. There is also a wide range of searchable business databases, many of which involve extra fees for use. The Business Database Plus holds over 2 million articles, available at fees that are quite reasonable in a business context. Many of the business services and databases use older-style plain text interfaces. They may take some getting used to, but their power lies in their content.

Like the other services, CIS offers unlimited service for a fixed monthly price. Although it's a few dollars more per month than some services, it's easily worth it if you need the kind of resources that are available only there.

Install CompuServe software by clicking the icon in the Online Services folder. Choose Express installation unless you want to be able to specify the drive and directory where CompuServe software will be installed or you're connecting through a network. The Custom option allows you to specify this and what type of connection to use.

TIP   CompuServe includes in its installation a request for a *virtual key*. This is essentially a word that's used to make the connection if you access CIS by way of the World Wide Web. The virtual key is the way CIS identifies itself to you. If you see the virtual key when you connect via the WWW, you know it's safe to provide your username and password.

After the installation is complete, you'll need to restart your computer to put the settings into effect. Clicking the CompuServe 4.0 icon at this point will start the software and open the Welcome screen.

Click the Signup button for a new account or Setup if you already have a CIS account. If your computer already has an older version of CompuServe software, the connection settings will be taken over automatically.

For a new account, read the Signup Wizard initial screen and click Next. The list that appears gives you an idea of CompuServe's world-wide access network. You should understand, however, that in many countries, access involves communications surcharges.

The Wizard then asks for information about your phone line and connects to a toll-free number to find the closest local access numbers. After choosing an access number, continue the sign-up process. When you are finished, the CompuServe opening screen will look like Figure 6.5.

NOTE   CIS has done an exemplary job in controlling junk mail. They have a strict policy against CIS members sending spam and they enforce it. If you receive spam from any source, inside or outside of CIS, forward it to FEEDBACK for action.

FIGURE 6.5: CompuServe's opening screen takes you directly to a variety of services.

Prodigy Internet

Though the original Prodigy service attempted to provide unique content to attract users, the current Prodigy Internet is basically a national Internet service provider with a few extras. If you want some guidance as you get started using the Web, Prodigy Internet may have what you want.

Prodigy's service uses your browser rather than special software. In the case of the setup included with Windows 98, that means Internet Explorer 4.0. It also adds a special configurable toolbar for faster access to your favorite features.

Prodigy's unique service is content aggregation. Under the motto "Untangle the Web," it assembles a collection of Web sites in 10 different subject areas. The subjects include music, travel, and computing, and the selected sites have been screened for the quality of their content and for reliability and ease of use. Prodigy users contribute to the ratings that are a part of this process. It can help you find excellent sites within some subject areas without getting lost on the Web.

Clicking the Prodigy icon in the Online Services folder starts Internet Explorer and opens a cached Web page with a variety of information buttons and one to Sign Me Up. Clicking it starts the Internet Connection Wizard and connects to Prodigy's secure server for the sign-up process.

Prodigy shows the strain of being number three or four in the Internet wars. Connections are geographically scant. For example, I live in a fairly densely populated suburb of San Francisco and could find only *one* phone connection in the entire county! If I happened to live in the town where the phone number is located, it would be great. But I don't, and if you don't live near one of the connection points, Prodigy is probably not a good choice.

NOTE   Prodigy has a pretty good history of fighting unsolicited ads (spam). If you receive junk e-mail, forward it to postmaster@prodigy.net—with a note explaining that it's unwanted and unsolicited junk.

The Microsoft Network

Microsoft's own entry into the online service arena, The Microsoft Network (MSN) is a very slick attempt to show what can be done in the field, making heavy use of animation and sound. Unfortunately, this pushes the limits of what can be done with a modem connection. You'll find the MSN icon on the desktop, not in the Online Services folder.

In addition, the content is fairly limited and uneven. Some of the best is on the channels in the area called On Stage. Some of the channel content, and much of the additional content created by MSN, is available to anyone at www.msn.com, or at specific sites such as cartalk.msn.com for National Public Radio's favorite auto mechanics.

There are several useful services in the Essentials area, including the well-known Expedia travel service. Here again, most of it can be reached without an MSN membership.

Click the MSN icon on the desktop to set up the basic MSN software. You'll then be instructed to reboot your computer. After rebooting your machine, the setup program will connect to MSN and sign you up for service as well as download more software to complete the installation. When the process is complete, the opening screen will look like Figure 6.6.

Like America Online and AT&T WorldNet, MSN makes changes to your system. For example, if you already have another Internet account, MSN changes your Internet Explorer home page to MSN. It also installs an icon on the Taskbar in the section called the System Tray (see Figure 6.7). Right-click on the icon to open a menu of choices relating to MSN.

MSN also does its best to counter junk mail. If you receive any while you're an MSN member or any spam originating from an MSN address, forward it to postmaster@msn.com. To save yourself from getting ads that originate on MSN, go to Member Services, click Your Feedback, and then click Communications Preferences. There you can check a box that says you don't want to receive any unsolicited advertisements.

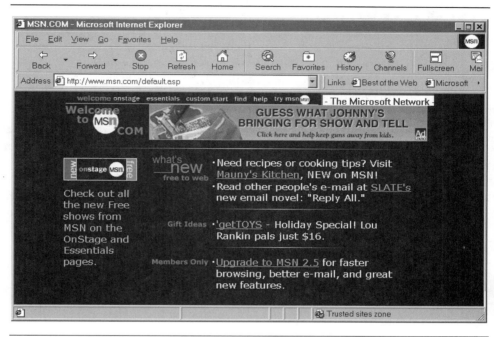

FIGURE 6.6: The Microsoft Network's welcome screen

FIGURE 6.7: Right-click the MSN icon to open a menu of choices relating to MSN.

AT&T WorldNet

Although its software is included in Windows 98's Online Services folder, AT&T WorldNet is not *quite* an online service in the way that the others reviewed here are. It has fewer resources of its own, but there are quite a few options available on the home page.

One of the big attractions of AT&T WorldNet is that the service is free for up to five hours of use a month for your first year—if you use it from a phone line that has AT&T as its long-distance service. Otherwise, the monthly, hourly, or unlimited access rates are similar to those of the online services.

Begin the sign-up process by clicking the AT&T WorldNet icon in the Online Services folder. Follow the instructions; eventually, if you decide to go ahead, the software will dial a toll-free number to carry out the enrollment procedure. Be sure to read the Service Agreement and Operating Policies. Then continue through the pages of the setup, providing requested information and clicking Next to move on.

When you are finished, you'll be using Internet Explorer as your Internet browser. When you log on, you will initially be connected to the AT&T World-Net home page.

Connecting to an Existing Account (Dial-Up)

If you're like most people, you have a *dial-up connection* to the Internet. This simply means that you use a modem to connect your computer with the ISP's computers by way of a regular telephone line. (The other way to connect is by way of a LAN—local area network—or through a dedicated high-speed line. Connecting via a LAN is covered later in this skill.) If your connection is through one of the online services already discussed, simply click the appropriate icon in the Online Services folder and follow the instructions.

If you have an existing account with another ISP that you need to set up on this computer, follow these steps:

1. Click the Connect to the Internet icon on the desktop to start the Internet Connection Wizard.

2. In the first dialog box (shown in Figure 6.8), select the second option, which is to set up an existing account on the current computer. Click Next.

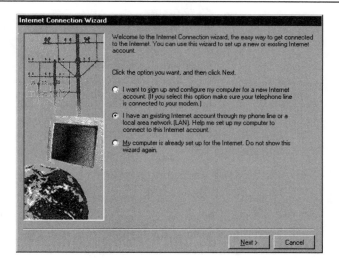

FIGURE 6.8: Setting up an existing account

3. Choose the first option on the next page. Click Next. (If your connection to the Internet is through one of the online services already discussed, simply click the appropriate icon in the Online Services folder or the MSN icon on the desktop and follow the instructions.)

4. On the next page (Figure 6.9), select *Connect using my phone line*. Click Next.

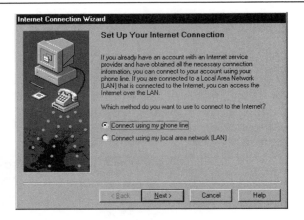

FIGURE 6.9: Setting up the type of connection

5. Next supply the phone number to dial to make the connection to the ISP. Click Next.

6. On the User Name and Password page type in the name and password that identifies you to the ISP.

7. Read the Advanced Settings page (see Figure 6.10). It's unlikely you'll need to change these settings, but if your connection fails, you may have to consult your ISP about making changes to the Advanced Settings.

FIGURE 6.10: Don't change the Advanced Settings unless you know what they're supposed to be!

8. Next provide a name for the connection. (In case you end up with more than one Internet connection, you'll want to be able to identify them easily.)

9. The next step is to set up your Internet e-mail account. If the information about your account is available on the computer, it'll be shown and you'll be asked to confirm it. If the account is unknown to the system, you'll be asked to supply your name, your e-mail address, your username, password, the name of the mail server (if any), and possibly other information.

10. On the Friendly Name page (see Figure 6.11), provide a name that you'll recognize that will sum up the information about this e-mail account.

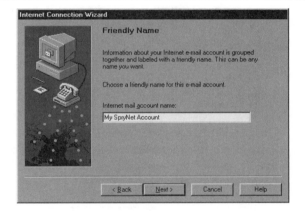

FIGURE 6.11: Providing a "friendly" name

11. On the following screens, you'll be asked for information about setting up a news account. (Your ISP can provide you with the name of your news server.)

12. The final step requires you to set up or skip to an Internet Directory Service. If you've already signed up for such a service with your ISP, provide the name of the server.

When you've provided all the information, click the Finish button. You can always return to change the information by clicking Start ➤ Programs ➤ Internet Explorer ➤ Connection Wizard.

Setting Up a New ISP Account (Dial-Up)

If you don't have an Internet account and don't want to use one of the online services described earlier in this chapter, you definitely have alternatives. To establish a brand new Internet account, follow these steps:

1. Click the Connect to the Internet icon on the desktop to start the Internet Connection Wizard.

2. The Wizard will dial and connect you to the Microsoft Referral Service, then show you a list of ISPs in your area. Choose an ISP and click Next. The information you'll need to provide will vary depending on the ISP. After you provide the information and click Next, you'll be connected to the ISP directly.

3. You'll be presented with a list of phone numbers. If possible, select one that is not a toll call from your location. Click Next.

4. Supply the information requested and follow the instructions to get signed up for the account you want.

   When the setup process is complete, an icon for Internet Explorer will replace the Connect to the Internet icon on the desktop. To connect to the Internet, click the Internet Explorer icon and your modem will dial the ISP, open Internet Explorer, and connect to your Home Page.

 NOTE   To set up an account with an ISP that isn't listed, contact the ISP directly for instructions (and perhaps additional software).

Connecting to an Existing ISP Account (LAN)

If you're working on a network, your Internet connection is probably what's called a *LAN* (local area network) connection. This means that instead of using a modem attached to your machine, the connection to the ISP is made either by a network modem or through a routing device that connects all the network's users to a high-speed communications line.

After you install Windows 98, you have to let the software know about your existing ISP account as well as the LAN connection. To set up the connection, just do the following:

1. Click the Connect to the Internet icon on the desktop to start the Internet Connection Wizard.

2. On the next page, select the second option which is to connect to an existing account. Click Next.

3. On the next page, select the first option and click Next.

4. In the Set Up Your Internet Connection dialog box, select *Connect using my local area network (LAN)*. Click Next.

5. The next page asks if you're connected through a proxy server. If you don't know the answer, ask your system administrator. (If you select Yes, the name of your proxy server(s) and port settings will have to be provided.)

6. To set up an Internet mail account, select Yes and click Next. On the Internet Mail Account page, your existing mail account may be listed (if the installation of Windows 98 was done over an older version of Windows that had the mail account installed). Select the mail account, and your settings will be confirmed.

7. If your account isn't listed, you'll have to opt to create a "new" account. This just means the account is new to Windows 98. On subsequent pages, you'll be asked to provide your name, your e-mail address, your username, password, the name of the mail server, the name of the news server (if any), and possibly other information.

8. The final step requires you to set up or skip an Internet Directory Service. If you've already signed up for such a service with your ISP, provide the name of the server.

When you've provided all the information, click the Finish button. You can always return to change the information by clicking Start ➣ Programs ➣ Internet Explorer ➣ Connection Wizard.

Skill 6

TIP   If your LAN runs an ISDN (or faster) connection to the Internet you can get a very speedy connection to CompuServe, MSN, Prodigy, AT&T, or AOL through your ISP (once you run the appropriate software for CompuServe, MSN, etc., in the Online Services folder). However, you won't be able to make an ISDN (or faster) connection to another ISP without specific system configurations that will inevitably involve your network's system administrator.

NOTE   Setting up a new ISP account on a local area network (LAN) is a task for the network administrator, involving as it does, routers, gateways, and various forms of permissions.

Are You Experienced?

Now you can...

- ☑ Select an Internet provider
- ☑ Sign up with an online service
- ☑ Connect to an existing ISP account
- ☑ Set up a new ISP account

SKILL 7

EXPLORING THE OUTSIDE WORLD

- Browsing the World Wide Web
- Saving links to your favorite Web sites
- Customizing the Internet Explorer screen
- Setting up your security on the Internet
- Publishing pages on the World Wide Web
- Holding meetings on the Internet

It's a big world out there, and to visit it, you don't even have to leave your office. Using the Internet brings the outside world to your desk. The Internet is a global network made up of thousands of networks that communicate with each other.

The Internet offers a diverse range of information and ideas. On the Internet, you'll find information about almost every topic you can think of, and you can share your knowledge and interests with others. With the Internet, you can read about scientific discoveries, publish your latest poem, or talk with friends and colleagues around the world.

Discovering the World Wide Web

The World Wide Web has become the most popular part of the Internet. The Web is made up of *hypertext* documents stored on servers around the world. Hypertext documents contain links you can click on to move to another section of the page, to different documents, or to another type of Internet resource, such as electronic mail (e-mail) or newsgroups.

Documents published on the Web show information that is rich in content and visually interesting. Web pages include text, graphics, animation, sound, and movies. This rich content, coupled with the ability to jump from page to page using links, has contributed to the explosive growth of the Web in the past few years. From what started as a way for scientists to move technical documents easily across networks, the Web has become a business tool, a research base for students, and a popular communication medium.

To start Internet Explorer and begin browsing the Web, use one of these methods:

- Click the Launch Internet Explorer Browser button on the Taskbar.

- Click the Internet Explorer icon on the desktop.

- Click the Start button and select Programs ➢ Internet Explorer ➢ Internet Explorer.

Browsing the Web

If you're not sure what you're looking for on the Web, you can start at one page and browse around from page to page by clicking on links. As you browse, a list of the pages you visit is kept automatically in Internet Explorer. To return to a previous page, you can:

- Click the Back button on the toolbar.

- Click the Back button down arrow, and select the page you want to see from the drop-down list.

- Click the History button on the toolbar, and select the page you want to see from your History list. (If the calendar entries are compressed, click the calendar icon to see the list of Web sites you visited that week or that day.)

It's easy to get lost wandering around the Web. That's why it's a good idea to designate one page as your home page. This is the page you return to when you click the Home button on the toolbar.

To specify the location of your home page, select View ➤ Internet Options, fill in the full address of the page, and click OK. If you're not sure which page you want to designate as your home page, consider the two pages suggested in Internet Explorer. Click the Use Current button to set the page you're viewing as your home page, or click Use Default to set `http://home.microsoft.com` as your home page.

Locating a Page by Its URL

Every page on the Web has a unique address, called a Uniform Resource Locator (URL).

Table 7.1 shows the components that make up a URL. The URL used as the example in the table is `http://www.microsoft.com/windows98/info/w98overview.htm`.

Skill 7

TABLE 7.1: Components of a URL

Example	Explanation	Description
http://	Protocol	A protocol is a set of rules that tells Internet Explorer how to transmit information. HTTP is the protocol used to transmit Web pages.
www.microsoft.com/	Domain name	The server where the page is located. Every domain name is unique. To obtain a domain name, you must fill out a request form, pay a fee, and record the name with a registration service.
windows98/info/	Directory path	The directory where the page is located.
w98overview.htm	Filename	The filename of the Web page.

To access a page by its URL, type the URL on the Address bar. You do not need to type the protocol (http://); Internet Explorer adds that for you automatically. For example, to access the Audio Highway page shown in Figure 7.1, type **www.audiohighway.com** on the Address bar.

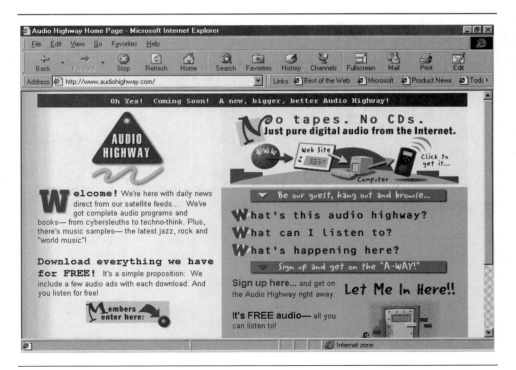

FIGURE 7.1: Accessing a Web page when you know the URL

It's not always necessary to know the full URL of a page to locate the page. For example, if you know the domain name, you can start at the home page of the site and click links until you find the page you want.

Most companies and organizations use domain names that are easy to remember. Often, you can make an educated guess to come up with the domain name. Each domain name ends with an identifier that tells you what type of Web site it is. Table 7.2 shows the identifiers commonly used today, and identifiers proposed (as of this writing) for use in the future.

TABLE 7.2: Domain Identifiers

Current Identifiers:	
.com	Commercial businesses
.edu	Educational institutions
.gov	Government entities
.mil	Military sites
.net	Internet service providers
.org	Organizations that do not fit any other category
Proposed Identifiers:	
.arts	Cultural and entertainment-related organizations
.firm	Businesses
.info	Information services
.nom	Web sites of individuals
.rec	Recreation-related organizations
.store	Stores and shops
.web	World Wide Web-related organizations

Skill 7

Browsing around the Web

Browsing from page to page can lead to some interesting discoveries. You might jump from a page about Kodiak bears to a page about Alaska state facts, then to a page describing tours of Denali. The author of a Web page will provide links to related information, or links that guide you through a Web site.

Links can be included within the text, marked as hot spots on graphics, or be the graphic itself. Links in text are easy to locate because they usually appear underlined and in a different color than the regular text. To determine if a graphic is a link, place the pointer on the graphic and look at the status bar at the bottom of the Internet Explorer screen. The status bar shows the destination of the link. If a destination is not displayed, it's not a link.

Graphics that contain multiple links are called image maps. Most image maps include a word or phrase you can click on to jump to the link. You can also drag your pointer across the image to find the hot spots.

The Web page shown in Figure 7.2 shows an image map, with links on the map and additional links spotlighted below the image. As an author, if you include an image map on your Web page, it is considered proper *netiquette* (a shorthand term for Internet etiquette) to include text links in addition to the image map. Some older browsers do not display image maps or graphics, and you don't want to exclude people using those browsers from moving around your site.

To browse around a page such as the one shown in Figure 7.2, use one of these methods:

- Click any word in the image. Remember, to see the destination or to determine if an area is a link, move the pointer across the image and, when the pointer changes to a cartoon hand, look in the status bar for the URL.

- Click any word in the text line at the bottom of the page.

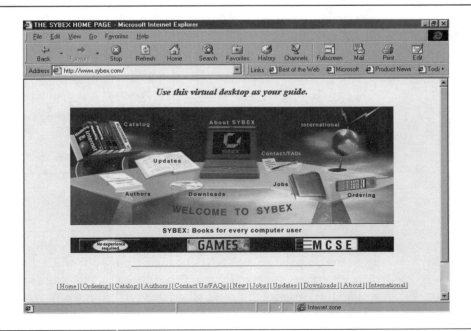

FIGURE 7.2: Browsing around the Web using links on an image map and text links

TIP Don't know the URL of a page to start browsing? Click the Search button on the toolbar, and look for a topic using the Search bar.

Printing Web Pages

As you browse, you'll come across pages containing information you want to keep. Although the actual letter of the law is still murky about this, information published on the Web is copyrighted by the author, and you cannot copy it or distribute it at will. Most Web pages include a copyright statement; if the author is picky about how content from the page is used by the public, the page might also include a legal disclaimer or notice. In general, unless it's otherwise stated on the page, it's acceptable to print Web pages for your own use.

There are a lot of print options available in Internet Explorer, and most of them will look familiar to you from other application programs. Options that allow you to select the printer, page range, and number of copies are available. Other options that pertain only to Web pages are available, too. These options include:

- Printing all documents linked to the current page
- Printing a list of links contained on the current page
- Printing selected portions of a page that has been constructed using frames

Frames are formatting options used by authors of Web pages to organize information on the page. Frames divide the page into sections. Figure 7.3 shows a Web page with a frame containing a graphic running down the left side of the page, a frame with the page title at the top of the screen, and a scrollable frame containing text on the remainder of the page.

The fastest way to print a Web page is to click the Print button on the toolbar. You won't be permitted to choose any options, and you'll receive a printout of the page as it looks on your screen.

Skill 7

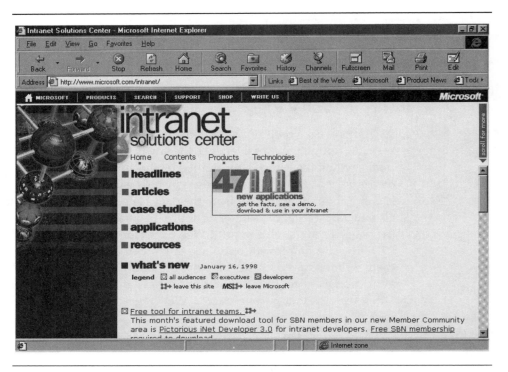

FIGURE 7.3: Web page constructed with frames

To print a Web page using the options in the Print dialog box, follow these steps:

1. Select File ➢ Print. The Print dialog box is displayed, as shown in Figure 7.4.

2. Select the printer, pages, and number of copies you want.

3. If the page is constructed in frames, select one of these options:

> **As laid out on screen**   Prints the entire page as it appears on the screen.
>
> **Only the selected frame**   Prints one selected frame. This option requires you to select a few words in the area you want to print, prior to printing.
>
> **All frames individually**   Prints each frame on a separate page.

4. Select one of the links options. The Print All Linked Documents option generates a printout of every document linked to the current page. The Print Table of Links option produces a short printout listing all the URLs mentioned in the document.

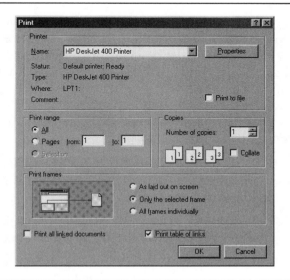

FIGURE 7.4: Selecting print options in the Print dialog box

 NOTE Not all pages that are divided into sections use frames. An author can use other formatting options to organize information on a Web page. If the Print Frames area in the Print dialog box is dimmed, the page is not constructed with frames, and the frames options are not available.

Downloading Files

All Web sites present information you can view. Some Web sites also offer files you can download to your computer. For example, distributing information on the Web is a timely and cost-effective way to make sure clients and customers have the most up-to-date information. Many companies have chosen to place instruction manuals or user guides on their Web sites for you to download and read at your convenience.

Companies, organizations, and individuals share a variety of information that's available for you to download. For example, there are many Web pages that offer items you'd use to format your own Web page, such as buttons, banners, and other graphics files. You can download these files and use them to format and spice up your Web page. Just be sure there is a statement somewhere on the page that indicates you're free to download the files and use them on your own page.

The steps used for downloading files differ from page to page. Some pages have files set up so that you just click a link to download the file automatically. Other pages require you to specify a file location and filename before downloading.

The following steps show how to download a font file from a Web page listed on your Links bar.

1.   Click the Web Gallery link on the Links bar. (If the Web Gallery link is not on the screen, click the right arrow on the Links bar until you see the link.) The Web Gallery page appears.

2.   Scroll down to the Fonts heading, and click the round icon next to the heading. Scroll down until you locate the Comic Sans heading.

3.   Click the Windows 95 & Windows NT link. The File Download dialog box is displayed, as shown in Figure 7.5.

4.   Click OK in the File Download dialog box to save the file to disk. Click Save in the Save As dialog box, and the download starts. You can monitor the progress of the download on your screen. When the download is complete, click the Comic32.exe icon on the desktop to install the fonts.

TIP   Most Web pages contain instructions on how to download a file. Before you do, check the page to see if there are special steps you need to take to download the file.

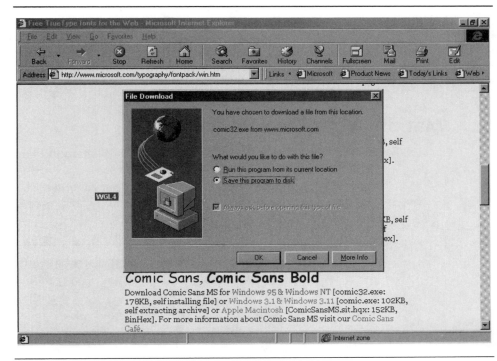

FIGURE 7.5: Downloading a font file from the Web Gallery

Keeping Track of Your Favorite Things

As you move around the Web, you'll find pages you want to revisit. Instead of keeping a written list of Web pages, or trying to memorize URLs, add the pages to your Favorites list. Then you can return to a page quickly, whenever you want.

TIP Your Favorites list is not restricted to just Web pages. You can add files or folders stored on your computer or your network to your Favorites list via Windows Explorer, then use the Favorites option on the Start menu to access them. The files are displayed in the program they're associated with.

Marking Your Favorites

When you add a Web page to your Favorites list, a shortcut to the page—not the content of the page—is stored in your Favorites folder.

To add the page you are currently viewing to your Favorites list, select Favorites ➤ Add to Favorites. Choose the *No, just add the page to my favorites* option, as shown in Figure 7.6, and click OK.

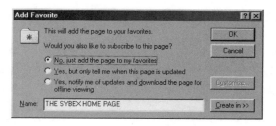

FIGURE 7.6: Adding a Web page to your Favorites list

  NOTE The two other options in the Add Favorite dialog box deal with setting up subscriptions to the Web page. You can add subscriptions to Favorites pages and to channels, which I'll discuss in Skill 11.

When you're ready to go to a page on your Favorites list, click the Favorites button on the toolbar. The Explorer Bar appears, and your Favorites are displayed, as shown in Figure 7.7. Click any link to view the page.

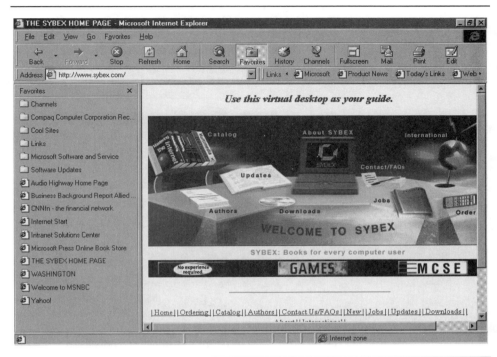

FIGURE 7.7: List of favorite Web pages

To remove the Favorites list from the screen, click the Favorites button again, or click the Close button at the top of the Explorer bar.

Keeping Things Organized

If you use your Favorites list a lot, it can become unruly. You can tame your list by creating subfolders on different topics and moving your shortcuts into an organized structure.

To organize your Favorites list:

1. Select Favorites ➢ Organize Favorites.

2. Click the Create New Folder button, and enter the name of the new folder, as shown in Figure 7.8.

3. In the Organize Favorites dialog box, drag one of your Favorites to the new folder.

4. Close the Organize Favorites dialog box, and display the Favorites list on the screen to see the changes.

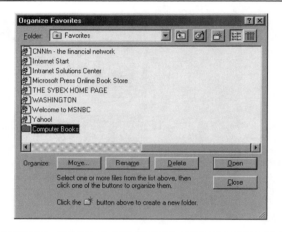

FIGURE 7.8: Creating a new subfolder to organize your Favorites list

Customizing the Internet Explorer Screen

You can change the screen display in Internet Explorer to make viewing Web pages more enjoyable and comfortable for you. To accomplish this, you can:

- Manage the amount of information you see on the Explorer bar
- Control the way bars are arranged on the screen
- Display as much information as possible in the viewing area on the screen

Managing the Explorer Bar

The Explorer bar is the area of the screen where you see your Search options, Favorites list, History list, and Channels list. When you click the Search, Favorites, History, or Channels buttons on the toolbar, the Explorer bar opens with the appropriate search information or list displayed.

You can control the amount of information you see on a list by expanding and compressing folders, and by deleting entries periodically. (The Search option is unique in that you can't control what information is displayed on the Search bar.)

To delete a listed entry, right-click the item and select Delete on the pop-up menu, as shown in Figure 7.9.

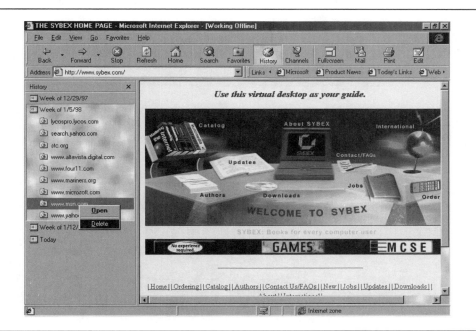

FIGURE 7.9: Deleting an item from the History list

> **TIP**
>
> If you want to delete all items on your History list, select View ➢ Internet Options and click the Clear History button.

You can also delete an item from the Favorites list by selecting Favorites ➢ Organize Favorites, choosing the item, and clicking the Delete button.

Reorganizing the Toolbar

The toolbar in Internet Explorer is made up of different bars you can resize and drag around the screen. Don't worry if your screen looks messy while you rearrange bars; you can always move the bars back to their original positions.

To resize a bar, place the pointer on the raised divider bar at the left end of the bar, until the pointer changes to a two-headed arrow. Drag the arrow to the left or right to resize the bar.

To hide a bar completely, select View ➤ Toolbars and clear the selection for the bar you want to remove.

To move a bar, drag the bar by its label to the new location on the screen.

TIP   The figures in this skill show the toolbars in the default arrangement. Use the screens in the figures as references, if you want to reset your screen back to its original appearance.

Full screen view is available if you don't want to see anything extra on the screen, except the smallest button bar. To switch to full screen view, click the Full Screen button on the toolbar. The Web page is displayed without the title bar, menu bar, status bar, or Taskbar, as shown in Figure 7.10.

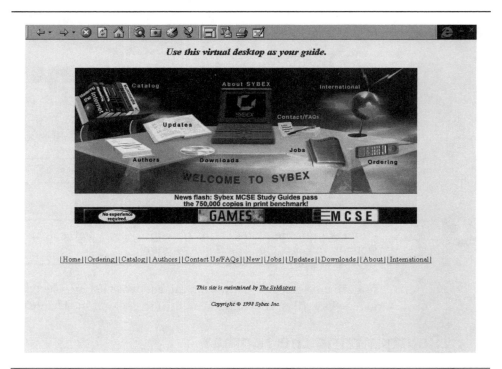

FIGURE 7.10: Full screen view of a Web page

To exit full screen view, click the Full Screen button on the toolbar.

Feeling Secure on the Internet

The Web is a free-wheeling place. There are no restrictions or censorship. People can post any kind of content they want, or offer files for downloading that could be damaging if they made their way onto your computer.

No system can guarantee that you'll be absolutely safe on the Internet, just as no system can guarantee you'll be absolutely safe in your home, your car, or at work. On the Internet, you need to set up the level of security that meets your comfort level. The more security you set up, the more restricted your access will be. In this section, I'll discuss the steps you can take to feel more secure while exploring the Web.

Activating a Ratings System

If everyone in your family uses your computer, or if you want to save yourself from stumbling onto Web pages you find insulting or offensive, consider activating the ratings system in Internet Explorer.

The ratings system warns you when you try to access a Web page that contains content you might find objectionable. Ratings are separated into four categories (Language, Nudity, Sex, Violence), and you can set the level you'll tolerate for each category. The ratings system is password protected to be sure only authorized people can enable or disable the system, or change the category levels.

To enable the ratings system and set up your ratings guide:

1. Select View ➢ Internet Options and click the Content tab.

2. Click the Enable button and enter your password. (Make sure the password is something that's not too easy to guess.)

3. Click Language and slide the rating bar to the level you find acceptable. Repeat for each of the other categories, and click OK until you are back at the Internet Explorer screen.

When you try to access a page that doesn't meet your ratings standards, a warning message appears. You might also receive a warning if the page is not rated. If you find you are getting too many warnings, try loosening the restrictions in the four ratings categories. If you don't want to see any warnings at all, select View ➢ Internet Options and click the Content tab. Click the Disable button, key in your password, and the ratings system is turned off.

Skill 7

Setting Up Security Zones

Another way to monitor your travels on the Web is to assign sites to *security zones*. Security zones are divisions that have been established in Internet Explorer. They're used to group Web sites of similar security levels together. For example, you can add the sites you trust completely to the Trusted Sites zone, or sites you distrust completely to the Restricted Sites zone. You don't have to add sites to security zones if you don't want to; by default, all Web sites fall into the Internet zone, which has a medium security level.

Table 7.3 describes each security zone.

TABLE 7.3: Internet Explorer security zones

Zone	Purpose
Local Intranet	Holds sites that are part of your company's intranet. You cannot add sites to this zone. Only the server administrator can make changes to this zone.
Trusted Sites	Intended for sites you download files or run programs from with confidence. For example, if your company maintains a site on the Web, add your company's site to this zone.
Internet	Contains all sites that do not fit any other category. You cannot add sites to this zone.
Restricted Sites	Intended for sites you do not trust. If you accidentally downloaded a file that contained a virus, add the offending site to this zone.

Let's say you want to add your company's site to the Trusted Sites zone so you don't get any more warnings when you run programs from the site. Select View ➤ Internet Options and click the Security tab. Select the Trusted Sites zone, click Add Sites, enter the URL, and click OK until you are back at the Internet Explorer screen.

 NOTE   Each security zone can be assigned a custom security level where you can choose the specific actions (such as enabling/disabling Java or ActiveX) you'll allow for sites in that zone. If you're not familiar with the options on the Custom list, leave the default security level settings as they are for each zone.

Protecting Your Privacy

Have you ever wondered how a Web page greeted you by name?

Your name was probably logged in a *cookies* file during a previous visit. Cookies are pieces of information that are stored on your computer in your Cookies folder. The information is used to customize your visit to a site. For example, if you shop from a Web site, your name and the items in your shopping basket are probably stored in a cookie. Cookies don't harm anything, but since they are stored on a local computer, many people like to be notified before a site sends cookies.

Cookies are only one of the security options you can control by selecting View ➤ Internet Options and clicking the Advanced tab (see Figure 7.11). The more security features you turn on, the more warning boxes you'll see when you access Web pages.

The amount of security you apply is up to you, but it's an impersonal world, and sometimes it's nice to be greeted by your name.

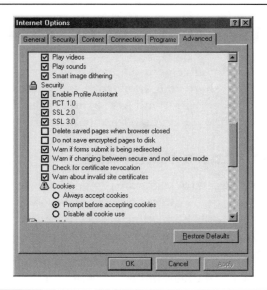

FIGURE 7.11: Selecting Advanced security options

WHAT ARE SECURITY CERTIFICATES?

Certificates guarantee you're getting information from the individual or company you *think* you're getting it from, and that information sent by you to a Web site is really from you and not an imposter. A personal certificate that verifies you are you is also known as a *digital ID*.

Certificates are granted only by certifying authorities. For information on how to obtain a Web server certificate or a digital ID, see the VeriSign Web site at www.verisign.com. There's more on digital IDs and how to use them in e-mail in Skill 9.

Making Web Pages with FrontPage Express

Now that you've perused the Web safely, it's time to create your own Web page and share your knowledge and interests with the world. The HTML editor included with Windows 98, FrontPage Express, allows you to create Web pages without having to learn or memorize HTML codes.

Personalizing a Web Page

Templates and Wizards are provided in FrontPage Express to get you off to a quick start. You can create your own Web page just by filling in answers to a few questions—the formatting has been done for you.

Suppose you wanted to create your own personal page to add to your company's Web site. Here are the steps you'd use to create your profile sheet:

1. Click the Start button and select Programs ➢ Internet Explorer ➢ FrontPage Express.

2. Select File ➢ New. In the New Page dialog box, select Personal Home Page Wizard and click OK. The Personal Home Page Wizard starts.

3. Answer the questions in each dialog box with as much or as little information as you want to include on your page. In the final dialog box, click Finish. Your page is displayed in FrontPage Express and looks similar to the page shown in Figure 7.12.

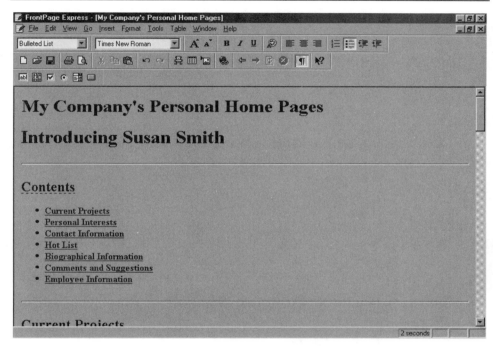

FIGURE 7.12: A personal home page in FrontPage Express

TIP

There are a couple of quick things you can do to spruce up your page. Select Format ➤ Background, and select a background image or a different background color. Select the first heading and click the Center button on the toolbar. Select the Contents heading and list, and click the Increase Indent button on the toolbar.

Creating from a Blank Canvas

As you get more comfortable in FrontPage Express, you'll probably want to stretch your creativity and create your own Web page without using a Wizard or template.

Web pages are like a jigsaw puzzle; they're made up of different pieces that look better when they're together than they do alone. The most common pieces used to create a Web page are:

Text The text can be plain, or you can apply familiar formatting commands such as Bold, Italic, Center, etc. to enhance the appearance. Short statements or statistical information can be presented in lists or in tables.

Pictures The two most common graphics formats used on the Web are Graphic Interchange Format (GIF) and Joint Photographic Experts Group (JPEG). As a rule of thumb, use GIF for logos, icons, and simple images, and use JPEG for photographs.

Hyperlinks When you set the color of your hyperlinks, be sure the color you select doesn't conflict with the text color or disappear against the background.

Memorizing all of the link types and HTML codes required to create a page from scratch would take a lot of time and energy. Luckily, you don't need to know all the HTML codes required to compose a page because FrontPage Express adds the codes for you. The toolbars in FrontPage Express give you quick access to the commands you need to construct a Web page. Many of the buttons that format text on the Web page, like the Bold button or the Center button, will look familiar if you use other Microsoft products.

Table 7.4 describes the Web-related buttons on the toolbars and the action that takes place when you click the button. There are three toolbars, and only two are displayed in the default setup. The box, button, and menu buttons are on the Forms toolbar, which you'll need to open before use.

TABLE 7.4: Web-related buttons in FrontPage Express

Button	Description
	Changes the color of the selected text.
	Adds a WebBot at the cursor position. WebBots are special components that are preprogrammed and ready to use. The WebBots in FrontPage Express are:
	Include Lets you include another file in your current file. You'll be asked to supply the URL of a Web page when you use this WebBot.
	Search Inserts a Search form into your Web page.
	Time Stamp Adds a date and/or time field that is updated automatically. You can select the date and time format you want to use.
	Before you use WebBots, check with your server administrator to make sure your server supports these options.
	Inserts a table on the page. To indicate the number of rows and columns you want, drag the pointer across the table grid that appears when you click this button.
	Adds a graphic file to your page. You'll be asked to supply the graphic's filename or URL.
	Inserts a hyperlink, or allows you to edit the selected hyperlink. You'll need to know the URL of the link you're adding and what type of link it is (http, ftp, etc.).
	Places a one-line text box at the cursor position. Text boxes are designated areas visitors can use to type information on your page. Text boxes are usually used to construct forms, such as a survey form or an online order catalog. To set the width of the box, right-click it and select Form Field Properties on the pop-up menu.
	Places a multiple-line text box at the cursor position. This box is used on a form when you want to allow the user to type more than one line of text. To set the width of the box and the number of lines allowed, right-click the box and select Form Field Properties on the pop-up menu.

Skill 7

TABLE 7.4 CONTINUED: Web-related buttons in FrontPage Express

Button	Description
	Creates a checkbox on your form. You use checkboxes when you want to list options and let respondents check as many options as they want. To indicate whether the box should be checked or unchecked by default right-click the checkbox and select Form Field Properties on the pop-up menu.
	Adds a radio button to your form. You use radio buttons when you want to create a list in which respondents can choose only one item. To indicate whether the button should be checked or unchecked by default, right-click the radio button and select Form Field Properties on the pop-up menu.
	Inserts a drop-down menu box on your form. To add menu options, right-click the box, select Form Field Properties on the pop-up menu, click the Add button, and type the menu option.
	Adds a button to the form. The most common buttons are Submit and Reset, but you can type any label on the button by right-clicking it and selecting Form Field Properties on the pop-up menu.

If you've added any of the form fields to your Web page, you won't be able to fill in the fields until you view the page in Internet Explorer.

 NOTE   There's more to publishing a form than just creating the Web page with text boxes and buttons. The information that respondents type on your form has to be processed. Contact your Web server administrator to find out what you need to do to process forms at your location.

To create a Web page in FrontPage Express:

1. Click the Start button and select Programs ➤ Internet Explorer ➤ FrontPage Express.

2. Type the text you want to include on your Web page. Use the formatting buttons on the toolbar to format the text.

3. Insert your graphics files at locations in the text. To specify how you want the text to flow around the graphic, right-click the graphic and select Image Properties from the pop-up menu. Click the Appearance tab, click the Alignment down arrow, and select one of the alignments on the drop-down list. If

you want the graphic flush left, with text flowing around it, choose Left. Try different alignments until you find the one you like.

4. Select File ≻ Save, then click the As File button. Select a location, enter a filename, and click Save.

5. Click the Launch Internet Explorer Browser button on the Taskbar. Type the filename of your Web page on the Address bar, and make sure everything on the page looks the way you want.

PUBLISHING ON THE WEB

For others on the Web to see your page, you must publish it on a *Web server*. A Web server is the computer that's connected to the Internet and holds Web pages. Although you can publish a Web page directly from FrontPage Express (instead of saving it to your computer), it's a good idea to preview the page in a browser before you turn it loose on the world.

When you select File ≻ Save in FrontPage Express and elect to post the page directly to the Web location (that is, you accept the assigned URL as a page location), the Web Publishing Wizard starts. The Wizard walks you through the steps to upload all graphics files and HTML files to the server. You'll need information from your Internet service provider or Web server administrator to complete all of the Wizard screens and publish your page on the Web.

Skill 7

Meeting on the Internet

NetMeeting is a conferencing program you use to meet with other people over the Internet or on a local network. In NetMeeting you can:

•   Talk to another person, if both of you have a microphone and speakers connected to your computers.

- Meet face-to-face with another person, if both of you have cameras connected to your computers. (Even if you don't have a camera, you can still receive video.)

- Send and receive messages among many people, by typing messages in a Chat window.

- Create a drawing on a whiteboard, and have others edit the drawing while you watch.

- Share an application program, such as Microsoft Word or FrontPage Express, with other people.

 NOTE   Using NetMeeting involves communicating with other individuals. Unless you don't mind talking to strangers, enlist a friend or co-worker to work through the steps in this section with you.

Sending and Receiving Messages in NetMeeting

You can communicate with one person voice-to-voice, or face-to-face. Using NetMeeting this way is similar to making a telephone call, except your transmission is routed via a server on the Internet or your local network, and there are no toll charges.

If you'd like to have many people involved in the conversation, use the Chat window. With the Chat window, you see each person's message as soon as they enter it. You can also save the messages from the Chat window to a file or generate a printout of the messages.

To start communicating with NetMeeting, follow these steps:

1. Click the Start button and select Programs ➢ Internet Explorer ➢ Microsoft NetMeeting.

2. If this is the first time you've used NetMeeting, the NetMeeting Wizard starts, and you're asked to supply some information like your name and e-mail address. These don't have to be your real name and e-mail address, but if someone is trying to call you, they should know what name and address you are using. Fill in all of the Wizard screens. If the Dial-Up Connection dialog box appears, connect to the Internet. You are logged

on to a Microsoft NetMeeting server automatically, and a Directory list of other people who are on the server is displayed. If the first server is busy, click the Server down arrow and select a different server.

3. On the Directory list, click the name of the person you want to call, and click the Call button on the toolbar. The person's name is displayed in the New Call dialog box, as shown in Figure 7.13.

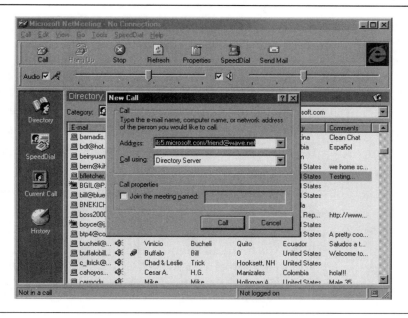

FIGURE 7.13: Placing a call in NetMeeting

4. Click the Call button in the dialog box to place the call. On the recipient's end, they'll be asked to accept or ignore the call. When they accept, you can talk to each other through the microphone and speakers. If you both have video cameras, you can see each other, too.

5. If you want to switch to typed messages, click the Chat button on the toolbar in the Current Call window.

6. When you're finished with the call, click the Hang Up button on the toolbar. If you want to call someone else, click the Directory button, and select a

name on the Directory list. As you use NetMeeting, you'll be able to build up addresses on your Speed Dial list so you won't have to scroll through names on the Directory list as often.

7. When you're finished with all calls, select File ➢ Log Off, and then exit NetMeeting. If necessary, disconnect from the Internet.

Sharing a Program in NetMeeting

NetMeeting allows you to share an application program with other people. For example, let's say you've been asked to co-author an article for your company's annual report. Your writing partner is at a regional site across the country. Using NetMeeting, you and your collaborator can share the application program the article is written in, and see each other's changes instantly on the screen.

To start collaborating, open the document in its original application program, and then follow these steps:

1. Click the Start button and select Programs ➢ Internet Explorer ➢ Microsoft NetMeeting.

2. On the Directory list, click the name of the person you want to call, and click the Call button on the toolbar. In the New Call dialog box, click the Call button.

3. In the Current Call window, click the Share button on the toolbar. Select the application program and click OK.

4. Click the Collaborate button on the toolbar. (You can still talk to each other while you're collaborating.) Click the mouse within the document to gain control of the document; your collaborator can do the same—control switches between the two of you. To stop collaborating, click the Collaborating button on the toolbar.

5. To close the call, click the Hang Up button on the toolbar.

6. Select Call ➢ Log Off to log off the server. Exit NetMeeting and, if necessary, disconnect from the Internet.

Are You Experienced?

Now you can...

- ☑ Browse pages on the World Wide Web
- ☑ Add Web pages to your Favorites list
- ☑ Adjust the Internet Explorer screen
- ☑ Set your security options
- ☑ Create Web pages in FrontPage Express
- ☑ Use NetMeeting to communicate with other people

SKILL 8

FINDING WHAT YOU WANT

- **Locating files and folders on your computer or on a network**
- **Finding a computer on a network**
- **Searching for pages on the World Wide Web**
- **Searching for e-mail addresses**

In Windows 98, you have information available to you from your computer, other networks you're connected to, and the Internet all within a few clicks of the mouse. In this skill, you'll learn how to find the information you're looking for, whether it's as close as a file on your computer or as far-flung as a page on the World Wide Web.

Locating Files and Folders

You can search for files or folders stored on your own PC or on any computer you have access to on a network. You don't need to know the name of the file or folder to locate it. If you created the file weeks ago, and only remember part of the name, use the part you remember to conduct your search. If the filename escapes you, try searching by the date the file was modified or by a word that's in the text of the file.

Don't worry if you can't find the file or folder on your first try! If you saved it, it's there somewhere, and you may just need to expand your search to locate it.

Searching by Name

To find a file or folder when you know at least part of the name:

1. Click the Start button, point to Find, and then click on Files or Folders.

2. In the Find dialog box, type part of the name in the Named box. Your search will find all files and folders containing the characters you type. It doesn't matter whether the characters you type in fall at the beginning, middle, or end of the filename. For example, Figure 8.1 shows the results of a search for "test."

3. The information in the Look In box tells you what area will be searched. When C: is displayed in the Look In box, your C: drive is searched. If you want to search a different area, click the drop-down arrow or the Browse button and select a drive from the list. To search all drives on your computer, select My Computer.

4. Click Find Now to start the search.

NOTE   Be sure the Include Subfolders checkbox is selected when you conduct a search. When you use this option, all subfolders in the location you specified in the Look In box are searched. If you want to narrow your search to files that contain a certain word or phrase, type the word(s) you are looking for in the Containing Text box.

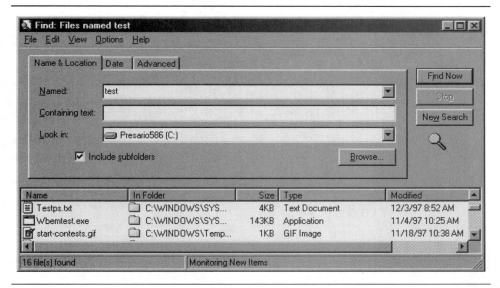

FIGURE 8.1: Searching for files and folders by name

Searching by Date or Type

What do you do if your search by name finds no files, or if you can't remember any part of the name or content of the file? Expand the search to other characteristics of the file. You can search for:

- Files and folders that were modified, created, or last accessed during a specific date range

- A particular type of file (such as Microsoft Word files, font files, NetMeeting whiteboard documents, etc.)

You can also search for a file by the file size, although this type of search is not used very often.

To search for files by date, open the Find dialog as described in the previous section, and click the Date tab. Select Find All Files, then click Between, and fill in the dates you are looking for as shown in Figure 8.2. If you'd rather search by the date the file was created or last accessed, click the Find All Files down arrow and make your selection.

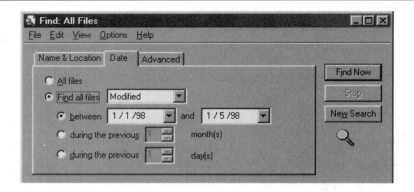

FIGURE 8.2: Searching by date

A handy pop-up calendar appears when you click the down arrow next to the date field. You can click the date on the calendar to select it, instead of typing in the date on the screen. Click the left and right arrows at the top of the pop-up calendar to go to the previous month or the next month.

To search for one type of file, select the Find dialog box's Advanced tab. Figure 8.3 shows a search for Microsoft Word documents.

You can refine the search by combining elements from the Name & Location, Date, and Advanced tabs. For example, if you want to find all Word files created from January 1 to 5 containing the word "Windows," fill in the information under all three tabs and then click Find Now.

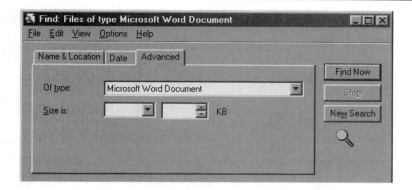

FIGURE 8.3: Searching for Word documents only

Searching Other Computers on a Network

When you are on a network, you may need to locate files or folders on other computers. Using the same techniques you used to search your own computer (described in the previous sections), you can hunt for files and folders on other computers on the network.

NOTE   To search drives on other computers, the drives must be shared and mapped to your computer. For more about setting up shared drives, see Skill 14.

To search for files and folders on other computers, select the Name & Location tab of the Find dialog box. Click the Look In down arrow, and select a drive on the drop-down list. If you want to search all drives you have access to, select My Computer on the drop-down list. Figure 8.4 shows the results of a search for files with names containing "txt" on another computer's M: drive.

TIP   When you find the file you are looking for (whether it's on your own computer or a computer on the network), click the name to open the file.

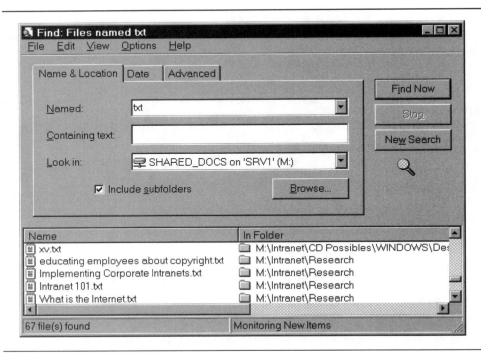

FIGURE 8.4: Searching for files on another computer

Saving Your Search

After you've completed your search, you can save the search criteria for use at a later time. Suppose you want to see a list of all files with "contract" in their file-names that were created within the last month. Conduct your search as usual (by typing Contract in the Named box, clicking the Date tab, selecting During the Previous 1 Month(s), and clicking Find Now). Then, select File ➢ Save Search. Your search selections are added as a shortcut on your desktop. The next time you want to conduct the search, click the shortcut on your desktop to open the Find window, and then click Find Now.

> **TIP**   To view the searches you've saved, open Start ➢ Find ➢ Files or Folders and click the Advanced tab. Click the Of Type down arrow, select Saved Search, and click Find Now. All of the searches you've saved will be displayed.

Locating a Computer on a Network

In addition to using Find to locate files and folders, you can use it to locate a computer on your network. The way you locate a computer is similar to the way you search for a file or folder—you don't have to know the full name of the computer to locate it. Click the Start button, point to Find, and select Computer. In the Find dialog box, type in the part of the name you want to search for in the Named box and click Find Now. Figure 8.5 shows the results of the search for computers with "ci" in the name.

If you want to see more information about one of the computers on the list, click that name. A list of folders and printers attached to the computer will be displayed. To open one of the folders or see the print queue for a printer, click the folder or printer.

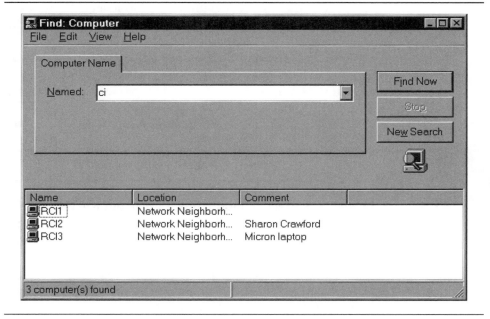

FIGURE 8.5: Searching for a computer on a network

Skill 8

Finding Information on the Internet

The Internet is a vast resource with information on almost everything. Finding what you want on the Internet is like picking out constellations in the sky—it's easy once you know how.

Searching for Web Pages

The most popular and fastest growing part of the Internet is the World Wide Web. The Web is made up of millions of pages of information, created and maintained by people around the world. Pages are grouped together to form sites, and sites are assigned unique names that act as addresses to help keep everything organized.

Site addresses are also known as Uniform Resource Locators, or URLs. The home page of the site is listed under the top-level URL (for example, Microsoft's home page is www.microsoft.com), with pages on specific topics listed under longer URLs that include the path or filename. If you don't know the specific URL of the page you are looking for, you can usually start at the home page and use links to jump to the page you want. Let's say you were looking for information on Windows 98. You could type www.microsoft.com/windows98/ to go directly to the Windows 98 page, or you could start at www.microsoft.com and follow links until you locate the Windows 98 page.

 NOTE   For more about locating a page by its URL, see Skill 7.

Using URLs to get to information is great, but what happens when you want to find other sources or don't know the URL? Use a search engine to locate what you want. A search engine is a database application that catalogues and indexes information from Web pages. (Some search engines have expanded their territory to let you search for information in newsgroups as well as Web pages, or to search for pages written in languages other than English if you feel like, oh, taking a tour of the Louvre museum in French.)

Looking for Information

There are many search engines available on the Web, and each one can give you slightly different results. If you don't find what you need with one search engine, try another.

To search for information:

1. Click the Start button, point to Find, and click On the Internet. Internet Explorer opens. If you see the Dial-Up Connection dialog box, fill in the User Name and Password boxes, and click Connect. When you are connected, The Microsoft Network search page is displayed.

 NOTE   If you don't have MSN, another page will be displayed, and even if you do have MSN, the page may look different.

2. Type **"Windows 98"** and select the AltaVista search engine. Figure 8.6 shows how the screen should look after you type in your selections. Putting quotes around a phrase means that the entire phrase must be found. Without the quotes, the search results will include *98 ways to caulk windows* and other irrelevancies.

3. Click Search to go to the AltaVista page. The search results are displayed, as shown in Figure 8.7. To view one of the pages you found, click the link. Scroll down through the list to see more results.

 NOTE   You can also use the Explorer bar in Internet Explorer to view a side-by-side display of your results list and each Web page. For more on how to use the Explorer bar, see Skill 7.

Skill 8

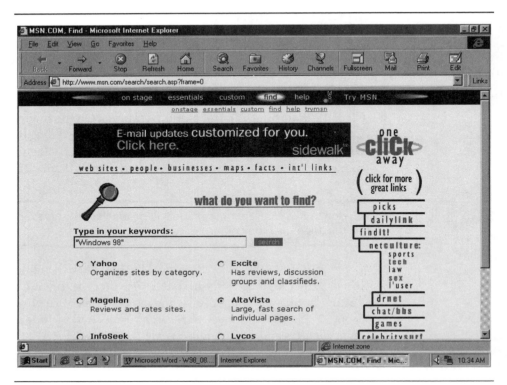

FIGURE 8.6: Searching for information using the default search page

Narrowing the Search

There is no lack of information on the Web. In most cases, a search will find too many pages for you to examine. (The search for *Windows 98* yields hundreds of thousands of pages on any given day.)

Internet slang refers to each page you find as a *hit*. If you get too many hits when you conduct a search, narrow the search to a more specific word, or a combination of words. For example, if you're a sports fan, you'll probably get better results by searching for a particular sport, like *baseball*, rather than searching for *sports*. If you really want to narrow the search, you can look up the rules the search engine uses to find multiple-word phrases (each search engine has its own rules, usually under the Help or Search Tips link), and restrict your search to pages about baseball and a specific team or player.

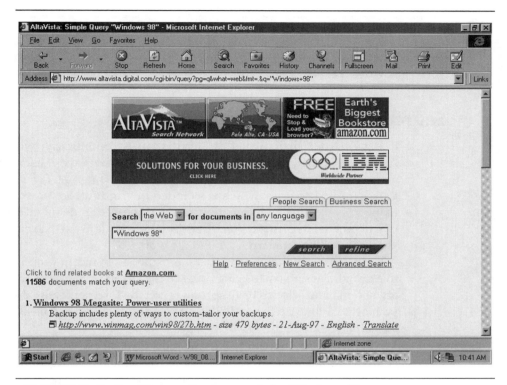

FIGURE 8.7: The results of a search for *Windows 98*

To narrow a search for sports information:

1. Click the Start button, point to Find, and click On the Internet.

2. Type **Olympics AND Sydney** to search for information on the Summer Olympics in Sydney, Australia. Select Magellan, and then click Search. Remember: You can use any search engine you want—Magellan happens to use the word *AND* when you want the results to include both words. Other search engines use different syntax and symbols, so be sure to check the engine's Help page or Search Tips page so you know how to format your request.

3. Click a link to view a page located by your search.

TIP   When you are on a Web page, you can search for a specific word to locate it quickly. Select Edit ➤ Find (On This Page), type the word, and click Find Next. Keep clicking Find Next to locate all occurrences of the word on the page.

Searching for E-Mail Addresses

Using electronic mail (e-mail) is a terrific way to communicate with other people. All you need to send or receive e-mail on the Internet is your computer, a modem, and an e-mail account that gives you access to the Internet. (You can use the Outlook Express program, which is included in Windows 98, to send, receive, and manage your e-mail. Outlook Express is discussed in detail in Skill 9.) Sending e-mail on the Internet is fast and convenient, and allows you to communicate inexpensively with people from around the world.

The use of e-mail on the Internet has exploded in recent years. To keep up with this growth, and to try to bring order to the chaotic expanse of addresses, a variety of e-mail directories have sprung up on the Internet. These directories help you locate Internet e-mail addresses for individuals, and some also help you locate personal or business Web pages.

When you find an e-mail address on the directory list, you can click the Add to Address Book button to add it to your own personal Address Book. The Address Book is stored on your computer, and it's your electronic record of phone numbers, addresses, and contacts.

Using Internet Directories

Internet directories are like phone books of e-mail addresses. Just as there are a number of different brands of phone books, there are a number of different Internet directories.

The directories are grouped together in one dialog box in Windows 98 for your convenience. Each directory is a separate entity, with its own Web site. If you can't locate an e-mail address in your initial search, click the Web Site button to go to the directory's Web page and conduct a more thorough search.

To search for an e-mail address in an Internet directory:

1. Click the Start button, point to Find, and click People. The Find People dialog box opens.

2. To select a directory, click the down arrow in the Look In box, and select Four11 on the drop-down list, as shown in Figure 8.8.

3. Type in the name you are looking for and click Find Now. If you see the Dial-Up Connection dialog box, fill in the User Name and Password boxes and click Connect. When you are connected to the Internet, the search begins, and the results are displayed in the dialog box (see Figure 8.9). To add a name to your Address Book, select the name and click Add to Address Book. Storing e-mail addresses in your Address Book is an easy way to access them when you're ready to send an e-mail message.

4. When you're finished, click Close and, if necessary, disconnect your dial-up connection.

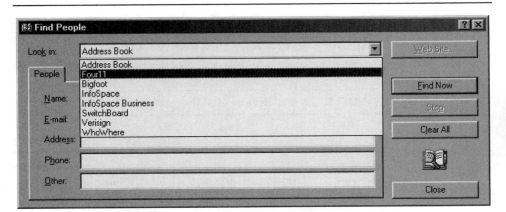

FIGURE 8.8: Selecting an Internet directory

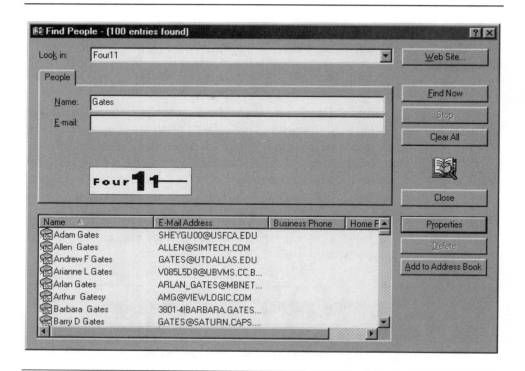

FIGURE 8.9: Results of a directory search

 TIP

No directory lists all e-mail addresses. If you want your e-mail address included in a directory, go to the directory's Web site and follow the directions on the page to add your name and e-mail address to their directory list.

Finding Names in Your Address Book

Your Address Book can be a useful resource for keeping track of e-mail addresses, home and business phone numbers, digital IDs, and contact information. You can enter information manually in your Address Book, or you can add entries automatically by:

- Setting up your options in Outlook Express, so all people you send replies to are added to the Address Book

- Importing an existing address book from another e-mail program

- Selecting a name from an Internet directory

The more information you include in your Address Book, the more search options you will have when it is time to locate a name. For example, if you use the Other field in the Address Book to record comments, you can search on any word(s) in that field to find entries. This is a helpful way to locate and organize entries that otherwise wouldn't have anything in common.

To search for an e-mail address in your Address Book:

1. Click the Start button, point to Find, and click People. In the Look In box, click the down arrow and select Address Book.

2. Type the name you are looking for and click Find Now. If you can't remember the exact spelling of the name, type in part of the name. You can also use any of the other fields to search for the record, as shown in Figure 8.10. If you need to add or change information, select the name on the list and click Properties to bring up the Address Book record.

3. To clear the screen and conduct a new search, click Clear All. When you are finished, click Close.

TIP Many people have multiple e-mail addresses. To record more than one e-mail address for a person in your Address Book, click Properties, fill in the new address in the Add New box, and click Add. The new address is added to the list of e-mail addresses on the person's record.

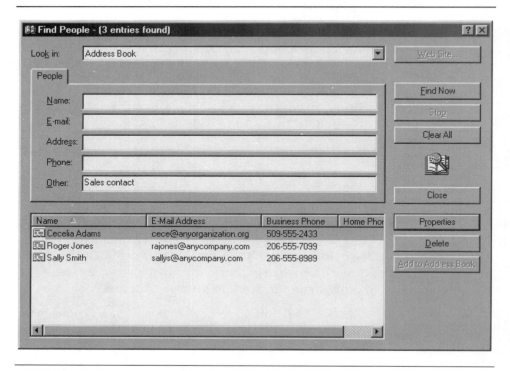

FIGURE 8.10: Searching in your Address Book

Are You Experienced?

Now you can...

- ☑ Find files and folders on your computer
- ☑ Find files and folders on your network
- ☑ Find computers on your network
- ☑ Search for pages on the World Wide Web
- ☑ Locate e-mail addresses

SKILL 9

USING OUTLOOK EXPRESS

- Sending and receiving e-mail
- Customizing your mail
- Encrypting mail
- Participating in newsgroups
- Maintaining an Address Book

Windows 98 comes with an entirely new mail system. As you might expect, this is both good news and bad news. In this case, it's mostly good. If you're upgrading from Windows 95, and you like or need the Windows Messaging System (Exchange), you can keep using it. If you haven't been using Exchange, you probably won't miss it.

Users who are connected to a local area network, including company intranet users, can continue using their current e-mail system. Home and small office users for whom e-mail means Internet mail will find the new Outlook Express far easier to set up and use than Windows 95's Exchange. Outlook Express also allows you to use Internet newsgroups (the Usenet).

 NOTE   The fax capability that was built into Windows 95 is gone in Windows 98—unless you installed over Windows 95 *or* saved the fax program using the method described in Appendix A.

Internet Mail

Windows 98 and Internet Explorer are designed to work with your preferred e-mail program. The installation routine checks your system for installed e-mail programs and lists them in the Mail drop-down box on the Programs page of the Internet Options dialog box (accessed from Internet Explorer's View menu). If you upgraded from Windows 95 with Microsoft Exchange installed, it will appear on the list as Windows Messaging. Outlook Express, which is part of the Windows 98 package, is also on the list. Of course, you can also open your mail program directly, either from the Start menu or from a shortcut on the desktop.

Starting Outlook Express

If you don't already have an e-mail program—and even if you do—Outlook Express can handle your Internet mail very nicely. If you have Microsoft Exchange (left over from Windows 95) but find it complicated and difficult to use, give Outlook Express a try.

 NOTE   In spite of the similar name, Outlook Express is not a scaled-down version of Microsoft Outlook. If you have Outlook (a part of the Office 97 suite), you can still use it for your e-mail.

To set Internet Explorer to start Outlook Express, do this:

1. Start Internet Explorer (click Start ➢ Programs ➢ Internet Explorer).

2. Choose View ➢ Internet Options ➢ Programs.

3. Set the Mail drop-down list to Outlook Express.

4. Set the News drop-down list to Outlook Express, unless you have another newsreader you prefer.

5. Click OK.

Now, Internet Explorer will open Outlook Express when you choose Mail from the Go menu or when you choose an operation from the menu under the Mail button on the toolbar. You can start Outlook Express from the Start menu (click Start ➢ Programs ➢ Internet Explorer ➢ Outlook Express) or, easiest of all, from its desktop shortcut.

The Outlook Express main window (see Figure 9.1) is designed like a Web home page.

Besides the usual menus and toolbar, six icons appear in the main window. Click any one of them for a quick route to the most common functions.

Read Mail   Opens your e-mail Inbox.

Read News   Opens your list of subscribed newsgroups. Newsreader functions are described later in this skill.

Compose a Message   Opens a window for creating mail.

Address Book   Opens your address book.

Download All   Connects to your Internet mail service and collects all your new mail messages.

Find People   Allows you to connect to an Internet directory service (white pages) to find someone's e-mail address.

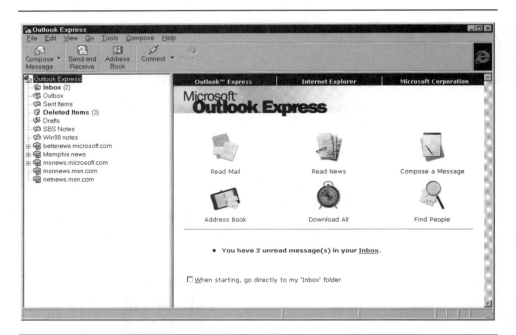

FIGURE 9.1: The opening window for Outlook Express

The three bars at the top of the window—labeled Outlook Express, Internet Explorer, and Microsoft Corporation—are links to Microsoft Web sites. The first two take you to the Outlook Express and Internet Explorer areas, while the third links to a more general page. Clicking one of the bars will start Internet Explorer and connect to the site.

The left pane of the Outlook Express main window gives you direct access to your Inbox, which holds received mail until you delete it, and the Outbox, which holds messages you have created until you connect so they can be transmitted. There are also folders for items you've sent, items deleted from your Inbox, and items you've composed but decided not to send yet (drafts). Also in the left pane are any news servers which you have set up in Outlook Express.

Adding an Internet Mail Account

Making a connection for Internet mail is covered in Skill 6. However, if you want to have a second mail account through Outlook Express, you'll have to enter it here. Read through the steps to make sure you have all the necessary information before you start.

1. Select Start ➢ Programs ➢ Internet Explorer ➢ Outlook Express to open Outlook Express.

2. In Outlook Express, choose Tools ➢ Accounts. The Internet Accounts dialog box will appear.

3. Click the Mail tab. Any accounts you have already set up will be listed here, as shown in Figure 9.2.

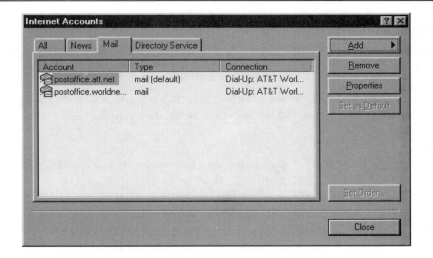

FIGURE 9.2: Mail accounts in Outlook Express

4. Click Add and choose Mail to set up a new account. The Internet Connection Wizard will start.

5. Enter the name you want to appear in the From field of messages you send from this account. Click Next.

6. Enter your e-mail address for this account. This is the address you chose when you established the account with your service provider. Click Next.

7. Enter the e-mail server names given to you by your service provider. There are separate servers for incoming and outgoing mail. Set the incoming mail

server type (in the drop-down box) to either POP3 or IMAP, to match the beginning of the server name. Click Next again.

8. Enter your logon name and password for this e-mail account. Click Next to continue.

9. Enter a "friendly name" for this Internet mail account. If you have multiple accounts, this name will help you tell them apart. For example, use names like "My Work Mail" or "Michael's NetCom." Click Next again.

10. Choose your method for connecting to the Internet. If you connect via a local area network or choose to connect manually, this is your last entry. Click Next, and then Finish.

    or

    If you want Outlook Express to dial automatically to connect, choose Connect Using My Phone Line, then click Next.

11. To use a connection which is already set up on your computer, choose it from the list and click Next, then Finish.

    or

    If you need to set up a new connection, choose Create a New Dial-up Connection, and click Next.

12. Continue through the Wizard. You will need to enter the phone number you dial to connect to your Internet service provider, your username and password, and a name for the connection. Don't change the advanced properties unless you know you need to. Finally, click Finish.

Outlook Express can now connect to your Internet mail account to send and receive mail. If you need to change (or just check) any of the information you entered, re-open the Internet Accounts dialog box (see step 2 above), highlight the account name, and click the Properties button. You can also use the Internet Accounts dialog box to remove an account you no longer need.

Reading Your Mail

Clicking the Read Mail icon in the Outlook Express main window takes you to your Inbox, shown in Figure 9.3. You can also get there by clicking the Inbox in the left pane of the Outlook Express window.

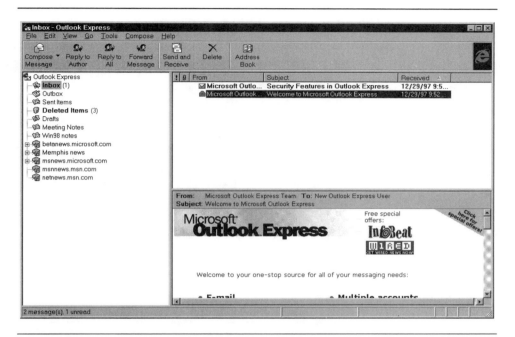

FIGURE 9.3: The Outlook Express Inbox

Click the Send and Receive button on the toolbar to tell Outlook Express to connect to your Internet service provider and get your mail. Outlook Express pops up a dialog box to show the progress of your e-mail connection (see Figure 9.4). The "look" of this box will vary depending on the ISP you're using.

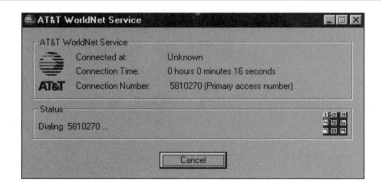

FIGURE 9.4: Connecting to AT&T WorldNet

Next, a dialog box opens showing the connection to the mail servers as your mail is sent and received (shown in Figure 9.5).

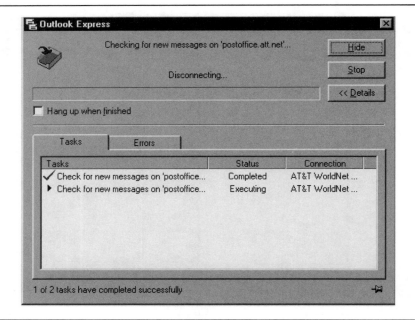

FIGURE 9.5: Mail being sent and received

Outlook Express won't automatically disconnect from your Internet service unless you check the Hang Up When Finished box. And if you have Active Desktop installed, it won't disconnect even then. Right-click on the networking icon on the Taskbar and select Disconnect.

In the Inbox, your messages are listed in the upper pane, with unread messages in bold. You can change the order of messages by clicking a column heading to sort messages according to that column. Click the heading again to reverse the sort order.

When you highlight a message header in the upper pane, the message itself appears in the lower preview pane. Double-click on a message header to open the message in its own window for easier viewing. As shown in Figure 9.6, Outlook Express is not limited to plain text e-mail. It also handles messages formatted in HTML, which means you can vary fonts and colors and include links and graphics. If people you are writing to use e-mail software that can handle HTML messages, they'll see all the formatting; otherwise, the message will be displayed in plain text.

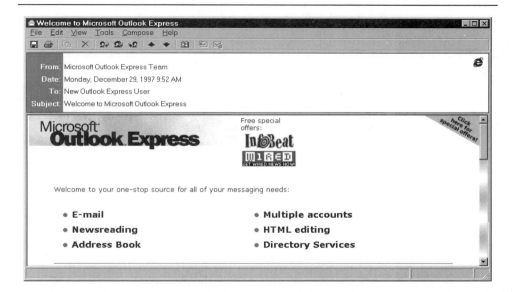

FIGURE 9.6: Viewing an incoming message with different fonts, links, and graphics in the mail reader window

The Inbox view will be most useful if you receive lots of mail and want to quickly check the subject and sender—reading important mail first. Otherwise, you may find it simpler to just double-click your first new message and work in the mail reader window (like Figure 9.6). The mail reader toolbar gives you quick access to the most common operations.

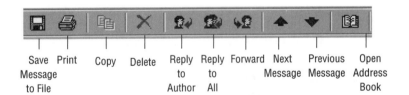

As you read each message, Outlook Express will mark it as Read in the Inbox by changing its entry to normal type instead of bold. To delete a message, click the Delete button instead of Next; Outlook Express will automatically move on to the next message.

 TIP   Deleted messages are stored in the Deleted Items folder. If you don't want these messages kept, click the Tools menu and select Options. On the General tab, mark the checkbox next to *Empty messages from the 'Deleted Items' folder on exit.* To manually empty the Deleted Items folder, right-click the folder and select Empty Folder from the pop-up menu.

Replying

To reply to a message, click the Reply to Author button. Outlook Express opens a reply window like the one in Figure 9.7. The sender of the original message is automatically entered in the To field, and the original subject is copied to the Subject field with "Re:" in front of it. Depending on your setup, the original message may be copied to the text area, so that the recipient knows what message you're replying to. (This may seem redundant, but many people send dozens, if not hundreds of e-mail messages a day and, for them, it's very frustrating to receive a message that simply replies "OK" or "I agree completely.")

 TIP   If you want (or don't want) the entire message copied to the text area of your reply, you can change the setting by selecting Options from the Tools menu. On the Send tab, check or clear the box next to *Include message in reply*.

On the other hand, if the message you are replying to is a long one, only quote back enough so that the sender understands what you're responding to. You can put >> and << around the parts of the original that you leave. In Figure 9.8, I've quoted back the relevant part of the message and added my reply.

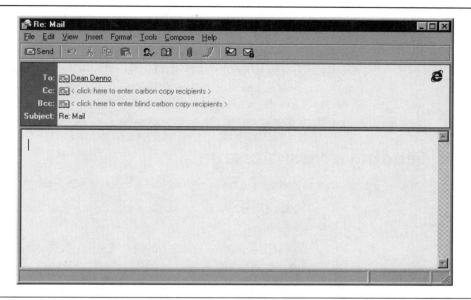

FIGURE 9.7: Generating a reply

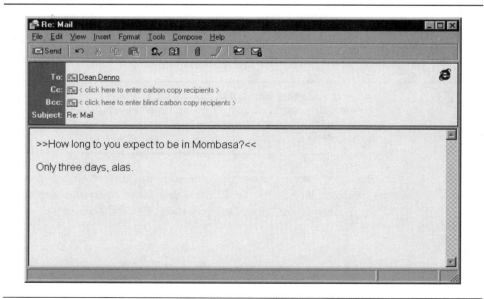

FIGURE 9.8: Quoting back part of a message

If you create your reply by clicking the Reply to All button (instead of Reply to Author), your reply will be sent to all the people listed in the To and Cc fields of the original message.

When you are finished typing your reply, just click the Send button on the toolbar to put the reply in your Outbox. The next time you click the Send and Receive button, the messages in the Outbox will be transmitted to your mail service. Since most of the controls in the reply window are the same as in a new message window, we'll discuss them in the next section.

Sending a New Message

There are several ways to open the New Message window:

- From the Outlook Express start-up window, click the Compose a Message icon.

- From the same window or the Inbox or Outbox, click the Compose Message button on the toolbar.

- If you're reading your mail in its own window, choose New Message on the Compose menu.

In the To field, you can directly type in the Internet mail address of the recipient. If the recipient has an entry in your Address Book, just start typing the name and Outlook Express will complete it. (We'll discuss the Address Book later in this skill.)

TIP As in many other parts of Windows 98, if you rest your mouse pointer on one of these fields, you will get a pop-up help message. In the To field, the message tells you that you can enter multiple names, separating them with commas or semicolons.

If you're not sure how you have someone entered in the Address Book, click the file card icon in the To field to see a list of everyone in your Address Book. Highlight the name in the list and then click the To button.

Back in the New Message window, fill in the Subject field, and then move on to typing the body of your message. Again, there's a toolbar to help you with the most common operations.

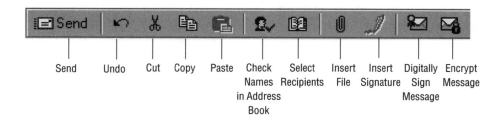

If you've entered one or more names in the To or copies (Cc and Bcc) fields, and want to be sure they are really in your Address Book, click the Check Names button. If you've entered a name for which there is no match or made a mistake typing, you'll be able to choose the correct name from your Address Book or create a new entry. The Select Recipients button offers an alternate way to fill in the To and copies fields. You may find it quicker when you need to fill in several names.

Use the Insert File button to attach a file to your message. The file will appear as an icon in a separate window below your message. Insert File attaches the file to your message, like most other e-mail programs you may have used.

When you finish typing your message, click the Send button to put it in your Outbox. Outlook Express will then connect to your Internet service to transmit it.

NOTE   If you prefer, you can use Send Later on the File menu to just put the message in your Outbox. It will be transmitted the next time you click the Send and Receive button.

Sending a Message with HTML

To dress up your messages, you can use HTML graphics and formatting abilities. Outlook Express comes with over a dozen types of "stationery," which include background, graphics, and appropriate fonts.

 **WARNING**   Adding HTML formatting to a message increases its size dramatically, so use such formatting judiciously. For example, you're bound to be chastised (if not severely flamed) if you send HTML to a newsgroup with many members who resent having to download a large message when a small one would have sufficed.

To compose an HTML message, follow these steps:

1. In the Outlook Express main window, choose Compose ➤ New Message Using.

    or

    Click the down arrow just to the right of the Compose Message button on the toolbar.

2. You will then see this menu, though the specific stationery items on it may vary. Choose the one you want to use.

You can also click More Stationery to open a browse window listing all the stationery files in the Stationery folder, or choose No Stationery to create a message with HTML formatting from scratch.

3. The New Message window will open with your chosen stationery (or none),
    and with a formatting toolbar at the top of the message text area, as shown
    in Figure 9.9. Fill in the To, Cc, Bcc, and Subject fields the same as for a plain
    text message. You can accept the ready-made text, add to it, or you can
    delete what's been provided and just use the background.

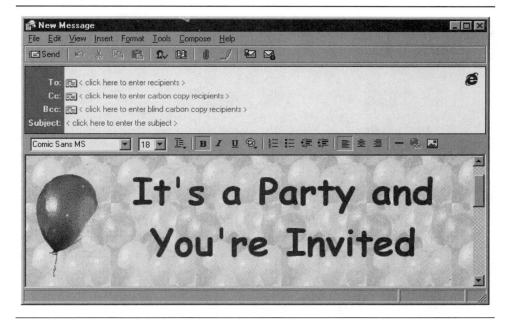

FIGURE 9.9: Sending a ready-made invitation

> **TIP**   Once you've started a message, you can change it from plain text to HTML by
> choosing Rich Text (HTML) on the Format menu.

Most of the controls on the formatting toolbar will be familiar to anyone who
has used a Windows word processor. The best way to discover the details is by
experimenting. Table 9.1 lists unfamiliar buttons.

TABLE 9.1: HTML shortcuts

Button	Description
	Style tags; select a defined paragraph style
	Font color
	Decrease indentation
	Increase indentation
	Insert horizontal line
	Insert hyperlink
	Insert picture

Signing Your Message

Of course, there's really no need to sign your messages. Anyone receiving e-mail from you will see your name in the From box. Nevertheless, signatures are a big deal on the Internet. Sometimes people simply type in their names. Other times, signatures are elaborate constructs—either of plain text characters or, in some cases, HTML.

To create your signature line, return to the Outlook Express main window.

1. Choose Tools ➢ Stationery.

2. On the Mail tab, click the Signature button. The Signature dialog box will appear. Figure 9.10 shows a plain text signature.

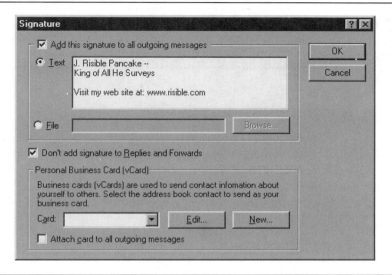

FIGURE 9.10: Setting up your signature

3. Check the box labeled *Add this signature to all outgoing messages*.

4. For a simple signature like the one shown, choose the Text radio button and enter the signature lines you want.

5. If your taste runs to the more elaborate, you can choose File to have a file inserted as your signature. You can also choose whether your signature should be used when you reply to or forward a message.

6. When you are finished, click OK twice.

Once you set up a signature, it's automatically included any time you open a new message window in plain text mode. The insertion point is placed above the signature, so you can just type your message and the signature will always be at the end. If you choose to also use your signature with replies and forwards, you should pay attention to where it's automatically placed in such messages.

If you only want to use the signature with *some* messages, don't check the box for adding the signature to all messages. When you do want the signature, just place the cursor at the end of your outgoing message and select Signature from the Insert menu.

NOTE If security is an issue, you can sign your message with a digital ID, by using the Digitally Sign Message button. We'll discuss digital IDs, which are also used for the Encrypt Message function, in the next section.

Adding a Business Card

In the Signature dialog box, you can also set up a business card to be transmitted with e-mail messages. The card is sent as an attachment in a standard format called vCard. The information included on your card comes from an entry in your Address Book. Since you may not want to include the same information you use for other purposes, you should create a special Address Book entry called My vCard (or some such).

1. In the Outlook Express main window, click Tools ➤ Stationery.

2. On the Mail page, click Signature.

3. In the Personal Business Card (vCard) section of the Signature dialog box, click New.

4. Enter whatever information you want included in your e-mail business card. You are creating an Address Book entry. For more information, refer to "Using Windows Address Book" later in this skill. Click OK when you are finished.

5. In the Signature dialog box, check *Attach card to all outgoing messages*, if that is what you want. Click OK twice.

If you don't want to attach your business card to all messages, you can attach it to individual messages by choosing Insert ➤ Business Card when composing a message.

When someone sends you a message with a vCard attached, you will see a file card icon in the header area of the message reading window.

Click it to open the vCard attachment, which will appear as an Address Book entry. There's also a button to add the information to your Address Book.

Digital IDs

A digital ID allows you to prove your identity to others with whom you correspond electronically. A part of your digital ID also allows others to encrypt messages they send you. Digital IDs work in conjunction with the S/MIME standard for secure electronic mail.

Personal digital IDs generally are tied to a particular e-mail address. If you have more than one e-mail account set up in Outlook Express, make sure the default account is the one for which you want a digital ID. Check this on the Mail tab of the Tools ➤ Accounts dialog box.

Here's one way to get a digital ID:

1. From the Outlook Express main window, open the Tools ➤ Options dialog box.

2. On the Security page, click the Get Digital ID button. This will connect you to the certification page of Microsoft's Internet Explorer Web site.

3. Read the information provided, then click the VeriSign Get Your ID Now button to connect to their site.

 NOTE   As of this writing, VeriSign is Microsoft's preferred provider of digital IDs, and is offering free 60-day trial digital IDs for use with Outlook Express.

4. When you get to the VeriSign site, your name and e-mail address will already be filled in. Read the explanation of the challenge phrase, and enter one (like a password).

5. There are several more options to decide on, including the possibility of getting a full-featured permanent digital ID for a modest fee. After you have chosen your options, click the Accept button at the bottom of the page.

6. After leaving the VeriSign site, wait a few minutes. Then click Send and Receive in Outlook Express. You will receive an e-mail with further instructions.

7. When you read VeriSign's message in Outlook Express, it will include a Next button. Click the button to connect again to the VeriSign Web site.

8. When you see the message that your digital ID has been successfully generated, click the Install button. After a few seconds, you will see a message that your digital ID has been installed in Outlook Express.

Skill 9

9. Return to Outlook Express and choose Tools ➢ Accounts.

10. Select the e-mail account for which you just obtained the digital ID, and click Properties.

11. Choose the Security tab, and check the box labeled *Use a digital ID when sending secure messages from: (your e-mail address)*, as shown in Figure 9.11.

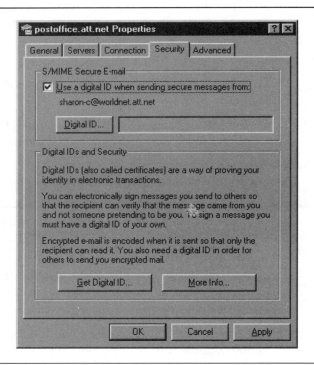

FIGURE 9.11: Associating your digital ID with your e-mail account

12. Click the Digital ID button. You will see a list of the personal certificates installed on your machine. If this is your first digital ID, there will probably be only one.

13. Highlight the new certificate and click OK twice, then Close.

You can now use the Digitally Sign Message button in a message compose window. The digital signature serves to prove your identity and the authenticity of your message to those who receive it.

When someone sends you a digitally signed message, its icon in the Inbox will include a red ribbon seal.

When you view the message, you'll first see a help message explaining the digital signature. You can check the box at the end of the help message if you don't want to see it in the future. Then click the Continue button to see the message content.

 NOTE   Digitally signed messages have an extra line in the message header that says, "Security: Digitally signed and verified."

Encrypted E-Mail

The chances of your e-mail being intercepted and read by an unauthorized person are miniscule. However, if you're sending business secrets, financial information, or other sensitive material out over the Internet, miniscule may not be small enough for your peace of mind. Outlook Express includes tools that, along with digital IDs, allow you to send and receive encrypted (that is, coded) messages that are virtually impossible to crack.

For encrypted mail, both sender and receiver must have a digital ID. After you've acquired digital IDs, you'll need to exchange digitally signed messages.

To send encrypted e-mail to the person from whom you have received a digitally signed message, you'll need to add that person's digital ID to their record in your Address Book.

1.   Open the signed message you've received and choose File ➤ Properties.

2.   On the Security tab, click Add Digital ID to Address Book. This opens the Properties sheet for the entry, if the person is already in your Address Book. Otherwise, it creates a new entry with the name, e-mail address, and digital ID.

3.   Click OK twice.

Skill 9

You can add or change whatever information you wish, as described in "Using Windows Address Book" later in this skill.

 **WARNING** If the person who sent the digitally signed message has more than one e-mail address, and the message was sent from an address not listed in your Address Book, you will need to manually enter the e-mail address in step 2. Also, the process is likely to fail if you have multiple address book entries for the same person. Multiple e-mail addresses for the same person are not a problem when adding the digital ID as long as they are stored in the same Address Book record. To send an encrypted message to someone with multiple e-mail addresses, you will have to set their default e-mail address to one for which you have a digital ID.

You can now use the Encrypt Message button on the compose window toolbar to encode messages to this person.

When someone sends you an encrypted message, it will be marked with a lock icon.

When you read the message, the first thing you'll see is a help message explaining encrypted e-mail. If the message has been properly encrypted by someone to whom you gave your digital ID, Outlook Express will decrypt it automatically. Click the Continue button at the end of the Help screen to view the message.

 TIP After you've seen the Help screen once, you really don't need to see it again, so add a checkmark in the box that says *Don't show me this Help screen again*.

Using the Mail Folders

The left pane of the Outlook Express main window offers a tree view of the folders used to organize your mail and newsgroup messages. Click any folder to open it. Here is a brief description of the folders:

Inbox Where incoming e-mail lands. Whether you read it or not, your messages stay in the Inbox until you put them somewhere else.

Outbox   Where outgoing e-mail and newsgroup messages are held. When the messages are transmitted (uploaded to your ISP and then to the recipients), they are moved out of the Outbox to the Sent Items folder.

Sent Items   Holds copies of messages you have sent.

Deleted Items   Keeps copies of items you have deleted from other folders. If you want this folder emptied automatically when you quit Outlook Express, you can set this option on the General page of the Tools ➤ Options dialog box.

Drafts   Holds messages you may or may not want to send in the future. To compose a draft message, open the folder and select Compose Message. Write the message and then save and close it. Later, you can open it again and send it, delete it, or modify it some more.

News Servers   Listed by the friendly name you assign, as described in the next section.

You can create new folders by right-clicking in the upper part of the pane (above the news servers). This is one good way to create a filing system to organize your e-mail. Move messages by dragging headers from the upper right pane to the folder where you want them. You can also create copies with the File ➤ Copy to Folder command in a compose window.

 NOTE   Outlook Express folders are not Windows 98 folders, and can only be used within Outlook Express.

Participating in Newsgroups

An important part of the Internet is the Usenet, composed of thousands of *newsgroups*. A newsgroup is like a community bulletin board: Anyone can post anything. Often the only restraints are self-imposed, based on the topic and decorum (or lack thereof) of the particular newsgroup. There is no assurance of accuracy, quality, or even authenticity of postings, though many newsgroups are reasonably reliable because the participants are, too.

Newsgroups are hosted on news servers, also called NNTP servers (for Network News Transfer Protocol). Your Internet service provider should give you access to at least one news server. The total number of public newsgroups on the Internet is near 20,000, but some news servers carry only a few thousand of these.

 NOTE   Some newsgroups are *moderated*. That is, totally off-the-wall or inappropriate postings aren't allowed, and advertisements are deleted. Also, many news servers are limited to special purposes. For example, as part of the beta test of Windows 98, Microsoft operated a news server open only to beta test participants. It hosted over a hundred newsgroups devoted to discussing various features of the operating system and its accessories.

Programs that allow you to read newsgroup postings and post your own messages are called newsreaders. Outlook Express is a newsreader as well as an e-mail program. If you have another newsreader installed, you can set which program Internet Explorer opens when you use its Go ➢ News command. In Internet Explorer, choose View ➢ Internet Options ➢ Programs. Set the News drop-down list to the newsreader you prefer.

Adding a News Server

The process of reading and creating newsgroup postings is very similar to e-mail, so it's appropriate that Outlook Express handles both operations. The first step in gaining access to newsgroups is to tell Outlook Express what news server to use.

1. Look at the left pane of the Outlook Express main window. Any news servers you have already set up will be listed here.

2. If you need to set up a new server, choose Tools ➢ Accounts.

3. Click the News tab.

4. Click Add and choose News. The Internet Connection Wizard starts.

5. Enter the name you want to appear in the From field of messages you post. Click Next.

6. Enter your e-mail address. This allows other newsgroup participants to send you private e-mail, as well as responding in the newsgroup. Click Next.

7. The dialog box shown in Figure 9.12 appears. Enter the news (NNTP) server name given to you by your service provider. If the server requires users to log on, check the box at the bottom. Click Next again.

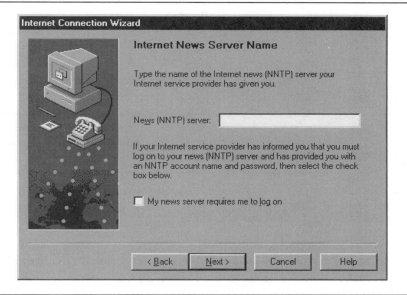

FIGURE 9.12: Entering your news server name

8. If you checked the logon box, a dialog box will appear where you enter your logon name and password. Fill these in and click Next, or skip to step 9 if you don't have to log on.

9. Enter a "friendly name" for this news server. This name will identify the server in Outlook Express. Click Next again.

10. Choose your method for connecting to the Internet. If you connect via a local area network or choose to connect manually, this is your last entry. Click Next, and then Finish.

    or

    If you want Outlook Express to dial automatically to connect, choose Connect Using My Phone Line, then click Next.

11. The necessary connection should already be set up on your computer, so choose it from the list and click Next, then Finish.

    or

    If you need to set up a new connection, choose Create a New Dial-up Connection, click Next, and continue with the Wizard.

 NOTE   If you need more information about setting up a connection, refer to Skill 6, *Connecting to the Internet*. Also, if you have trouble making a new connection, read Skill 12, where we do it without benefit of a Wizard.

Searching Newsgroups

Once you've set up your news server, you'll want to know what newsgroups it carries. Highlight the news server in the left pane of Outlook Express, and answer Yes to the question that appears about viewing a list of available newsgroups. Outlook Express will connect to the server and download the list (see Figure 9.13). This may take a few minutes because the major news servers (like those used by the online services) carry many thousands of newsgroups.

When it's done, the list of newsgroups will appear, as shown in Figure 9.14.

FIGURE 9.13: Downloading a list of newsgroups

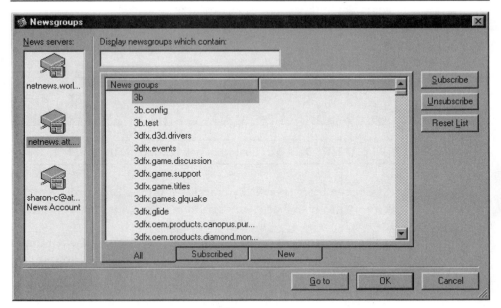

FIGURE 9.14: Viewing a list of newsgroups

Considering that there are almost 20,000 entries on this particular list, you could spend a long time just browsing through it even once. To shorten the process, enter a keyword in the box at the top. For example, a sports fan might enter *sport* in the text box (see Figure 9.15). That shortens the list dramatically, but it's still pretty long.

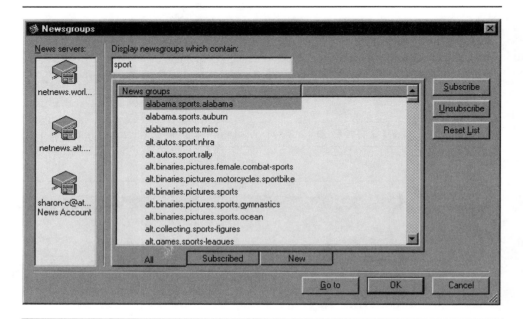

FIGURE 9.15: Listing of newsgroups with "sport" in their names

Get even more specific by entering multiple keywords, separated by spaces, to see only groups whose names contain all of your keywords. In Figure 9.16, the listings have gotten a lot more focused.

Some experimentation may be necessary because the naming of newsgroups is only occasionally systematic. When you find newsgroups you want to check out, highlight them and click Subscribe.

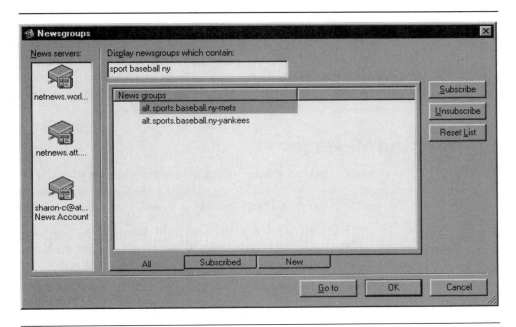

FIGURE 9.16: Adding more words narrows the list

When you'd like to look at the newsgroups, click the Subscribed tab and check over your list. Then click OK. The news server should still be highlighted in the left pane. Now go to the Tools menu and choose Download This Account. Outlook Express will connect to your server and download the headers of approximately the last 300 messages posted in each newsgroup to which you have subscribed.

 TIP   You can return to the Newsgroups dialog box to change your subscriptions by clicking the News Groups button on the toolbar. If a newsgroup turns out not to be what you're looking for, simply Unsubscribe.

Skill 9

Now click the + beside the news server name in the left pane of Outlook Express. This will expand the folder to list all the newsgroups to which you subscribed. Click a group and the upper right pane will list the message headers. You can change the sort order of the list by clicking the column headers. If you are still online, clicking any message header will download the text, which will appear in the lower right preview pane. A + beside a message header indicates there are replies. Click the + to see the list of replies.

Getting Messages

If you disconnected after getting the headers, clicking a header will produce a message in the preview window that the message is not cached and you need to connect to the server. Here's how to do it efficiently and minimize online time:

1. With the list of headers in view, hold down Ctrl as you look through the list. Click each header that interests you. Don't expand the lists of replies; just click the one visible header (for the original posting).

2. When you are finished, choose Tools ➢ Mark for Retrieval ➢ Mark Message.

3. Choose Tools ➢ Download This Newsgroup.

4. In the dialog box that appears, accept the default Get Marked Messages, then click OK.

5. Outlook Express will again connect to your news server and will download the full text of the messages you selected, including replies.

6. On the list of headers, the icon for the messages you chose to download has changed from a half page (header only) to a full page, indicating that the full text has been downloaded and cached for you to read when you wish.

7. As with e-mail, click on a header to read the message in the preview window. Double-click to open the message in a separate window.

 NOTE   If you want to keep messages after you've read them, go to the Advanced tab of Tools ➢ Options, and remove the checkmark from the box labeled Don't Keep Read Messages.

Reading and Replying

There are several ways you can read newsgroup messages, depending on your Internet connection and your preferences. If you have a full-time connection or don't mind staying online, you can use the header pane to select messages, which will appear in the preview pane. Or you can double-click a header to open the separate message reading window. Navigate by using the Next and Previous buttons on the toolbar, or equivalent menu commands or hotkeys. There are also Next Unread Message and Next Unread Thread commands under Next on the View menu.

If you prefer to download selected messages as described in the "Getting Messages" section, you still have two ways to view them. You can use the header pane to select and the preview pane to read. If you prefer to read messages in a separate window, first go to the View menu in the Outlook Express main window. Under Current View, choose Downloaded Messages. Now when you double-click a header to open the message reading window, you can navigate just among the messages you downloaded, without having to bother with all the other headers.

 NOTE   There are many possible ways to organize your reading of newsgroups. For additional helpful hints, look at Outlook Express's Help, especially the Tips and Tricks section.

In replying to a newsgroup posting, you must first decide whether you want to reply with a posting in the newsgroup or by private e-mail. To reply with a posting, click the Reply to Group button on the toolbar. If you are using the Outlook Express main window, the button is labeled.

In the message reading window, it looks like this:

The Reply to Author buttons mean that you're sending a message to the author by e-mail that will not be posted in the group.

Either way, the reply window is very similar to the one used for replying to e-mail, as discussed earlier in this skill. When you click the Post button, the message will be placed in your Outbox. It will be transmitted the next time you connect to your news server.

Posting a New Message

To post a new message in a newsgroup, open Outlook Express. In the main window, be sure the appropriate newsgroup is highlighted in the left pane. Click the Compose Message button.

The cursor is already in the Subject field, so you can just enter the subject, then use the Tab key to move to the text area and start typing your message. If you want to post to multiple newsgroups, click the icon in the Newsgroups field and select from a list of the newsgroups to which you subscribe. You can use the Cc field to send copies as e-mail to anyone listed in your Address Book.

When you're finished, click the Post button on the toolbar. The message will be placed in your Outbox, to be posted to the newsgroup the next time you connect.

TIP Newsgroup etiquette is sometimes a delicate matter. Pay attention to the tone of discussion if you want to be sure that your contributions will be welcome. As the new person, it's always best to read a newsgroup ("listen") for a while before you post ("speak").

Using Windows Address Book

Though the Windows Address Book can serve broader purposes, its most effective use is likely to be limited to Internet-based communications. For example, it is nicely integrated with Outlook Express and Internet Explorer, but it can't use the Windows Phone Dialer to dial a phone number.

You can open the Windows Address Book from the Start menu by going to Programs ➢ Internet Explorer ➢ Address Book. It can also be opened from Outlook Express's main window toolbar, or from the Go menu in Internet Explorer. Figure 9.17 shows how Address Book opens.

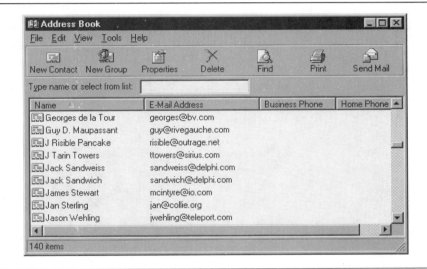

FIGURE 9.17: The Outlook Address Book

As in similar Windows programs, you can sort based on a column's subject by clicking the column header button. Click the button again to reverse the order. A small pointer indicates which column is sorted, and whether it is ascending or descending. You can also go to View ➢ Sort By to set whether sorts on the Name column are done by first or last name.

Skill 9

Adding Contacts

Click the New Contact button to create a new entry in the Address Book. This opens the dialog box shown in Figure 9.18.

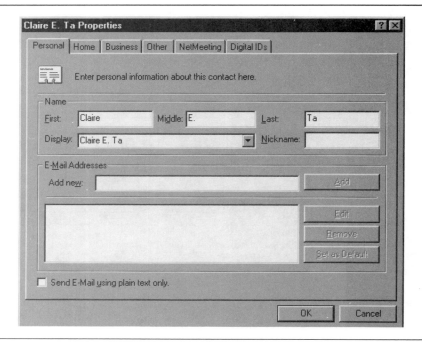

FIGURE 9.18: Adding a new entry to the Address Book

On the Personal page of this dialog box, you can enter the person's name and nickname. The display name will identify this record in the Address Book. Also on this page, enter the person's e-mail address. If there is more than one, click Add after entering the first e-mail address; this will put the address in the list box and allow you to enter the next address.

On the Home and Business pages, you can store the person's home and business addresses and phone numbers, including fax, pager, and cellular numbers, as well as company, job title, and department. There are also fields for personal and business Web page addresses.

The Other page allows you to include free-form notes about the person, and the NetMeeting page stores information needed for Internet phone calls and conferencing, using the Microsoft NetMeeting software that is part of the Internet Explorer 4.0 package. Finally, the Digital IDs page stores the codes used for digital signatures and encrypted e-mail.

Besides storing information about individuals, you can create groups to use as mailing lists. Click New Group on the Address Book toolbar. Give the group a name and select the individuals you want to be part of the group.

Using Address Book Information

You will probably most often use Address Book information in Outlook Express. When composing a new message, clicking the Address Book button on the toolbar or any of the file card icons in the To or copies (Cc and Bcc) fields allows you to choose recipients from your Address Book. If you choose a group, all of the group's members will receive the message.

On the General page of the Outlook Express Tools ➢ Options dialog box, you can choose the option *Automatically put people I reply to in my Address Book*. The default is Yes. Unfortunately, there's no way to do this on a case-by-case basis, except by entering the information manually.

Internet Explorer's Profile Assistant uses Address Book to store information about you. You can then use Profile Assistant to quickly send such information to Web sites that request it. More details on this are in Skill 7.

You can open Address Book itself to make use of the full range of information you have stored there. The initial view shows only the person's name, default e-mail address, and business and home phone numbers. For any other information, you must double-click the entry and choose the tab you need in the Properties dialog box. Once there, you can copy out information you need, or edit the entry. If you have entered personal or business Web page addresses, you can use the Go button beside the entry to open the page.

Are You Experienced?

Skill 9

Now you can...

- ☑ **Send and receive e-mail**
- ☑ **Customize your mail**
- ☑ **Digitally sign and encrypt mail**
- ☑ **Participate in newsgroups**
- ☑ **Use your Address Book**

SKILL 10

INSTALLING AND RUNNING PROGRAMS

- Installing a program
- Finding a program
- Removing programs
- Making programs easy to find

Programs—also called applications—have become easier and easier to install in recent years, but there are still occasional pitfalls. In this skill, we'll cover the steps for installing programs, whether or not the program is one designed for Windows 98. Later in the skill, you'll find information on how to set up the programs you use most to be available when you want them.

Installing a Program

In general, computer programs are easy to install. If you're going to have a problem, it's most likely to happen when you try to *run* a program. Programs that are genuinely compatible with Windows 98 or Windows 95 are the easiest to install.

Installing from a CD

If the program is supplied on a CD-ROM, it may almost install itself. Some CDs are self-starting. Put the CD-ROM in the drive, and in a few seconds you'll see a window like the one shown in Figure 10.1.

In the window that opens, you choose what you want to install from the choices presented. After that, you answer the questions that are asked as you go along. You're often asked to supply your name, approve the location for files, and perhaps supply other information.

 TIP   If you put the CD-ROM in the drive and nothing happens, go to "Installing from the Control Panel" later in this skill.

Most applications will copy some files to your hard drive, and when the setup procedure is completed, you remove the CD-ROM. You won't need it again until and unless you need to reinstall or you later decide to install some piece of software on the CD that you skipped the first time.

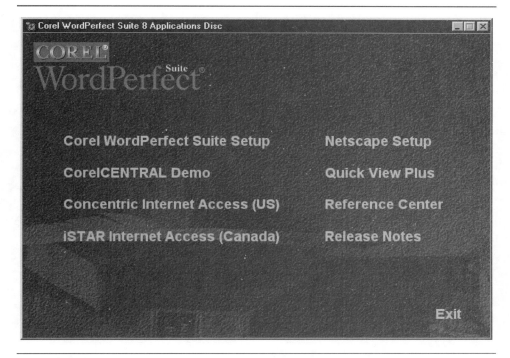

FIGURE 10.1: Corel's WordPerfect Suite on a CD-ROM automatically starts and lets you choose what to install.

Running from a CD

Some programs are so large that you may not be able to install all their data files for space reasons. Or you use them only infrequently and don't want to clutter your hard drive with a zillion graphics files. In that case, you can often *run* the program from the CD. For example, WordPerfect (see Figure 10.2) offers the option of running the program from the CD.

Skill 10

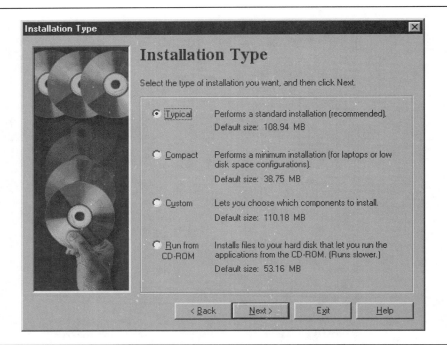

FIGURE 10.2: Selecting the installation type for WordPerfect

While this type of installation uses only minimal hard drive space, it will also cause the program to run much more slowly. For a word processing program, which you presumably use for extended periods, this will be both annoying and frustrating. Getting and using files from the hard drive is much faster than even the fastest CD-ROM drive. And you won't be able to run the program at all unless the CD is in the CD-ROM drive.

 TIP   If your hard drive space is severely limited, try a laptop installation rather than running a frequently used application from the CD-ROM drive.

Many programs that are designed to be run from the CD-ROM don't give you any other option. These are often games and reference works (dictionaries, encyclopedias, catalogs of graphics, etc.). These programs will set up by copying some

files to your hard drive, but they will still require the CD-ROM to be in the CD-ROM drive in order to work.

For example, The Encarta World Atlas copies about 10MB to your hard drive (see Figure 10.3). These are the files used, for the most part, to make accessing the CD-ROM faster.

FIGURE 10.3: Installing files for a program to be run from the CD-ROM

The Encarta World Atlas runs speedily enough from the CD-ROM drive because you're looking at a series of maps with at least a second or two between each. This is a positively restful pace for acquiring images from a CD. In the case of games, perhaps 80MB or more will be copied to the hard drive. All the files necessary to keep the action moving will be on your hard drive with only backgrounds or help files retrieved from the CD.

TIP   If you have plenty of space, you can copy the entire contents of a CD to your hard drive and run the program from there. For example, I sped up searches through the Encyclopedia Britannica by copying all 601MB to my local hard drive. With hard drive space selling at an average of 4 cents per megabyte, that isn't as much of an extravagance as it might seem.

Skill 10

Installing from the Control Panel

All programs, whether on a CD or on floppy disks, can be installed using Add/Remove Programs in the Control Panel. Put the CD in the CD-ROM drive or the first floppy disk into the floppy drive and follow these steps:

1. Click the Start button and select Settings ➢ Control Panel.

2. In the Control Panel, click the Add/Remove Programs icon.

3. In the Add/Remove Programs Properties box, click the Install button. Click Next.

4. The application will search for a setup program, first in the floppy drive and then in the CD-ROM drive. Usually it will find setup and proceed with the installation. If it doesn't, you'll see a dialog box like the one in Figure 10.4.

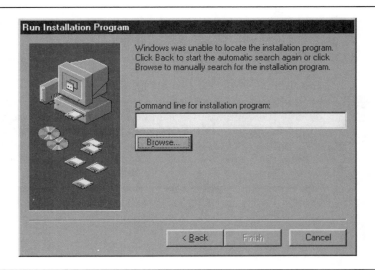

FIGURE 10.4: Add/Remove Programs is unable to find the new program's setup file.

5. If you know exactly where the setup program is on the CD or the floppy disk, you can, of course, type the path into the Command Line text box. But more likely, you'll need to click the Browse button.

6. The Browse window opens showing your C: drive. Use the Look In drop-down box to move to your floppy drive or CD-ROM drive.

7. Find the setup file (the program's documentation will be helpful here) and select it (see Figure 10.5). Click the Open button.

FIGURE 10.5: This program's setup file is in a subdirectory on the CD-ROM.

8. You'll return to the installation process with the path for the setup file shown in the Command Line text box (see Figure 10.6). Click Finish.

9. The setup program will be run and the actual installation of the new program will start.

 TIP   Programs downloaded from the Internet or other sources are installed in a similar fashion. You can use Add/Remove Programs, pointing to the setup file location on your hard drive. Or you can click the setup file directly to start the installation process.

Skill 10

FIGURE 10.6: With the setup file located, you can click Finish to move on in the installation process.

Removing a Program

The process of removing a program (also called uninstalling) varies depending on whether the program is a true 32-bit program written for Windows 95 or Windows 98, or something older.

A software producer who wants the license to put a Windows 98 or 95 logo on a product is required to make sure the program can uninstall itself. This proviso is intended to correct a problem in Windows 3.1. When using Windows 3.1, it was very difficult to completely get rid of some programs because their files could be spread all over the hard drive. The average person has no way of knowing whether a file called, let's say, fxstl.dll is disposable because it belonged to a long gone program or whether deleting it will cause the entire system to fail!

A few programs that claim to have been written for Windows 95 or 98 can be uninstalled and still leave bits of themselves cluttering your hard disk. How the major programs written for Windows 98 or 95 handle Add/Remove varies widely. Some will just uninstall themselves without a fuss; others give you the option of removing all or just part of the program. *Nothing* will be uninstalled without your OK.

To remove a Windows 98 or Windows 95 program, follow these steps:

1. Click the Start button and select Settings ➤ Control Panel.

2. Click the Add/Remove Programs icon.

3. In the dialog box that opens (shown in Figure 10.7), you'll see a list of programs that can be automatically removed. If the program you want to uninstall is in the list, highlight it and then click the Add/Remove button.

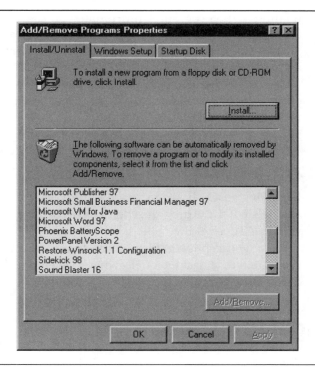

FIGURE 10.7: In this window, select a program to uninstall.

4. A dialog box will open describing what will be removed by this step. Click Yes to continue.

5. The program will be uninstalled.

Sometimes after the removal, you'll get a message to the effect that not all parts of the program could be deleted. Since you're not told *which* parts, this is something less than helpful. For the ultimate in hard drive tidiness, look into one of the third-party programs like Uninstaller or WinDelete, which are very good at getting rid of stray files with safety.

Removing a Windows 3.1 Program

Programs written for Windows versions prior to Windows 95 don't have an uninstall capability. These programs aren't hard to get rid of—at least superficially. Just find the directory for the program and delete it. Delete shortcuts relating to the program. Unfortunately, these early Windows programs have an unhappy tendency to deposit files in the main Windows directory, the System subdirectory, and anywhere else that the program's designers thought appropriate.

Getting rid of every trace of such a program is very difficult unless you have a program like Uninstaller. Most of the time, however, it's not absolutely necessary to track down and delete every stray .dll file. You can survive quite well even if bits and pieces of a program remain.

Removing a DOS Program

Removing a DOS-based program is the easiest of all. Find the program's folder and delete it. DOS programs don't have roaming files, so if you delete the folder, you delete everything.

The only exception to the nonwandering file is if you have a shortcut to the program on the desktop or elsewhere. Delete the shortcuts at the same time you delete the program folder.

Finding a Program

There are times when you've installed a program only to be abruptly returned to the desktop with your new application nowhere in sight. Or you inherit a computer that you know has certain programs on it—but they're likewise nowhere in sight.

Starting with the easiest method, here are some ways to find a program hiding on your system.

Program Menu   Your application may be in the easiest place of all. Click the Start button and select Programs. If it's not in the first menu, look for something that might be a "parent" to the one you want. For example, Figure 10.8 shows the Encarta World Atlas under the more general heading of Microsoft Reference.

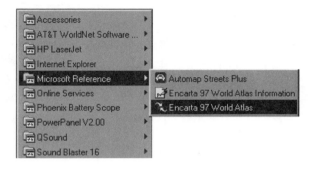

FIGURE 10.8: Finding the Encarta World Atlas program under a more general heading

Shortcuts   Look for a shortcut on your desktop. If all you want to do is launch the program, clicking on the shortcut should do the job. If you want to find the physical location for the program's files, right-click the shortcut and select Properties from the pop-up menu. In the Properties dialog box, click the Find Target button. The folder containing the program will open.

Find   Knowing the name of the program is usually enough to use the Find feature. Click the Start button and select Find ➢ Files or Folders. In the Named text box, type in what you know. In Figure 10.9, I'm looking for a program made by Starfish. Sure enough, the search turns up a folder called Starfish, and inside is the program I'm looking for.

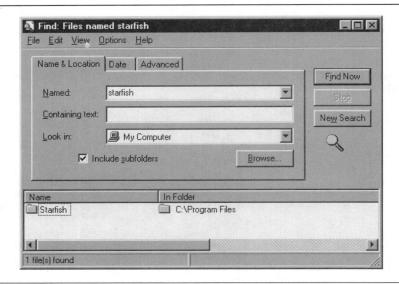

FIGURE 10.9: The Find function turns up a folder named Starfish.

I could just as easily search using a partial filename or program name. Sometimes it takes two or three tries to find what you're looking for.

Windows Explorer When all else fails, you can simply open Windows Explorer and browse. Be sure to look in the Program Files folder as well as any Temp folders. The folder may be clearly named or it may not. In Figure 10.10, it's not hard to figure out what might be in Internet Mail and News, but what about NAVHMI or the even more cryptically named NC? Once you get to this stage of searching, you'll just have to poke around.

TIP If you're in an unhelpfully named folder looking at even more unhelpfully named files, look for a file that really might help (it'll have the .hlp extension) and click it. You'll be looking at a help file that—with the addition of some thought—will tell you what program you're dealing with.

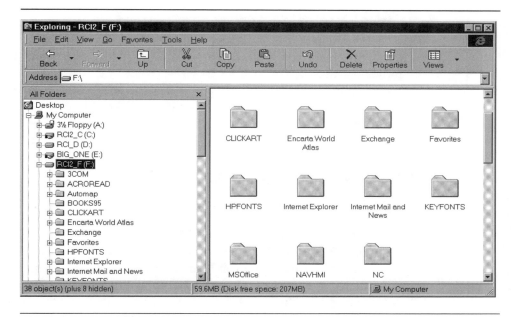

FIGURE 10.10: Searching for program files in Windows Explorer

Making Programs Easier to Find

Once you've been through a few searches like the ones just described, you realize the importance of making your programs easy to find. In the next sections, you'll see how to put your programs in convenient locations. When you're deciding, do give some consideration to how often you use a given application. If you put shortcuts to all your programs on the Start menu or on the desktop, the resultant clutter will immediately cancel out any gain.

To make a shortcut to a program on the Programs menu, you need to first locate the program file. This is the file you click on to start running the program. In general, this file will have the extension .exe and will have the same name (or a shortened version) as that of the overall program. As an example, the program file for Word for Windows is Word.exe and that for WordPerfect 8 for Windows is wpwin8.exe. On the other hand, the program file for Quicken for Windows is qw.exe, and for InfoSelect it's is.exe.

Skill 10

Desktop Shortcuts

As described in Skill 3, shortcuts are easily made. For a shortcut to a program, right-click the program file in Windows Explorer and select Send To ➤ Desktop As a Shortcut.

If you already have a shortcut on the desktop or in a folder, you can make a copy of it to use somewhere else. Even if you make a shortcut to a shortcut, the second shortcut will point back to the original file, *not* to the first shortcut. So you needn't worry that deleting a shortcut will somehow disrupt the connection.

Programs Menu Shortcuts

To put a shortcut on the Programs menu, follow these steps:

1. Right-click the Start button and select Open.

2. Click Programs. A window like the one in Figure 10.11 will open. Each item on this list corresponds to an entry on the Programs menu (shown on the left in Figure 10.11). Items that appear as a folder in the window are the items on the Programs menu with an arrow (➤) next to them—indicating that there are additional items to be found if you follow the arrow.

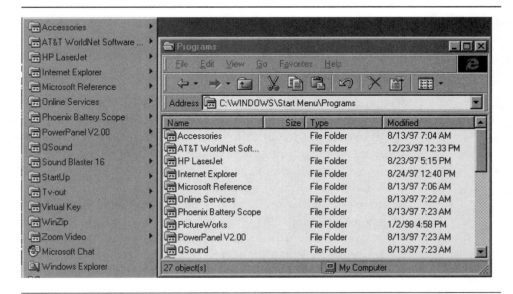

FIGURE 10.11: Comparing the Programs window to the Programs menu

3. If the shortcut is to be at the first level of the Programs menu, drag and drop the shortcut you've made into the Programs window.

4. To put the shortcut at the next level down, drag it into one of the folders in the Programs window. For example, drag and drop a shortcut to a game in the Accessories folder.

You can also easily move a program that's a level or two down up to the first Programs menu level:

1. In the Programs window, find the shortcut you want to move.

2. Right-click on the shortcut and select Cut from the pop-up menu.

3. Click the Up icon on the Programs window toolbar to move up one level in the Programs menu.

4. Right-click in a blank area of the new window and select Paste from the pop-up menu.

The program shortcut will move to its new location.

Start Menu Shortcuts

Adding a shortcut to the Start menu is as easy as drag and drop. In fact, that's what you do. Drag the shortcut to the Start button and drop it. When you open the Start menu, your shortcut will be listed among the programs at the top.

Toolbar Shortcuts

Even quicker access to a program can be had if you add a shortcut to the Quick Launch toolbar. By default, the Quick Launch toolbar comes with shortcuts to Internet Explorer, Outlook Express, Channels, and the desktop already in place.

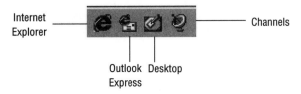

Internet Explorer — Channels

Outlook Express   Desktop

Add any shortcut to the toolbar by dragging the shortcut to the toolbar and dropping it there. You can remove shortcuts from the toolbar by reversing the procedure. Click the icon on the toolbar and, holding the mouse button down, drag the icon to the desktop. When you release the mouse button, the icon will be moved, and it's a simple matter to delete it using the right mouse button menu.

TIP　The Show Desktop icon on the Quick Launch toolbar is a great new addition in Windows 98. It acts as a "minimize all" button—minimizing all open windows to the Taskbar, even dialog boxes that won't ordinarily minimize. If you'd like to have other copies, right-click on the icon and drag it to the desktop (or to an open folder). Release the mouse button and select Copy Here from the pop-up menu.

Send To Shortcuts

A right-click on a file or almost any other object will produce a menu that includes Send To ➢. When you follow the arrow, you'll see a list of shortcuts to possible file destinations such as the floppy drive, mail recipient, or My Briefcase.

To modify the Send To list, follow these steps:

1. Right-click the Start button and select Explore from the menu.

2. In the Windows Explorer window that opens, look for the SendTo folder in the left pane (see Figure 10.12).

3. Click the SendTo folder to open it.

4. Add to, delete, or rename any of the shortcuts. The changes will be shown as soon as they're made.

NOTE　If a program—any program—doesn't want to run or hangs or crashes, see Skill 17 for troubleshooting tips.

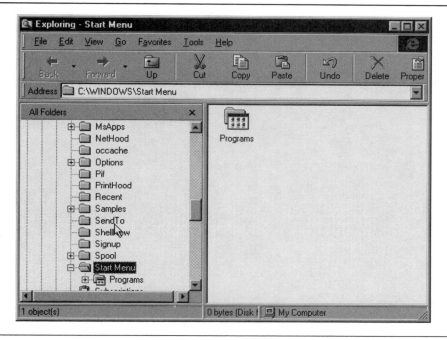

FIGURE 10.12: The mouse pointer shows the location of the SendTo folder.

Are You Experienced?

Now you can...

☑ Install and remove programs

☑ Find programs on your computer

☑ Make programs easily available

SKILL 11

RECEIVING INFORMATION BY SUBSCRIPTION

- Previewing channels
- Subscribing to a channel
- Subscribing to a page on your Favorites list
- Changing your subscription options
- Managing content delivered to your computer

Browsing is a fun way to find information on the World Wide Web, but it can be time-consuming. There's so much exciting information available on the Web that, before you know it, you've spent an hour or more just browsing around!

The solution? Subscribe to a channel, or to a page on your Favorites list, and have the information delivered to you.

You've already learned how to compile a Favorites list in Skill 7. In this skill, you'll learn how to view channels, how to subscribe to channels and to pages on your Favorites list, and how to manage your subscriptions.

Subscribing to a channel is like subscribing to a newsletter or magazine; information is delivered to you, on a schedule set up by the publisher of the page. Subscribing to a Favorites page is like running to the corner newsstand to pick up the newspaper; the information is there, but you have to go and get it. There are no fees involved for either type of subscription.

Reviewing Channel Selections

Channels are selected Web sites that deliver updated information to you, usually on a regular schedule. Any Web site can be set up to work as a channel, if the author of the site creates a Channel Definition Format (CDF) file.

A CDF file is an easy-to-code file that contains instructions on how the channel should deliver content. For example, a CDF file can contain a list of pages to be delivered to subscribers, a delivery schedule, and an abstract of each page. The CDF file is invisible to you when you're reading a Web page—you won't even know it is there. It's just a tool the author of the site can use to manage the information that is downloaded when people subscribe to the channel.

Using the Channel Guide

Any Web page can be a channel, but not all channels are listed on the Channel Guide. The Channel Guide shows channels that are preselected to be included with Windows 98.

The Channel Guide is listed on the Channel bar. To access the Channel Guide, use one of these methods:

- On the desktop, click the Channel Guide icon on the Channel bar.

- On the Taskbar, click the View Channels button.

- On the Internet Explorer screen, click the Channels button on the toolbar.

The Channel Guide groups channels into categories. You can roam around the categories as much as you like. When you see information you want to receive regularly, enter a subscription to the channel (described later in this skill).

Previewing Channels

There are a lot of channels to choose from on the Channel Guide, covering topics from News & Technology to Lifestyle & Travel. Before you subscribe to a channel, you'll want to preview the available channels to see what's out there.

To preview channels on the Channel Guide, follow these steps:

1. Click the Channel Guide icon on the desktop. If the Dial-up Connection dialog box appears, enter your username and password and connect to the Internet. Categories on the Channel Guide are displayed, as shown in Figure 11.1.

FIGURE 11.1: Selecting a category on the Channel Guide

2. Click the News & Technology category.

3. Click the CNET: The Computer Network logo on the News & Technology screen. If you don't see the CNET logo, click the Next 7 arrow to display more logos. Many channel previews move through a series of screens to show you what kind of information the channel carries. Figure 11.2 shows one of the CNET screens.

4. When you're finished in the News & Technology category, click the Today button on the toolbar. The Channel Guide is displayed, and you can select other categories to preview.

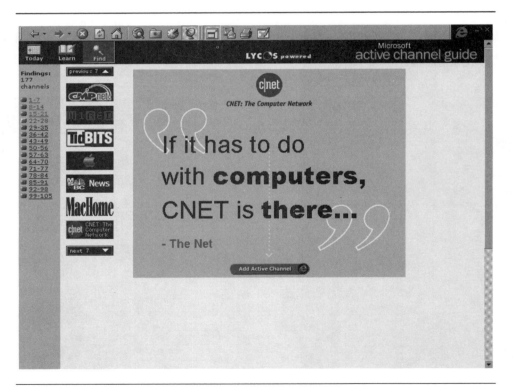

FIGURE 11.2: Previewing a channel. Reprinted with permission from CNET, Inc. Copyright 1995-7. www.cnet.com.

Subscribing to a Channel

While previewing channels, you probably noticed an Add to Channels button, or a similarly worded button, on almost every channel page. The buttons are there to help you subscribe to the channel. Subscribing to a channel does the following:

- Adds the channel to your Channel bar, so you can access it quickly.

- Sends an e-mail message to your Inbox to notify you when new information is available at the site (this is an optional feature).

- Downloads the updated information to your computer so you can read it offline (another optional feature).

- Allows you to set up a specific time when information is downloaded to your computer, according to your Daily, Weekly, Monthly, or Custom subscription schedule.

THE MECHANICS OF SUBSCRIPTIONS

What's the difference between subscribing to a channel and subscribing to a page on your Favorites list in Internet Explorer? The screens you'll go through to set up both types of subscriptions are almost the same. Where the subscriptions differ is in how information is gathered for you.

- When you subscribe to a channel, the author of the Web site determines what new information will be made available to you. The author can specify a lot of different options about how and when content is made available. This helps keep subscribers from being overwhelmed with information.

- When you subscribe to a Favorites page, a *crawler* program goes through the sites, looking for new information. The information is not screened; anything new is marked as updated information.

You might prefer the managed flow of information you get with channels, or you may find you like to sift through the new information yourself.

continued ▶

> Personally, I'd rather see all the new information and decide for myself what interests me. Experiment and see which type of subscription you prefer. It's not an all-or-nothing commitment—you can mix it up and subscribe to as many channels *and* Favorites pages as you like.

Adding the Channel Subscription

Signing up for a subscription is a simple process. If you use the default schedules set up in Windows 98, adding a subscription takes only a few clicks of the mouse. If you customize your schedules, you're presented with a few more options and screens to complete.

You can change a subscription or delete it at any time, so don't worry if a subscription isn't exactly right the first time you enter it. You have a lot of options to make subscribing to Web sites as flexible as possible.

To add a subscription to a channel from the Channel Guide:

1. Open the Channel Guide (see the previous section "Using the Channel Guide") and click the News & Technology category.

2. On the News & Technology screen, click the CNET: The Computer Network logo.

3. On the CNET: The Computer Network screen, click the Add Active Channel button. The Add Active Channel[TM] Content dialog box is displayed, as shown in Figure 11.3. Notice that you can elect to just add the channel to your Channel bar, to be notified when new content is available, or to be notified and have the content downloaded.

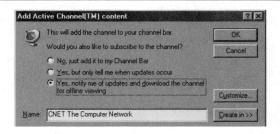

FIGURE 11.3: Subscribing to a channel

4. Select the third option on the list and click OK. When you select this option, the content is downloaded to your computer (on the day and time listed in your update schedule), and you can read it without connecting to the Internet.

5. To keep your current screen saver, click No in the Channel Screen Saver dialog box. Your subscription is added, and the full CNET: The Computer Network page is displayed, as shown in Figure 11.4.

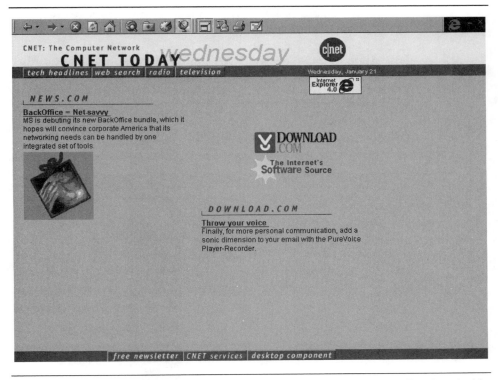

FIGURE 11.4: CNET: The Computer Network's channels page. Reprinted with permission from CNET, Inc. Copyright 1995-7. www.cnet.com.

Viewing Channel Content

Tomorrow, or the next day, or whenever you're ready to go back and see the content on your subscribed channels, all you have to do is click the channel on the Channel bar. If you set up your subscription to download information to your computer, you'll be able to view information without connecting to the Internet. You can view the channels you've subscribed to from any of these places:

- The Channel bar on the desktop

- The Channel bar in Internet Explorer

- Your Favorites list in Internet Explorer

- The View Channels screen (To get to this screen, click the View Channels button on the Taskbar. When the screen appears, be ready to click the push pin icon on the Channel bar to keep the Channel bar from sliding off the screen.)

After adding the CNET: The Computer Network channel, the Channel bar on your desktop should look like Figure 11.5.

FIGURE 11.5: Channel bar showing one channel subscription

As you can see, there's plenty of room to add more channels to the Channel bar. Filling in the Channel bar is a good way to access channels quickly, even if you don't subscribe to all of the channels you place there.

Subscribing to a Page on the Favorites List

Putting Web pages on your Favorites list in Internet Explorer gives you quick access to the pages you visit the most. If you want to go beyond that, add a subscription to the Favorites page, and you'll either receive notification when the page changes, or have the page downloaded to your computer.

Subscribing to a Favorites page saves your time—you won't have to visit each Favorites page looking for new information. You can let the crawler program do that for you at regularly scheduled update times.

To add a subscription to a page on the Favorites list:

1. Open Internet Explorer.

2. Click the Favorites button on the toolbar.

3. On the Favorites list, right-click the page you want to subscribe to, and select Subscribe on the pop-up menu.

4. In the Subscribe Favorite dialog box, choose the option to download information, as shown in Figure 11.6, and click OK. If you want to be notified by e-mail, click the Customize button, and answer the e-mail questions.

 TIP   You can also subscribe to a page as you add it to the Favorites list. Select Favorites ➤ Add to Favorites, and choose one of the "Yes" options.

In the future, when there is updated information on the page, you'll see a gleam—a small red splash—on your Favorites list.

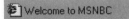

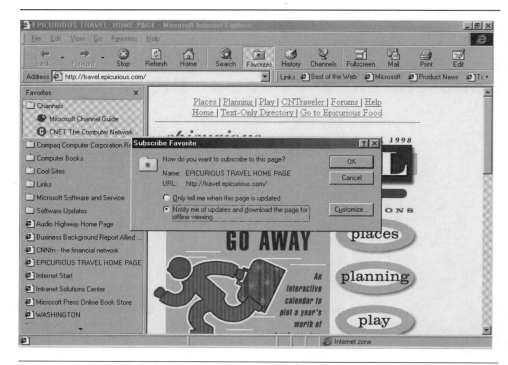

FIGURE 11.6: Subscribing to a Favorites page. Reprinted with permission from CondeNet, Inc. `http://travel.epicurious.com`.

To view an updated page, click the page on the Favorites list.

TIP   You can also see your Favorites list by clicking the Start button and selecting Favorites.

Revising the Update Schedules

Regular updates keep your subscriptions current. Even if there isn't any new information on a page, it's nice to know the subscription feature went out and looked for it.

You assign subscriptions to a Daily, Weekly, or Monthly update when you first subscribe, and specify the frequency and time of day (or night) for each schedule.

If you're connected to the Internet all day at work, you can schedule updates for any hour during the day. However, if you have dial-up access to the Internet, you can either manually update your subscriptions or set them to dial up automatically. To set automatic dial-up updates, follow these steps:

1. Open Internet Explorer, click the Favorites menu, and select Manage Subscriptions.

2. Right-click the subscription and select Properties. Click the Schedule tab and put a check in the box next to *Dial as needed if connected through a modem*.

3. Click OK. Repeat for other subscriptions you want updated this way.

You do not have to be at your computer for the update to be made, but the computer and modem must be turned on.

When updates start, you can watch the progress of the update in a status box on the screen. (See the section "Updating a Subscription Manually" later in this skill for more on watching the progress of an update.)

To change an update schedule:

1. Open Internet Explorer and select Manage Subscriptions from the Favorites menu.

2. In the Subscriptions list, right-click the one you want to change and select Properties.

3. Click the Schedule tab and set an automatic update or a manual one (see Figure 11.7).

Skill 11

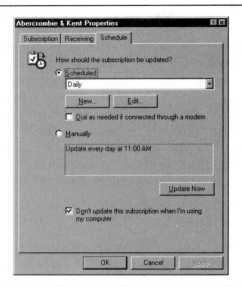

FIGURE 11.7: Changing the Daily schedule

Changing a Subscription

The update schedule isn't the only part of a subscription you can change. The options you selected when you added the subscription can be revised as well.

To change the options on a subscription, follow these steps:

1. Open Internet Explorer and select Favorites ➣ Manage Subscriptions. The Subscriptions folder is displayed, as shown in Figure 11.8. The Subscriptions folder shows when the next update is scheduled to occur, the schedule assigned to the subscription, and the size of the downloaded files. A new subscription that has not been updated yet shows "Unknown" in the Last Update field.

2. Right-click any subscription and select Properties on the pop-up menu. From the Properties dialog box, you can change the following information:

    *   The way you are notified when a subscription is updated. (To change the notification method, click the Receiving tab.)

- The amount and type of information you receive when the page is downloaded (To enter a change, click the Receiving tab, and then click Advanced.)

- The schedule assigned to the subscription (Click the Schedule tab.)

- The Daily, Monthly, or Weekly schedule (Click the Schedule tab, and then click Edit.)

3. Enter your changes in the Properties dialog box and click OK.

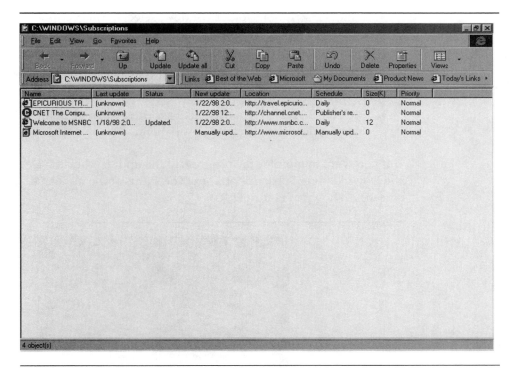

FIGURE 11.8: Viewing all subscriptions in the Subscriptions folder

 TIP To delete a subscription, right-click the subscription and select Delete on the pop-up menu, or click Unsubscribe in the Properties dialog box.

Updating a Subscription Manually

Even if you have a subscription scheduled to update every few hours, you won't always want to wait for the automatic update to kick in—you need the most current information, and you need it now.

When this happens, update the subscription manually. You can update a subscription at any time and as often as you want. Use one of these methods to do so:

- In Internet Explorer, select Favorites ➤ Manage Subscriptions. Right-click the subscription and select Update Now on the pop-up menu.

- In the Subscriptions folder window, select the subscription and click the Update button on the toolbar.

- In Internet Explorer, click the Favorites button on the toolbar. On the Favorites list, right-click the subscription and select Update Now on the pop-up menu.

- Click the Start button and select Favorites. Right-click the subscription and select Update Now on the pop-up menu.

If you want to monitor the progress of the update, click the Details button on the Downloading Subscriptions box. The status of the update is charted on the screen, as shown in Figure 11.9.

FIGURE 11.9: Monitoring the progress of a manual update

Updating All Subscriptions

If you want all of your subscriptions updated immediately, open Internet Explorer and select Favorites ➤ Update All Subscriptions.

TIP   If you have the Subscriptions folder open, click Update All on the toolbar to update all subscriptions.

Deleting the Temporary Internet Files

The Temporary Internet Files folder holds all of the information you download from the Web, as well as pages from your History list. The size of this folder increases quickly. To conserve storage space on your computer or the drive that holds this folder, you should clean out the folder periodically.

When you delete the contents of the folder, you won't be able to view information offline until your subscriptions are updated again, or until you visit Web pages in Internet Explorer and build up a History list.

Cleaning out the Temporary Internet Files folder deletes only the Web pages stored in the folder. Your subscriptions and links on your Favorites list are not touched.

To delete the temporary internet files:

1. Open Internet Explorer and select View ➤ Internet Options.

2. In the Temporary Internet Files section on the General page, click the Delete Files button.

3. Select the Delete All Subscription Content checkbox, as shown in Figure 11.10, and click OK until you are back at the Internet Explorer screen. The temporary files are deleted.

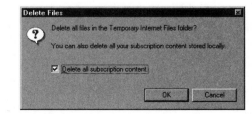

FIGURE 11.10: Deleting subscription content in the Temporary Internet Files folder

Are You Experienced?

Now you can...

- ☑ **Use the Channel Guide to preview channels**
- ☑ **Subscribe to channels**
- ☑ **Subscribe to pages on your Favorites list**
- ☑ **Modify a subscription**
- ☑ **Manage subscription content downloaded to your computer**

SKILL 12

DIAL-UP NETWORKING

- Configuring a dial-up connection
- Connecting to another computer over a phone line
- Allowing another computer to connect to you

Methods for setting up an account with an Internet service provider were covered in Skill 6. However, there's another dial-up connection you may be called upon to make. If you travel on business or work at home, it's very handy—perhaps necessary—to be able to connect to your company's network, if only to check your e-mail.

The network administrator (and company policy) determines the kind of access you can have. That same administrator will provide you with technical data that you'll need. But when you're trying to dial-up from a motel in Boise or access the office network from home at 2 A.M., you're pretty much on your own. This skill aims to give you the information needed to make a successful connection.

Calling a Network from Your Computer

Windows 98 comes with all the software you need to make a successful dial-up connection, but not all of it is installed by default. To install a dial-up connection, you'll need the following:

- A modem, preferably 28.8Kbps or faster. You can connect using a slower modem, but unless you're merely transferring a few text files now and then, a slower modem will be dreadfully slow.

- A regular telephone line

In addition, your network administrator at work will provide you with:

- A username and password for the network

- The phone number you call to make the connection

- Any special instructions if the network connection doesn't support PPP (Point-to-Point Protocol)

 NOTE   Remote Access Services (RAS) and Dial-Up Networking (DUN) are often used interchangeably, but they're not the same. When you call to connect to another computer, you're using dial-up networking. When that computer allows you to connect, it's performing Remote Access Services. This may seem like a distinction without a difference, but careful use of terminology can save you a lot of trouble when you're talking to technical support or getting advice from your know-it-all neighbor.

Checking Network Components

You'll also need to have some network components installed, namely:

- Client for Microsoft Networks
- TCP/IP -> Dial-Up Adapter

To check if these are installed, right-click the Network Neighborhood icon on the desktop. Select Properties from the pop-up menu. On the Configuration page you'll see a list of the installed network components. You may have additional adapters (such as a network card) and additional protocols listed.

The configuration list in Figure 12.1 shows that a TCP/IP dial-up adapter is not installed.

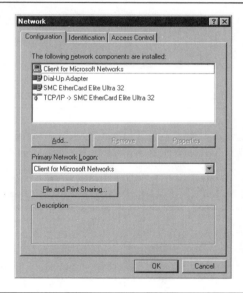

FIGURE 12.1: Viewing a list of the installed network components

To install a dial-up adapter for TCP/IP, follow these steps:

1. On the Configuration page of the Network dialog box, highlight Dial-Up Adapter and click the Add button.

2. In the Select Network Component Type box, select Protocol and then click Add.

3. In the next window (shown in Figure 12.2), select Microsoft in the left pane, TCP/IP in the right pane, then click OK.

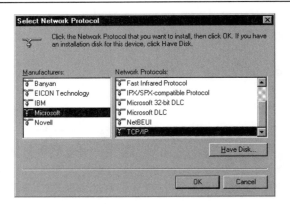

FIGURE 12.2: Select the manufacturer and then the type of protocol.

After a pause, you'll be returned to the Network Configuration page, and the new dial-up adapter will be in the list of installed components.

 TIP   Changes to network configurations require a reboot to take effect.

If there are other dial-up adapter protocols (such as NetBEUI), simply delete them. Don't delete the plain Dial-Up Adapter.

You can install the Client for Microsoft Networks in a similar way. On the Configuration page, click Add and then select Client in the Network Component Type window.

Configuring the Connection

In Windows 98 (as in Windows 95) an icon in the Dial-Up Networking window represents the settings for a connection. To start the process of making the connection, first click My Computer, click the Dial-Up Networking folder, and then follow these steps:

1. Click the Make New Connection icon.

2. The Wizard starts with a window like the one shown in Figure 12.3. Provide a meaningful name for the connection, so if you add others you'll be able to keep them straight in your mind.

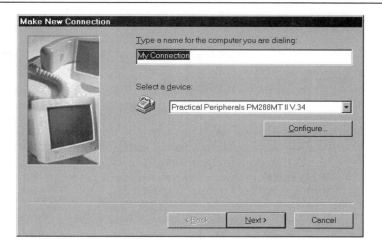

FIGURE 12.3: Supply a name for the connection you're about to make.

3. Select the modem you want to use (if you have more than one) and click the Configure button.

4. On the modem's property sheet, set the maximum speed to 115,200 for 28.8 modems and 57,600 for 14.4 modems. Don't check the box that says *Only connect at this speed*. Click OK and then Next.

5. Type in the area code and phone number you're calling. Click Next and then Finished. An icon with the name you selected will appear in the Dial-Up Networking Folder.

6. Right-click the new icon and select Properties. You shouldn't need to change anything on the General properties page (see Figure 12.4)—assuming you entered the correct information in the first place.

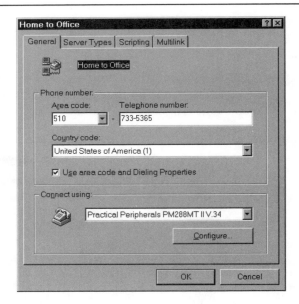

FIGURE 12.4: The properties pages for the new connection

7. Click the Server Types tab. Change the server type only if you have specific instructions from the network administrator to do so. Clear all the other options except Enable Software Compression and TCP/IP (see Figure 12.5).

8. Click the TCP/IP Settings button. The network administrator for the server you're connecting to determines the settings on this page. You may have a regular IP address or you may be assigned one by the server each time you log on. You also may have a regular names server address or you may be assigned one by the server you're connecting to. Click OK when the TCP/IP settings are established.

FIGURE 12.5: Making more settings for the connection

9. Click the Scripting tab and supply a path to a script (if necessary). See "Using a Script" next for more information. Click OK when you're finished.

Using a Script

Some connections require a complicated login procedure that you won't want to do manually. In that case, you'll use a script—which is really no more than a very simple program—to automate whatever secret handshakes and signals are necessary.

Generally, the person running the server should supply you with the script. However, Windows 98 comes with several script examples (files with the .scp extension in the Accessories folder inside the Program Files folder). Also, inside the main Windows folder is a document called script.doc that contains information on writing scripts to be used by Dial-Up Networking.

Skill 12

266 Skill 12 • Dial-Up Networking

Making the Call

To dial up to the network and connect, click the Connection icon in the Dial-Up Networking folder. Enter your username and password (see Figure 12.6).

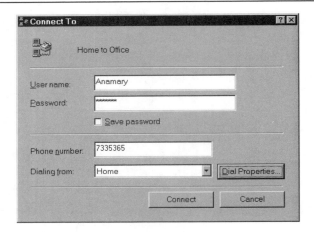

FIGURE 12.6: Enter your username and password for the connection.

Click the Save Password box if you don't want to enter it every time you make the call. Then click the Connect button.

You'll see a box like the one in Figure 12.7 showing the progress of the call. It may take a few seconds or as long as a minute for the connection to be made.

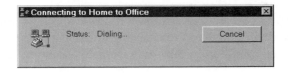

FIGURE 12.7: Making the connection

At the server end of the connection, remote access can be figured in a number of different ways.

- You call, your username and password are validated, and you're connected to the files and resources to which you've been granted permission.

- You call, log in, and the server calls you back at a previously fixed number (to reduce the chances of unauthorized access).

- You call, log in, and the server prompts you for a telephone number. After you enter it, the server calls you back, thus incurring the telephone charges for the session (easy for people who travel a lot).

- You call, log in, and you're passed through to a second login. This may require a second name and password, or it may not.

Indeed, there are even more ways that a login from a remote computer can be handled. The important point is that these methods are determined by the computer you're logging in to, so if you run into difficulty, consult the person who manages that server.

Dialing Manually

To make a connection manually, click My Computer ➤ Dial-Up Networking and then follow these steps:

1. Highlight the icon for the connection you want to make.

2. Select Properties from the File menu.

3. On the General page, click the Configure button.

4. Next, click the Options tab.

5. Put a checkmark in the box next to *Operator assisted or manual dial*.

6. Click OK twice.

7. Click the icon for the connection. When prompted, lift the receiver and dial the telephone number. When you hear the tone from the receiving computer, hang up.

 TIP   When you first set up your modem, you put a phone wire between the line socket on the modem and the wall socket. Plug your phone into the modem's phone socket, and you can use the phone to dial manually.

Disconnecting the Call

Once the connection is made, an icon that looks like two small computers will appear on your Taskbar.

To disconnect the call, right-click that icon and select Disconnect from the pop-up menu.

Letting a Computer Dial Up to You

Just as you can be a dial-up client, with Windows 98 you can also be a server—allowing another computer to dial up and connect to whatever files and resources you choose to share.

Although Dial-Up Networking is installed by default, Dial-Up Server is not. To install it and allow access to your computer, follow these steps:

1. Click Start ➢ Settings ➢ Control Panel ➢ Add/Remove Programs.

2. Click the Windows Setup tab.

3. Highlight Communications and click the Details button.

4. On the Communications page, place a checkmark next to Dial-Up Server. Click OK twice. You may have to provide your Windows 98 CD-ROM to set up Dial-Up Server.

5. Click My Computer and then Dial-Up Networking. From the Connections menu, select Dial-Up Server (see Figure 12.8).

6. In the Dial-Up Server dialog box (shown in Figure 12.9), click Allow Caller Access and then the Change Password button to set a password that will be required from incoming callers.

7. Click OK when you're finished.

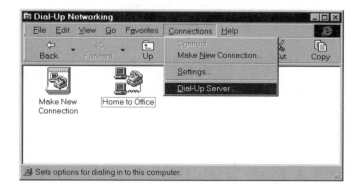

FIGURE 12.8: Connecting to the Dial-Up Server configuration

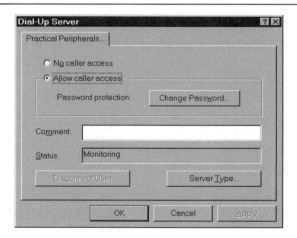

FIGURE 12.9: The dialog box for setting up Dial-Up Server

While Dial-Up Server is active, you won't be able to dial out because the server holds the port open to receive calls. To use your modem to dial out, you'll need to open the Dial-Up Server window and click No Caller Access. This turns off Dial-Up Server, and you'll need to restart it after you make your call out.

 **WARNING**   As you can see in Figure 12.9, the configuration is simple—and therefore not particularly secure. You can allow access or not allow access, and the only thing between your machine and everyone else in the world is a single password. Realistically speaking, this is probably enough if only one person is dialing up to your computer, but it is completely inadequate otherwise. If you want to be a full-fledged dial-up server, upgrade to Windows NT Server, which includes considerably more security features.

Are You Experienced?

Now you can...

- ☑ **Configure a dial-up connection**
- ☑ **Make the connection automatically or manually**
- ☑ **Let another computer make a dial-up connection to your computer**

SKILL 13

MAKING OTHER CONNECTIONS

- Making a direct cable connection
- Understanding Briefcase
- Using HyperTerminal
- Using Phone Dialer

In previous skills, we talked about connecting to the Internet and using e-mail. Later, in Skill 14, we'll discuss how to put together your very own network. In this skill, however, we'll cover all the other ways of making connections that are built into Windows 98. There's a direct cable connection, useful for linking two machines for the transfer of files. You'll also see how to use Briefcase, a very handy tool for keeping the files on two machines synchronized. Finally, you'll learn about two connectivity applets that have been part of Windows for some time: HyperTerminal and Phone Dialer.

Making a Direct Cable Connection

Networks and floppy disks are two ways to move files from machine to machine, but sometimes a network is overkill, and a floppy disk is inadequate. Let's say you've bought a new computer. It's all new from the ground up, but you have files and applications on the old computer that have taken you ages to configure *just so*. An easy way to transfer files from hither to yon is a *direct cable connection*.

For a direct cable connection to work, you'll need either a serial or a parallel cable. The types of ports that are free on the two machines determine which type of cable you need. The connection must be from serial port to serial port or from parallel port to parallel port.

For a serial-to-serial connection, you'll need a null modem cable. For a parallel port connection, you'll need what's commonly called a "LapLink" cable (LapLink is the name of a software package that also does a direct cable connection and much more). It's a pass-through cable with a centronix connector at each end.

> **TIP**   At a minimum, every computer comes with one parallel port (LPT1—customarily assigned to the printer). The PC will also have two serial ports (COM1 and COM2). If your modem is external to the computer box, it's undoubtedly plugged into one of the serial ports. If your mouse doesn't have its own port, it will be plugged into the *other* serial port. If you can use the parallel connection, do so. It's faster by a substantial margin.

To use Windows' Direct Cable Connection, both machines must be running either Windows 98 or Windows 95. Before you start, decide which computer is the *Host* (the computer that has the files you want to access) and which is the *Guest* (the one being used to access the files on the Host).

Connect the cable to the machines and then follow these steps, starting with the Host computer.

1. Click the Start button and select Programs ➤ Accessories ➤ Communications ➤ Direct Cable Connection.

2. Designate this computer as the Host. Click Next.

3. Select the port to be used for the connection. (There may be a short delay while the system looks for available ports.) Click Next.

4. Indicate if you want the Guest to supply a password. This isn't necessary unless this is an ongoing connection in an environment where security is advisable.

5. Direct Cable Connection will initialize the port and announce that it's waiting to be called (see Figure 13.1).

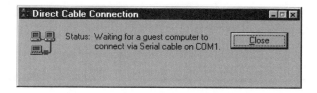

FIGURE 13.1: Waiting to be called by the Guest computer

6. Go to the Guest computer. Click the Start button and select Programs ➤ Accessories ➤ Communications ➤ Direct Cable Connection.

7. Once the connection is made, the Guest computer will look for shared folders on the Host. You can copy, move, delete, or do whatever you wish to the shared resources.

Once the connection has been set up, subsequent connections are much more quickly done. Just select Direct Cable Connection on the Host and click the Listen button (see Figure 13.2).

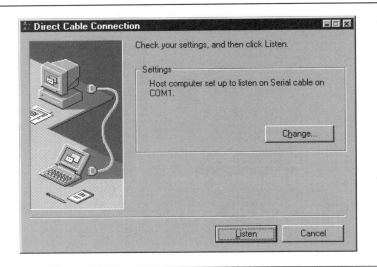

FIGURE 13.2: The Host is ready to resume the connection.

Do the same on the Guest computer and click Connect.

 A direct cable connection has a serious limitation in that all communication is strictly one way. If you want to be able to connect two computers on a regular basis and don't want to set up a simple peer-to-peer network (my choice), you can invest in the LapLink program, which is a good deal more flexible and useful than a plain cable connection.

Understanding Briefcase

The Briefcase is an odd little device that's on every desktop and pops up in various menus, and yet very few people actually use it. That's a shame, because if you work on two computers, Briefcase can be an efficient way of keeping your files synchronized so that you always have the latest version in front of you.

For example, let's say I'm working on a book called *Windows 98: No Experience Required*, and I have to travel for a week. I copy the chapters I'm working on and the related art work and notes from my desk computer to my laptop computer. While I'm on the road, I send completed chapters to the editor via e-mail and receive edited chapters back. I also start a new chapter, change some old ones, leave some alone, and delete some illustrations I've decided not to use.

All this is fabulously efficient—until I get home and start trying to figure out what's what. Without Briefcase, it's a painstaking file by file examination, comparing dates and file sizes, and getting increasingly annoyed, especially when I accidentally delete a chapter I've been working on.

With Briefcase, I make synchronized copies of my files on the laptop before I leave home. When I get back, the program compares the files in my laptop Briefcase with the Briefcase on the desk computer and reports on the differences.

Briefcase works especially well for a laptop with a network docking station. The Briefcase can be as large as you need it to be. But you can even use Briefcase for files that will fit on a floppy disk and move files back and forth that way.

Here's how to make a Briefcase for a networked portable computer:

1. Open Briefcase on the laptop (or make a new one by right-clicking on the desktop and selecting New ➤ Briefcase from the pop-up menu).

2. Open the shared folder(s) on your main computer and copy files into the Briefcase on the laptop.

3. While the laptop is disconnected from the network, be sure to work on the files in the Briefcase. In other words, open them from there and save them back to the Briefcase location.

4. When you want to synchronize the files, connect the laptop to the network and click the Briefcase. Select Update All from the Briefcase menu. Or highlight some files and click Update Selection.

5. In the Update window (shown in Figure 13.3), the files that have changed are shown. You can accept all the changes by clicking Update.

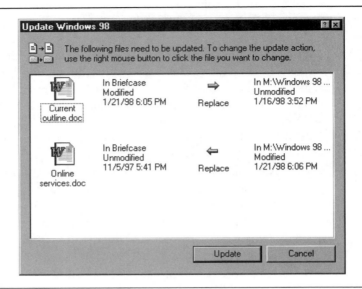

FIGURE 13.3: Showing the files that have been changed since the last update

6. You can also right-click a file and reverse the direction of the change, or skip any updating altogether.

For computers that aren't connected, you can still put a Briefcase on a floppy disk and keep files synchronized. Follow these steps:

1. Insert a disk into a disk drive on your main computer.

2. Open a Briefcase and copy files to it.

3. Click the Start button and select Programs ➢ Windows Explorer. Click the floppy disk icon in the left pane.

4. Drag the Briefcase icon to the right pane of Windows Explorer. The contents of the Briefcase are copied to the disk.

5. Put the disk into a disk drive on your laptop computer, and then edit the files in the Briefcase on the laptop.

6. To synchronize the files, reinsert the disk containing the Briefcase into a disk drive on your main computer, and then click the Briefcase on the desktop.

7. On the Briefcase menu, click Update All. Or, to update only some files, highlight the files you want to update, and then click Update Selection.

To separate a file in a Briefcase from the original, highlight the file and select Split from Original from the Briefcase menu. The file is now an orphan and can't be updated.

 TIP   You may create a new file while traveling and save it in the Briefcase. When you go to update the Briefcase, the program will refuse to update the new file, labeling it an orphan. To get around this, before you update, move the new file into the source folder on the main computer. Then drag and drop it into the Briefcase, making a synchronized copy. Update the Briefcase.

Using HyperTerminal

The most common way to transfer files these days is probably through e-mail. However, there may come a time when you need to do a dial-up connection to a non-Windows computer or a bulletin board. HyperTerminal will let you do that fairly easily.

As a demonstration of how to use HyperTerminal, let's create a hypothetical scenario. Suppose you are a travel writer—always on the go—and you need to periodically send your stories back to your publisher and retrieve your new assignments.

We'll create a fictional connection to your publisher, Skinflint Travel, send files back and forth, and save the configuration for future use.

1. Click the Start button and select Programs ➤ Accessories ➤ Communications ➤ HyperTerminal. Click the HYPERTRM icon.

2. Type **Skinflint Travel** in the Name text box.

3. Scroll through the icons until you locate one that resembles a briefcase and umbrella—what better icon for a traveler?

4. Click the OK button. You will see the Connect To dialog box shown in Figure 13.4. If the number you want to dial is located in a country other than the one shown in the Country Code box, click the downward-pointing arrow at the right end of the list box and select the correct country.

FIGURE 13.4: Supplying the connection phone number

5. Enter the area code and phone number in the appropriate text boxes and click OK.

6. The Connect dialog box opens, but since this is the first time we've run this application, click the Dialing Properties button to check your settings. Look over the options in this dialog box (shown in Figure 13.5) and make sure that they're correctly set.

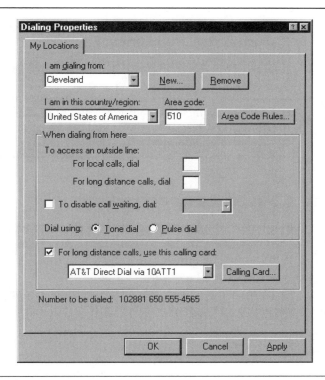

FIGURE 13.5: Checking dialing properties

7. If you click the Calling Card button next to *For long distance calls, use this calling card*, a dialog box will open for you to enter your telephone credit card number. After you enter the calling card information, click OK.

8. If you have to dial a number (typically 9 or 7) to get out of your business or hotel phone system, enter it in the box next to the text that reads *To access an outside line, for local calls, dial*. Enter the number (or numbers) you dial for long distance access in the next text box.

9. When you are through filling out this dialog box, click OK. At this point, all you need to do is click Dial to make the connection. If all the settings you made in the previous dialog boxes are correct, the call will go through, and you can upload your story to the publisher.

10. When you're through placing your call, pull down the Call menu and select Disconnect, or click the icon that looks like a handset being hung up, and the connection will be broken.

11. When you close the window, you will be prompted to save the session.

 NOTE　HyperTerminal includes setups to call CompuServe, AT&T, and MCI Mail in terminal mode. A terminal connection is totally interactive—you have to provide all the codes and parameters.

Using a Saved Connection

We just created a connection with a name and an icon. This connection appears in the HyperTerminal program group. Any time you want to use this connection in the future, simply click the icon, and all the settings (telephone number and so forth) will be in place for you.

Any time you want to change the settings in a particular connection, open the connection, pull down the File menu, and select Properties.

Sending Files

Once you've connected with a remote computer, you can upload or download files. This is the principal reason for making this sort of connection. Hyper-Terminal supports the following file-transfer protocols:

- 1K Xmodem
- Kermit
- Xmodem
- Ymodem
- Ymodem-G
- Zmodem
- Zmodem with Crash Recovery

Binary Files

To send a binary file, follow these steps:

1. After the connection is made (as described in the previous sections), pull down the Transfer menu.

2. Select Send File. A dialog box will open.

3. Using the options in this dialog box (see Figure 13.6), specify the file to send. (Click the Browse button to locate and identify the file to be sent.)

4. Select the protocol for file transfer. Zmodem with Crash Recovery is the best choice because it combines speed and excellent error correction.

5. Click the Send button. The file will be transferred.

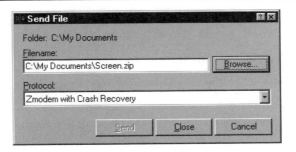

FIGURE 13.6: Selecting a file to send and the protocol to send it

---

TIP   Make sure the receiving computer can receive files in the protocol you choose. Zmodem and Xmodem are almost universal, but if you have a problem transferring a file, check this first.

Text Files

Text files are a little different from binary files. Most file transfer software distinguishes between binary files and text files, sending one in Binary mode and the other in ASCII mode or Text mode. HyperTerminal is no different.

To send a text file, follow the steps for a binary file, except choose Send Text from the Transfer menu. When you specify the file to send and click the Open button, the file will be sent as if you had typed it into the terminal program.

TIP Unless you're transferring files to a UNIX system, you should send *every* file as a binary file. Even a little bit of formatting in the file can cause a text file transfer to fail, while any file can be sent as a binary transfer.

Receiving Files

To receive a file being sent from another computer, follow these steps:

1. While you're still connected, pull down the Transfer menu and select Receive File. That will open a dialog box that looks very like the Send File dialog box shown in Figure 13.6.

2. Click the Browse button to specify a filename and location for the received file.

3. Select a file transfer protocol.

4. Click the Receive button to start receiving the file from the remote location.

NOTE Take the above steps when you hear the incoming call from the other computer. You have to do this yourself, because HyperTerminal is not smart enough to answer the phone.

Saving a Session

To help you remember how to navigate the complexities of a service you don't use very often, terminal programs provide *logging*—a way to save everything you do in a particular session to disk and/or print it on paper.

To save everything to disk:

1. Pull down the Transfer menu and select Capture Text.

2. By default, all the screen information in a session will be saved in a file called capture.txt in the HyperTerminal folder inside the Accessories folder. Of course, you can use the Browse button to save the file in a different location. Click Start when you're ready.

3. Pull down the Transfer menu again. Now you will note that there is a tiny triangle next to the Capture Text option. Select it, and you will see a sub-menu with Stop, Pause, and Resume options to give you control over the capture.

4. If you prefer to send the session to the printer rather than to a file on your disk, pull down the Transfer menu and select Capture to Printer.

Using Phone Dialer

If you make a lot of phone calls, you can turn over the connection task to Phone Dialer's capable, if virtual, hands.

To use Phone Dialer, you need a telephone on the same line you're using for your modem. If you have a separate phone line for data, you'll need an actual telephone on that line to use Phone Dialer. Since modems all have a jack for a phone in addition to the line jack, this is easily done.

To access Phone Dialer, click the Start button and select Programs ➤ Accessories ➤ Communications ➤ Phone Dialer. You'll see the window shown in Figure 13.7.

FIGURE 13.7: Use Phone Dialer to prevent digit woe.

The Phone Dialer gives you two simple ways to make phone calls using your computer, described in the next two sections:

Speed Dialing   If you have a number you need in an emergency or one you call constantly, you can enter it in the Speed Dial list.

Telephone Log   If you have a long list of numbers you call periodically, you can simply type those numbers into the Number to Dial text box and they will be added to a telephone log. You can access your log by clicking on the downward-pointing arrow at the right end of the Number to Dial box.

Speed Dialing

To create a speed dial number:

1. Click the Start button and select Programs ➤ Accessories ➤ Communications ➤ Phone Dialer. Pull down the Edit menu and select Speed Dial. You will see the dialog box shown in Figure 13.8.

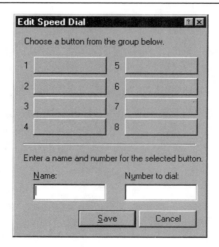

FIGURE 13.8: Speed Dial puts you on the telephone fast track.

2. Click the speed dial button you want to assign.

3. In the Name text box, type the name of the person or place you will dial with that button.

4. In the Number to Dial text box, type the number to dial.

5. Click Save. (You'll be returned to the Phone Dialer dialog box, and the name you entered in the Edit Speed Dial dialog box will appear on the speed dial button you selected.)

6. To speed dial the number, just click the button and lift your telephone handset.

The Telephone Log

As mentioned earlier, there are two ways to use the Phone Dialer. The quick and easy way is to use the speed dialer, but as you'll have noted, the speed dialer is limited to eight numbers. If you have more than eight numbers that you call on a regular basis, you'll have to use your log. Here's how:

1. Click the Start button and select Programs ➢ Accessories ➢ Communications ➢ Phone Dialer.

2. Either type the number in the Number to Dial box or use the telephone keypad to punch in the number.

3. When the number's completely entered, click the Dial button and pick up your telephone. In a moment, you will be connected with the voice mail system at the number you are calling. (No one ever talks to real people anymore.)

4. To call the number again, pull down the Tools menu and select Show Log. This displays a list of all the numbers you have called.

5. To redial one of these numbers, click its entry in the log.

Are You Experienced?

Now you can...

- ☑ **Make a direct cable connection between two computers**
- ☑ **Use Briefcase to synchronize files on two computers**
- ☑ **Connect to another computer using HyperTerminal**
- ☑ **Use Phone Dialer to connect your phone calls**

SKILL 14

BUILDING A NETWORK

- Installing and configuring a peer-to-peer network
- Sharing resources on your own computer
- Mapping shared drives on other computers
- Selecting good passwords

Windows 98 comes with all the software you need to make a simple peer-to-peer network. All you have to do is add a network card for each machine, connect the network cards with some cabling, and do a little software configuring.

In this skill, I'll show you the basics of peer-to-peer networking—setting up two or three computers to share a printer and one (or more) common drives. We'll go from the easy to the hard stuff, so when you get what you need, just skip over the rest and get on with your life.

 NOTE   A few words of advice: Network terminology is intimidating until you get used to it. Don't be intimidated. At this level, there's nothing very difficult to master.

Pick a Network

There are essentially two ways to design a network: client/server, or peer to peer.

Client/Server   This type of network uses one or more computers exclusively as servers. This means a server can't be used for anything else, and it runs a special operating system. While there are very definite advantages to this kind of network, they really don't become compelling until a network starts to get bigger than what we are talking about here. The costs in hardware, software, and general complexity also make client/server networks uninviting for someone just trying to connect a few computers.

Peer to Peer   This second network type is what we're going to spend some time on in this skill. In a peer-to-peer network, every computer is equally important. For connecting a couple of computers together to share some files and a printer, this is the way to go. It's easy to set up, it requires almost no complicated network administration to maintain, and the cost is minimal. No additional hardware is needed except for the actual networking boards themselves and the cable. You don't need any special software, either, since the networking is built right into Windows 98.

Even if you think your setup might grow into one that will require a client/server network, you can still start with peer to peer. When your network reaches 10 computers or more, you can easily upgrade it to something like Microsoft's Small Business Server—an all-inclusive client/server networking product that includes server software for e-mail, proxy, and fax services.

Selecting Hardware

You'll need one network card per computer, enough pieces of network cable to connect them all, and the actual connectors, terminators, and so on for the cable.

Before buying network cards and cabling, decide what kind of cabling to get and how you are going to arrange your network. Only two cabling options make sense in a small network situation.

Thin Ethernet

Up until the last couple of years, the most common way to connect personal computers in a network was to use a thin piece of coaxial cable run from computer to computer. The cable *looks* a lot like cable-TV wire (although it isn't the same stuff), with a single, often solid, copper wire down the center and a braided shield like that shown in Figure 14.1. This is easily the simplest (and cheapest) way to connect two or three computers in close proximity to each other.

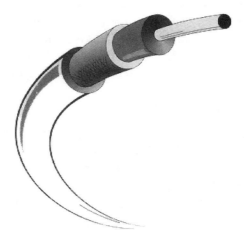

FIGURE 14.1: Thin Ethernet uses a coaxial RG-58 cable with a single central conductor and a braided shield.

NOTE   The cable for this connection method can be called thinnet, 10Base-2, co-ax, or thin Ethernet.

The total cost to connect two computers, including all cabling, cards, terminators, and connectors, can easily be under $200, and if you are careful, you could manage it for under $150.

The Thinnet Advantage

Thinnet has some definite advantages besides simplicity. Because the cabling is shielded, it's fairly resistant to electrical noise, and the maximum practical total distance your network can span is higher than with its primary competitor: unshielded twisted pair. Of course, distance isn't likely to be a major concern with a small network of the type we're talking about here. Thinnet becomes a requirement when 100 feet of cabling or more separates computers.

Hooking It Up

The most common method of hooking up a thinnet network is to hook each computer to the next one with a piece of cable between them, as shown in Figure 14.2.

Hooking one computer to the next in a series is called *daisy chaining*. Daisy chaining is simple, easy to understand, and requires no extra hardware. Once you get everything set up (assuming good quality cable and connectors), you generally don't have to think about it again.

One Shortcoming

A disadvantage of daisy chaining is that one bad piece of cable or a single bad connector in the network can bring the entire network down. (That's the main reason you don't buy the cheapest possible hardware.) Finding the bad connector or bad piece of cabling can be a very frustrating task. Of course, the smaller the network, the fewer pieces of hardware have to be ruled out when finding a problem.

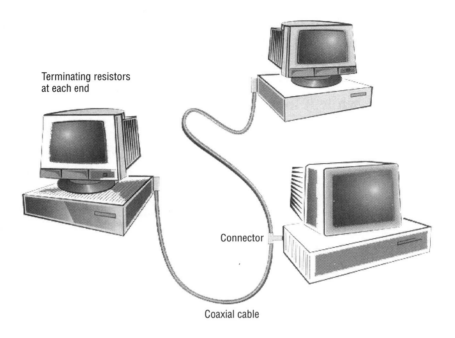

Terminating resistors
at each end

Connector

Coaxial cable

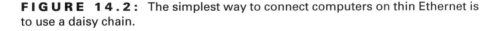

FIGURE 14.2: The simplest way to connect computers on thin Ethernet is to use a daisy chain.

Or Twisted Pair

Wiring based on twisted pair—or more properly, unshielded twisted pair cable—has started to replace thin Ethernet cable as the network cabling of choice. It's easy to install, requiring essentially the same skills as installing phone cable. Because it is smaller and flatter, it's easier to hide, and more wires will fit through a given space.

The cable, called variously 10Base-T, twisted pair, unshielded twisted pair, and UTP, looks a lot like standard phone cable and uses four pairs of wires twisted together, as shown in Figure 14.3. It has no shielding other than the inherent shielding effect of the twisted wires themselves. While it looks a lot like standard phone cable, the two are not interchangeable.

FIGURE 14.3: Twisted pair, or 10Base-T, wiring resembles a standard phone cable.

The Star Connection

Unlike thin Ethernet's daisy chain, UTP cables connect in a star configuration, as shown in Figure 14.4. The cabling to each individual workstation radiates out from a central hub. This has the distinct advantage of keeping a single bad cable or connector from disrupting the whole network. This makes troubleshooting easier, and in case of a cable failure, only one machine is out of service.

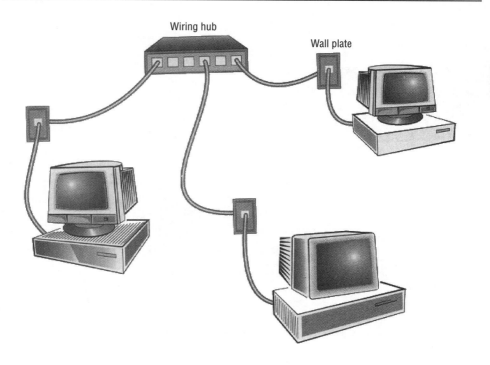

FIGURE 14.4: A star configuration means that a single bad connector or piece of cable won't bring down the entire network.

Some Disadvantages

The disadvantage of UTP, however, is that it requires at least one hub for the center of your star, and hubs aren't cheap—ranging from $300 to thousands of dollars for intelligent, stackable hubs. Of course, this cost is spread across the number of computers attached to the hub, so that cost is more on the order of $50 to $200 per workstation. Nevertheless, it's a lot of money just to connect a couple of machines.

The other disadvantages of UTP are not particularly important for most small networks. The effective maximum cable length from the hub to an individual workstation is substantially less than the maximum length between workstations with thinnet, and the cabling itself is somewhat less resistant to physical abuse and electrical noise. Neither of these will likely be major factors.

Buying Network Cards

You can't have a network without some way for your computers to connect to the cable. This takes a network card of some sort, or one of those network gizmos that attach to the parallel port of your laptop or plug into the laptop's PC Card slot.

First decide what cable you'll be using. Network cards come with one or more connectors on them, and you want to make sure that your card supports the connection you'll need. You can also get combo cards that support multiple types of cabling, but they cost a bit more than single interface types.

 TIP   Combo cards let you easily change your mind about cabling without having to buy all new network cards. Since permanent cable installation is such a major undertaking, however, you are unlikely to be changing it very often.

Should you get a 16-bit card, or a 32-bit card? Should it be a standard ISA bus card, or a VLB or PCI card? The answers to these questions have a lot to do with how you intend to use your network, but here are some general rules:

16-bit ISA bus card   For most purposes, this is more than adequate. On a small network, you are unlikely to need a bigger bandwidth than this card can handle, and they tend to be pretty cheap. However, if you buy the cheapest no-name card, you may find them to be very slow in transmitting data.

PCI network card   You might want to consider getting one of these for machines that will support them. They're fast and relatively cheap, and Windows 98 supports them as full plug-and-play devices.

EISA bus card   If you have an EISA bus computer, there are excellent and very fast network cards available. If you expect to use your network a lot or have more than a couple of machines on it, you will probably want to consider this option. Like all EISA cards, however, an EISA network card is going to cost you substantially more than a simple ISA card from the same manufacturer.

IRQs, Addresses, Memory, and Such

Old fashioned network cards required you to manually configure their IRQs, addresses, and other nerdy stuff. Every time you bought a new piece of hardware, you ran the risk of it interfering with your network card, and having to go through the whole process again. If you got it wrong, you were out of business—usually your computer wouldn't even boot, much less work properly if it did manage to struggle to life. You had no choice but to open the box, pull the card out, take another guess about what jumper to change to what position, and try the whole process again.

Well, those days are gone. The modern network card, even a simple 16-bit ISA card, uses an EEPROM (Electrically Erasable Read Only Memory) or Flash ROM to control its settings. A simple software program included with the card can configure the settings. (There are still some of the old cards around, so make sure you don't get one.)

Connectors and Terminators

Connectors and terminators are often given short shrift in the planning of a network. The most common point of failure on a network, however, isn't the cable or the network cards themselves but the means of connecting them to each other and the actual cable terminations.

For a typical small network, these little pieces will cost perhaps ¼ of the cable, and they are the first place that people tend to get cheap. After all, a $2.95 generic T-connector at the local Computers 'R Us looks just as good as an $8.75 AMP brand one from Black Box. Wrong answer! Don't get cheap here. Get the best ones you can. It will save you time, aggravation, and grief.

In the long run, it will actually save money.

Adding Cards and Protocols

Before you can actually use Windows 98 as a network, you need to install the network card into your computer and bind one or more network protocols to use the card.

NOTE   A *protocol* is just a fancy word for the method that your software (Windows 98 in this case) uses to talk to your hardware—and through cabling, to other computers.

The Add New Hardware Wizard

When you physically install the card, Windows 98 will notice the change the next time it boots up, and it will run the Add New Hardware Wizard to configure it. This process should happen automatically, but you can do it manually if for some reason it doesn't happen by itself. Just click the Add New Hardware icon in the Control Panel.

The Add New Hardware Wizard (see Figure 14.5) will walk you through the process of adding your new network card to your system. In addition, it will automatically install the minimal level of network support—adding the Microsoft client layer, so you can use files on someone else's Windows 95 or 98 computer—and both the NetBEUI protocol and the IPX/SPX compatible protocol.

NOTE   NetBEUI is an older Microsoft protocol that still has merit in small network systems or where the primary access is over slower dial-up lines. IPX/SPX is the protocol used on Novell NetWare networks and is installed by default by Windows 98.

The Network Wizard

If the Add New Hardware Wizard doesn't open the Network property pages shown in Figure 14.6, then you can run it yourself. Just open the Control Panel and double-click the Network icon.

FIGURE 14.5: The Add New Hardware Wizard will help you add and configure your new network card.

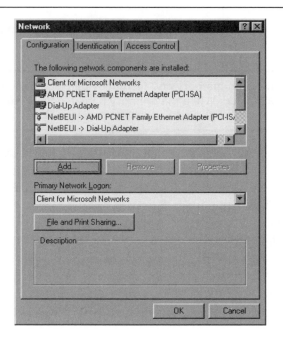

FIGURE 14.6: The Network property sheet lets you add, remove, or configure networking hardware and software.

Some network components may have been added in already when you installed the new network card. Additional client protocols, hardware adapters, networking "stacks" or protocols, and networking services can be added here.

Client Choices

Network clients let you use the services being provided by another machine on your network. The default network configuration includes clients for both Microsoft Networks and Novell NetWare Networks. If you're just using Windows 98 as a peer-to-peer network, you can delete the Client for NetWare choice since you will only be using the built-in Microsoft networking.

 NOTE   To remove the NetWare client, just highlight it and then click the Remove button. Don't worry, you can always add it back in later if you need to.

If you are connecting to other networks, such as Banyan VINES or Sun's PC-NFS, you will need to add them in here as well. For these, however, you will need disks (and instructions) from the manufacturer. In this skill, we'll stick to just adding in the Microsoft networking client.

 TIP   Save both memory and resources by installing only the network protocols you really need. While the memory hit is hidden better by Windows 98, there's still no such thing as a free lunch.

If you don't see the Client for Microsoft Networks listed in the Network dialog box under the heading *The following network components are installed*, click the Add button, and then double-click the Client icon in the Select Network Component Type box, as shown in Figure 14.7.

Clicking the Client icon opens the Select Network Client box shown in Figure 14.8. Highlight Microsoft, select Client for Microsoft Networks, and then click OK.

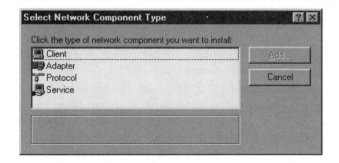

FIGURE 14.7: The Select Network Component Type box lets you add clients, adapters, protocols, and services to your network.

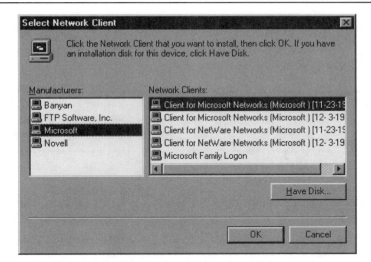

FIGURE 14.8: Adding the Microsoft client for Microsoft's own network is easy.

Service Choices

The default installation doesn't install any services at all, which is fine if you never want anyone else to be able to use the resources on your computer. If you were setting up your local network to have one main machine everyone else would share—the one with the fax modem, the big hard drive, the printer, and such—then you could leave this choice alone. But if you are going to distribute your resources across the network, you will need to add services to all the workstations to allow them to share their resources with others.

Double-click the Service icon in the Select Network Component Type box shown in Figure 14.7. Again, highlight Microsoft in the resulting Select Network Service dialog box, select *File and printer sharing for Microsoft Networks*, and click OK. This will add the necessary network services to allow others on the network to use your documents and folders as well as any printers or fax modems attached to your computer.

The previous actions should be enough to get your network configured and ready to go. You will need to reboot each machine when you get done adding the necessary hardware and software components since these changes are more than Windows 98 can do on the fly.

 TIP   If you have a notebook computer with PC Card support, once you have done the initial installation of the network components, you can insert or remove the network PC Card, and Windows 98 will detect the change without rebooting.

Using Your Network

OK, you got all the hardware up and configured, the cables are in, the whole thing is connected, and now you actually want to do something with your network like sharing files—or, in Windows 98 speak, documents.

Sharing and Mapping Drives

The simplest way to share files on your new network is to first share the drive or drives they reside on, then others on the network can map your drive to look like a local drive on their own computer. This is a two-step process. First you must *share* the drive (allow others to see and use it). Then the other network users can *map* the drive (if they use it a lot).

To share a drive with others in your workgroup:

Skill 14

1. Right-click the drive letter in the Explorer or in My Computer, and select Sharing from the pop-up menu. The Properties page for the drive, with the Sharing tab in front, will open.

2. Just click the Shared As radio button, and the rest of the options on the tab become available, as shown in Figure 14.9.

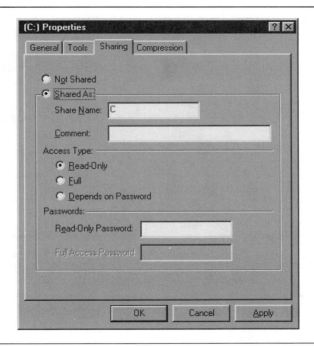

FIGURE 14.9: You can let some users have full access to your drives while others have read-only access.

3. By specifying different passwords for different access levels, you can allow full access to some users and read-only access to others.

Once you've got things set up the way you want them, other users can access these shared files by double-clicking the icon that represents your computer in Network Neighborhood. When someone using another computer on the network does this, it opens a window on their computer showing the drives or folders being shared by you.

If a shared drive on another computer is being used a lot, mapping it so that it appears to be a drive on your own computer makes sense. To map a shared drive, click Network Neighborhood. Find the shared drive you want to map and right-click it. Select Map Network Drive from the pop-up menu to get the dialog box shown in Figure 14.10.

FIGURE 14.10: Here's where you map drives on other computers to look just like another computer.

 NOTE   Mapping is necessary if you're using older programs that don't recognize the network. After mapping, a network drive looks (to the program at least) just like any other hard drive on your computer.

Sharing Printers

A network can also give everyone access to a printer without having to shell out the money to put a laser printer next to everyone's desk. Windows 98 makes this easy and painless. The person who has the printer attached to a PC simply shares it the same way they would share a drive or folder.

The Universal Naming Convention

Drive letter mapping provides complete compatibility with applications written before Windows 98, but it goes against the concept of documents and folders as being the central things we work with—not drives and files. After all, I don't really care where the outline for this book is stored. What I care about is getting at it quickly, so I have a shortcut directly to it on my desktop. Clicking on it starts the application that created the outline, and then opens the outline.

This method doesn't require any drive mappings at all, thanks to something called the Universal Naming Convention (UNC). Under this convention, the outline is known as: \\Rciserv\Windows98\outline.doc. The UNC is being used more and more. It lets any new machine added to the network to be able to find \\Rciserv\Windows98\outline.doc with no further information.

From the remote user's standpoint, using someone else's printer is no different from using one attached to your computer. Here's how to set it up:

1. First you add it as a new printer. (Like most things in Windows 98, you can do this from several different places. I like getting it off the Start button.) Select Settings ➢ Printers to open the Printers folder, and then click the Add Printer icon.

2. This opens the Add Printer Wizard and tells it that the printer is on the network. Type in the UNC location (see the sidebar "The Universal Naming Convention") for the printer if you know it, or just use the Browse button to find it. You'll end up with something like Figure 14.11 after you select the network printer.

3. If you'll ever need to use this printer from within a DOS program, make sure you click the Yes button for *Do you print from MS-DOS-based programs?* Click the Next button again, and select a printer port to capture for your DOS programs, since most of them need to think they are printing to a specific port.

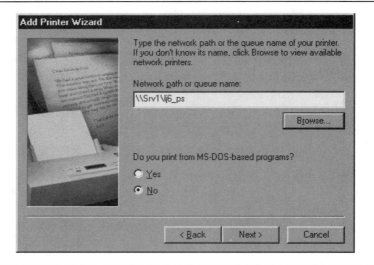

FIGURE 14.11: Adding a network printer is just as easy as adding a local printer.

4. Give the printer a name, and you are done.

SUPPORT FOR MULTIPLE NETWORKS

Windows 98—like Windows 95—includes support for more than one network at a time. You can be logged onto your Windows workgroup at the same time you are connecting to the Internet without bringing your entire system to a crashing halt. You can even log onto a Novell NetWare server without having to reboot or even cancel your other connections.

So, what does this mean for the small network user? Probably the biggest plus is the ability to link up to the Internet at the same time you are running your local network and sharing your documents and folders. With the built-in TCP/IP support in Windows 98, you don't need anything extra either.

Now you can use this printer exactly like a printer directly connected to your computer, as long as the computer that has the printer attached to it is up and running.

All about Passwords

One topic I haven't talked about yet is passwords. Everyone hates passwords. They're a pain. I know that. And if you don't want a password on your PC, that's your call.

You need a password if:

- There are more than two people on the network.

- You ever intend to connect to the outside world.

- You ever have business-critical data stored on any of the machines on your network.

If your needs are minimal, you can make the password easy to remember, but the best password is one that can't be easily guessed. If you will be directly connecting your computer to the Internet, I strongly urge you to adopt strict password guidelines and stick to them.

Here are some rules for bad passwords:

- Your name, nickname, or logon name

- Your spouse's, child's, or parent's name

- Your pet's name

- Your license plate or Social Security number

- Common swear words or combinations of them

- Any word in the dictionary

- Any of the above, spelled in reverse

Ideal passwords are a mixture of upper and lowercase letters and numbers or other nonalphabetic characters that don't spell anything obvious, yet are easy to read, pronounce, type, and are at least six characters in length—something like "NusSpot!".

TIP   If you don't use a password, and being prompted for one every time you boot your machine annoys you, here's how to skip that prompt. Open the Network applet in the Control Panel. On the Configuration page, look for Primary Network Logon. Open the drop-down list and select Windows Logon. Now you can boot your machine without having to enter a password.

Are You Experienced?

Now you can...

- ☑ Install and configure a peer-to-peer network
- ☑ Share resources on your own computer
- ☑ Map shared drives on other computers
- ☑ Select a good password

SKILL 15

CONFIGURING THE SYSTEM

- Date and time settings
- Regional settings
- Configuring special keyboards
- Managing fonts
- Setting passwords
- Setting up multiple users
- Enhancing security

In this skill, we'll cover several of the areas that can be configured, although not all changes will be appropriate to your system. Some areas may never apply to how you use Windows 98, but you may have need of them in the future.

Date and Time Settings

Windows 98 keeps track of the date and time based on the information provided at installation. It even makes the correct adjustment for daylight-saving time. If you elect to show the clock on the Taskbar, positioning the pointer over the time will produce a flyover box with the date inside.

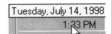

To display the clock on the Taskbar   Right-click on the Taskbar in a blank spot. Select Properties from the pop-up menu. On the Taskbar Option page, put a checkmark in the box next to Show Clock.

To change the date or time settings   Click the Start button and select Settings ➤ Control Panel. Click the Date/Time icon to open the Date/Time Properties dialog box (see Figure 15.1). Change the month or year with the drop-down lists. Change the day by simply highlighting it. To adjust the clock, highlight the portion to be changed in the text box and click the up and down arrows until the time you want is displayed. Click the Time Zone tab to change the time zone, selecting the one you want from the drop-down list.

 TIP   You can also access the Date/Time properties by right-clicking the time display on the Taskbar and selecting Adjust Date/Time from the pop-up menu. Or double-click the time display if you're truly impatient.

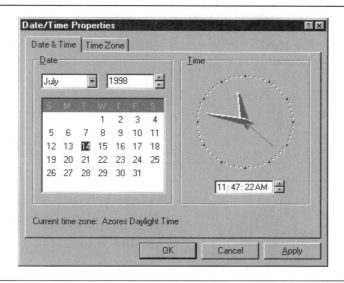

FIGURE 15.1: Change the date, time, or time zone in the Date/Time Properties pages.

Regional Settings

If you use programs that support international settings, the Regional Settings icon in the Control Panel is where you go to choose how these settings will be displayed.

Click the Start button, then select Settings ➤ Control Panel ➤ Regional Settings. In addition to being able to choose from dozens of different countries, you can also get very specific about how dates, time, and currency are displayed.

Some of the settings will require a reboot of the computer to take effect, but others, such as the date and time, will change immediately.

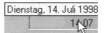

Keyboard Settings

The installation routine of Windows 98 finds the keyboard plugged into your computer and recognizes it. If you need to change keyboards, adjust the keyboard's speed, or install a keyboard designed for another language, click Start ➤ Settings ➤ Control Panel, then click this icon:

Keyboard

The two tabs on the Keyboard Properties dialog box cover these different types of settings—explained in the following sections.

Keyboard Speed

In the Keyboard Properties dialog box, click the Speed tab to adjust keyboard rates. Here are the available settings:

Repeat delay   Determines how long a key has to be held down before it starts repeating. The difference between the Long and Short setting is only about a second.

Repeat rate   Determines how fast a key repeats. Fast means you can hold down a key and almost instantly get a stream of letters. (Click in the practice area to test this setting.)

Cursor blink rate   Makes the cursor blink faster or slower. The blinking cursor on the left demonstrates the setting.

Keyboard Languages

If you need multiple language support for your keyboard, click the Language tab in the Keyboard Properties dialog box. Click the Add button to select languages from Afrikaans to Ukrainian—including 15 varieties of Spanish. If you have more

than one language selected, the settings on the Language tab let you choose a
keyboard combination to switch between languages (see Figure 15.2).

FIGURE 15.2: Set your keyboard for a different language or for multiple
languages.

Highlight the language you want as the default (the one that's enabled when
you start your computer) and click on the Set As Default button. Check Enable
Indicator on Taskbar, and an icon will appear on your Taskbar. Click the icon, and
you can instantly switch between languages.

Changing Keyboards

If Windows 98 doesn't seem to know what keyboard you have, or you change keyboards, highlight the installed keyboard on the Language tab of the Keyboard Properties dialog box and click the Properties button. In the Language Properties box, click the down arrow next to the Keyboard Layout box (see Figure 15.3) and choose the appropriate keyboard layout. Click OK.

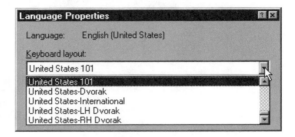

FIGURE 15.3: Choose a specific layout to match your keyboard.

Managing Fonts

TrueType fonts are easily managed in Windows 98. Click Start ➤ Settings ➤ Control Panel and click this icon to see the list of fonts installed:

Selecting and Viewing Fonts

The menus in the Fonts folder are slightly different from the usual folder menus. In the View menu, you'll find, in addition to the choices for viewing icons and lists, an option called List Fonts by Similarity. Choose that option to see a view like that shown in Figure 15.4.

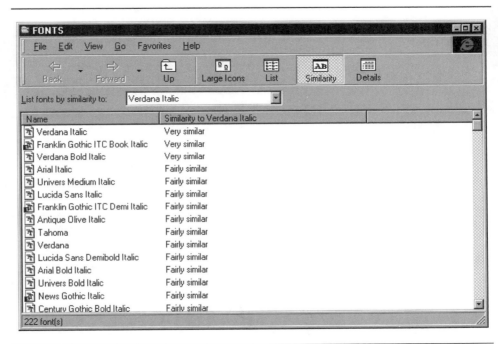

FIGURE 15.4: Viewing fonts by similarity

  TIP   If your font list is very long and unwieldy, select View ➢ Hide Variations. That will conceal font variations such as Italic and Bold, and make the list easier to look through.

Select a font in the drop-down box at the top, and the other fonts will line up in terms of their degree of similarity. To see just how similar, you can right-click any of the font names and select Open from the pop-up menu. A window will open with a complete view of the font in question (see Figure 15.5).

TrueType fonts located elsewhere can be moved into this folder. Figure 15.6 shows a newly acquired font being dragged into the folder.

FIGURE 15.5: Getting a look at a font

Fonts don't have to be physically located in the Windows/Fonts folder to be recognized by Windows 98. You can make a shortcut to a font in another folder and put the shortcut in the Fonts folder. The shortcut is all you need for the font to be installed.

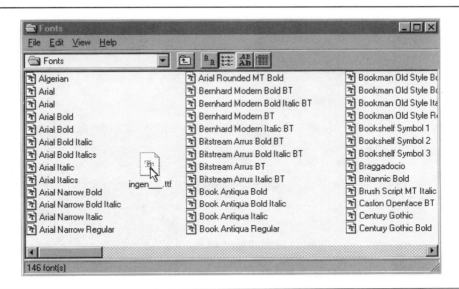

FIGURE 15.6: Move fonts into the Fonts folder just as you'd move any object—drag and drop or cut and paste.

Fonts that are identified with an icon like this are not TrueType fonts:

Windows 98 uses them as system fonts, so don't delete them.

Installing New Fonts

Installing new fonts is a pretty easy project. Just click Start ➤ Settings ➤ Control Panel and click the Fonts icon. Select Install New Font from the File menu. In the Add Fonts window (shown in Figure 15.7), you can tell the system the drive and directory where the font(s) reside. If TrueType fonts are at the location you specify, they'll show up in the List of Fonts window.

Highlight the font or fonts you want installed and click the OK button.

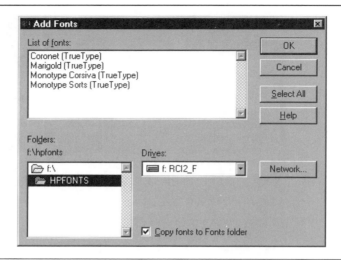

FIGURE 15.7: Installing new fonts

 TIP   Other types of fonts—not TrueType—like those installed by the Adobe Type Manager, will reside elsewhere on your hard drive, depending on the location you select at installation. You can't put them in the Fonts folder or view them by double-clicking. However, numerous applications can display fonts, and most font installing programs have their own viewers.

Passwords

These days it seems like everything requires a password or a code of some sort. You can't get money from the bank or messages from your answering machine without producing a password. Computers are even *more* rampant with passwords. Every online service and every commercial Web site asks for one.

That's why you want to avoid all unnecessary passwords. Who needs more complications in their lives?

One Computer, One User

When you sign on to Windows 98 for the first time, you're asked to provide a name and password. If you're the only one using a computer and you don't want to deal with a password every time you turn the machine on, leave the password blank. Then click Start ➤ Settings ➤ Control Panel and click the Network icon. Under Primary Network Logon (on the Configuration page), make sure Windows Logon is selected. You won't be troubled with a request for a password again.

On the other hand, if you later want to start using a password or change the one you have, click the Password icon in the Control Panel. Click the Change Windows Password button and enter the information requested. (If you had no previous password, leave the Old Password field empty.)

One Computer, Multiple Users

Everyone sets up Windows in a different way. This is great—until you have to share your computer with another person (or even persons). Fortunately, Windows 98 allows you to set up a profile for each user. You'll each have to log on with your name and particular password, but once you do, the desktop that appears will be the one you set up—programs, shortcuts, colors, and so forth, all just as you arranged.

Setting Up a User Profile

To allow user profiles, you'll need to follow these steps:

1. Click Start ➤ Settings ➤ Control Panel and click the Passwords icon.

2. In the Password Properties dialog box, select the User Profiles tab. Click the button for the second choice, *Users can customize their preferences*.

3. Select the kinds of settings you want individual users to be able to change and save:

   - Desktop icons and Network Neighborhood
   - Start menu and Program groups

   You can allow either, both, or none of these. Changes that other users make will affect only their profiles.

4. Click OK when you're finished.

Once user profiles are enabled, every user will have to sign on using a name and password. The first time a new user signs on, the desktop will look like it did at the time user profiles were enabled. But all changes, subject to the restrictions you set in step 3 above, will be saved for that user.

Removing a User Profile

To get rid of a user profile, sign on under a different name and password. Use the Find function to search for the user's name. For example, if the user signed on as Alfie, you should find alfie.pwl in the Windows folder and a folder named Alfie in the Profiles folder. Delete both the file and the folder to get rid of the profile and all things associated with it. (Don't be alarmed if you get a message about deleting user.dat; it's just a copy, and the original is still in the Windows directory.)

To eliminate all user profiles, log on and go back to the Password Properties dialog box (as described in the previous section, "Setting Up a User Profile") and change the User Profile setting.

You can also bypass all user profiles at startup by clicking Cancel in the dialog box that asks for name and password—don't be misled into thinking these are *security* devices; they're strictly for convenience.

Security Issues

Windows 98 is not a high-security system, although there are a few security provisions. User profiles and passwords provide some security, but they can easily be bypassed. Even a networking password can be bypassed. All someone has to do is boot in Safe Mode by pressing F8 during the boot process (instantly upon hearing the first boot beep) and then selecting Safe Mode from the menu.

To prevent this short-circuiting of your passwords, follow these steps:

1. Open Windows Explorer (click Start ➤ Programs ➤ Windows Explorer) and find the file msdos.sys on your C: drive. Right-click on the file and select Properties.

2. On the Properties page, remove the checkmark from the Read Only attribute. Click OK.

3. Open msdos.sys in a text editor such as Notepad. Under the Options section, add the line

   ```
   BootKeys=0
   ```

   then save the file.

4. Open Windows Explorer again and reinstate the checkmark for the Read Only attribute of msdos.sys.

5. Shut down and restart your computer.

On a network, you can improve the security for your computer by using some or all of these suggestions:

- Share resources selectively.

- Don't enable remote administration (in Password Properties).

- Always use a password.

- Prevent others from having physical access to your computer.

This last option is probably the most important, because that's how most security breaches occur. It's all very much like the old saying that "locks are for honest people." The security measures in Windows 98 will not discourage a knowledgeable person determined to make mischief, but they can help protect against inadvertent misuse.

 TIP   If you're in a situation where you need maximum security, you should investigate running Microsoft Windows NT—a system that can be made very secure.

Are You Experienced?

Now you can...

- ☑ **Set the date and time**
- ☑ **Make international settings**
- ☑ **Configure keyboards**
- ☑ **Manage fonts**
- ☑ **Use or avoid passwords**
- ☑ **Set up multiple users**
- ☑ **Enhance security**

SKILL 16

MAINTAINING THE SYSTEM

- Using ScanDisk
- Defragmenting hard drives
- Using Disk Cleanup
- Doing a system tune-up
- Setting up regular maintenance
- Converting to the FAT32 file system
- Using hard drive compression

Computers appear to be intelligent but, as we all know, they're only as smart as their software. Computers still have problems with internal errors—frequently caused by conflicts among programs—and require regular maintenance to operate at their best. In this skill, I cover the tools that perform that maintenance. In addition, I describe the merits and demerits of FAT32, a newly developed Windows file system that can make efficient use of your available hard drive space.

Running ScanDisk

Whenever a computer is turned on and operating, a lot of complicated tasks are going on inside. Fortunately, you're spared specific knowledge of these goings on, but you still have to deal with the consequences. As in most complex systems, errors are made, and, if not corrected, they tend to pile up into serious problems.

ScanDisk is protection against the accumulation of serious problems on your hard drive. It's a direct descendant of the CHKDSK utility in DOS, with many added features much like those in the justly famous Norton Disk Doctor.

You should run ScanDisk frequently—at least weekly. Once a month you should run its Thorough testing procedure, so the hard disk surface is checked for problems in addition to the standard checking of files and folders.

 NOTE You may have seen ScanDisk when you installed Windows 98, because part of the installation routine is to do a quick check of the hard drive to look for errors. Also, if you turn the computer off or reboot without the proper sign-off routine, ScanDisk runs automatically when the computer starts up again.

Starting ScanDisk

To run ScanDisk, follow these steps:

1. Click the Start button and select Programs ➤ Accessories ➤ System Tools ➤ ScanDisk. This will open the window shown in Figure 16.1.

2. Highlight the drive you want tested.

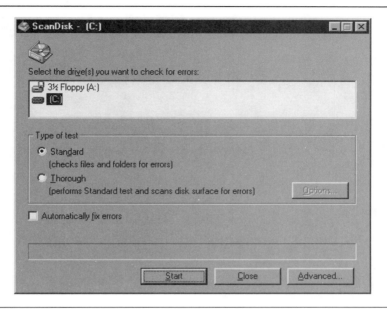

FIGURE 16.1: The basic ScanDisk window

3. Select the type of test and whether you want ScanDisk to automatically fix all errors or prompt you.

4. Click Start to run.

NOTE   If the *Automatically fix errors* box is checked, ScanDisk will repair most errors without consulting you again. Such corrections are made based on the settings you can review by clicking the Advanced button.

Changing ScanDisk Settings

Click the Advanced button to see (and change) the settings that ScanDisk uses.

Display summary   This setting controls whether you see a summary of ScanDisk's findings after a check (see Figure 16.2).

FIGURE 16.2: This is ScanDisk's summary report on the drive just scanned.

Log file   By default, ScanDisk creates a new log detailing its activities every time it's run. If you want one long continuous log or no log at all, change the setting.

Cross-linked files   A cross-link occurs when more than one file tries to use the same area (cluster) on the hard drive. The information in the cluster is probably correct only for one file (although it might not be correct for either of them). The Make Copies setting attempts to make some order out of the mess by copying the information in the cluster to both of the files that are contending for the space. This is the best of the three settings—it may not save your data, but the other two options definitely won't.

Lost file fragments   File fragments are a fact of computer life. You can leave the default setting to convert them to files. (They'll be given names like FILE0001 and FILE0002 and deposited in your root directory.) The odds are very high that these fragments aren't useful, and they do take up valuable disk space. I always set this to Free, and I have never lost anything valuable—but you can be extra cautious and leave it at Convert to Files. (Just remember to go look at these files periodically and delete the junk.)

Check files for   The default is to look just for invalid names, although you can add dates, times, and duplicate filenames if you want. It will slow down ScanDisk's progress, but not dramatically.

Check host drive first   If you have a compressed drive, errors are sometimes caused by errors on the host drive. Leave this box checked so the host drive will be examined first.

Report MS-DOS mode name length errors   What with the mixture of long filenames and the eight-plus-three filenames used in MS-DOS mode, errors can result. Check this box for a report on name length errors.

WHY SCANDISK RUNS AUTOMATICALLY

When you turn off your computer using the Start ➤ Shut Down procedure, Windows 98 goes through an orderly process of closing open files, deleting temporary files, and ending its own internal operations. That's what is going on between the time you order the shut down and the time you see the screen telling you it's OK to turn off the computer.

However, if you turn the computer off without going through the shut down procedure, when you start up again, ScanDisk will run automatically *before* Windows 98 is launched.

Why? Whether you turned the computer off by accident or because applications caused a lock-up, the results will undoubtedly be file fragments, lost files, and other detritus left on the hard drive. It's even possible that a crash could produce errors that could prevent a normal reboot. ScanDisk finds and fixes those sorts of serious errors *and* minor problems that could accumulate and cause trouble in the future.

Fixing Disk Fragmentation

Windows 98 is like its Windows and DOS predecessors in that when it writes a file to your disk, it puts it anywhere it finds room. As you delete and create files, over time a single file can have a piece here, a piece there, another piece somewhere else. When a file is spread over multiple places, it's said to be *fragmented*.

This isn't a problem for Windows 98—it always knows where these pieces are. But it will tend to slow file access time because the system has to go to several locations to pick up one file. The Disk Defragmenter in Windows 98 addresses this problem, plus it can rearrange the files on your hard disk to improve the speed at which programs start up.

 NOTE   If you are upgrading from a previous version of Windows, you'll notice that Disk Defragmenter no longer reports the fragmentation percentage of a drive. Some specific fragmentation of program files may be desirable for better performance, so the percentage of fragmented files is less important.

As a matter of good housekeeping, you should probably run Disk Defragmenter about once a month. Here's how it's done:

1. Click the Start button and select Programs ➤ Accessories ➤ System Tools ➤ Disk Defragmenter.

2. In the dialog box shown in Figure 16.3, use the drop-down list to choose the drive you want to defragment.

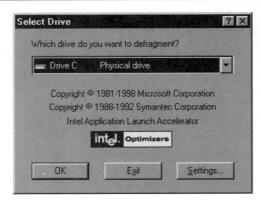

FIGURE 16.3: Select the drive you want to defragment or select All Hard Drives from the drop-down list.

3. Click OK to start Disk Defragmenter. Once the process starts, you can click Show Details to get a cluster-by-cluster view of the program's progress. Or you can just minimize Disk Defragmenter and do something else. If you write to the hard drive, Disk Defragmenter will start over—but in the background and without bothering you.

TIP If you have Microsoft Office 95 or 97 installed, pause Find Fast while Disk Defragmenter runs. Do this by opening Find Fast in the Control Panel and clicking Find Fast Index ➢ Pause Indexing.

If you want to check out Disk Defragmenter options, click the Settings button rather than OK. The dialog box is shown in Figure 16.4.

FIGURE 16.4: The Disk Defragmenter options

Here's what the options mean:

Rearrange program files so my programs start faster   Windows 98 keeps track of how often you start each program on your machine and what files are required. Disk Defragmenter can use this information to optimize the location of program files for faster startup. In the process, it deliberately fragments some program files, so you should not use a third-party disk defragmenter (such as Norton Utilities) if you use this option.

Check the drive for errors   Disk Defragmenter checks the drive before defragmenting. If it finds errors, you'll be advised of this fact, and Defragmenter won't continue.

NOTE   When Disk Defragmenter finds an error on your disk, run ScanDisk to repair the problem, and then run Defragmenter again.

Select whether these options are for this session only or should be saved for future sessions.

Disk Cleanup

The Windows operating system creates a mass of temporary files and cached files—all designed to speed up the performance of the graphical interface. These files do a pretty good job of it, too, but there are too many of them, and they often don't get deleted when they should be. The result is a lot of files cluttering up your hard drive—files that have inscrutable names and an unknown purpose.

Disk Cleanup is a new tool included with Windows 98 that is aptly represented as a small broom.

When you run it, Disk Cleanup checks for files that can be safely deleted and then presents a listing of such files.

To start Disk Cleanup, click the Start button, then select Programs ➢ Accessories ➢ System Tools ➢ Disk Cleanup. First the program will run a check on the hard drive and then open a window like the one shown in Figure 16.5.

 TIP   To run Disk Cleanup on a drive other than the C: drive, open My Computer. Right-click on the drive you want to check and select Properties from the pop-up menu. Click the Disk Cleanup button on the Properties sheet.

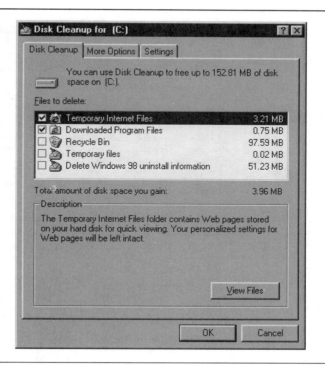

Skill 16

FIGURE 16.5: Disk Cleanup reports on files that can be deleted.

Understand that just because a file *can* be deleted doesn't necessarily mean it *should* be deleted. It all depends on your needs. Some of the categories that Disk Cleanup finds are listed below. Options will vary in each Cleanup window.

Temporary Internet files   These are from various Web sites that you've visited, and they can make reconnecting to a Web site much faster. But there's no point in keeping them around forever. Click the View Files button. Choose Details from the View menu, then click Last Accessed (see Figure 16.6). Delete anything with a Last Accessed date of more than six months ago.

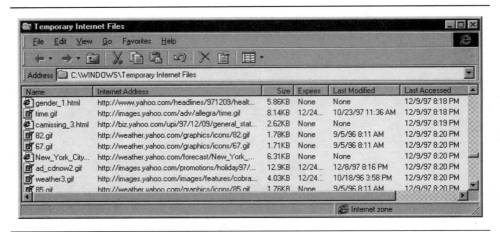

FIGURE 16.6: Delete Web files that you haven't used for a long time.

Downloaded program files   These are files also downloaded from Web sites. They are ActiveX or Java applets that produce effects on the Web pages you've visited.

Old ScanDisk files in the root folder   These are the recovered file fragments converted into files described under "Running ScanDisk."

Recycle Bin   If the Recycle Bin settings are correctly configured, you shouldn't need to empty the bin to clear space on your hard drive. If the Recycle Bin is too large, reset it to some smaller size (see Skill 4).

Temporary files   These are files created by Windows and Windows programs. In the normal course of events, these are routinely deleted by the operating system. Any that remain to be found by Disk Cleanup can be safely deleted. If you're at all unsure, use Windows Explorer to look at the files in the Temp folder inside your Windows folder. Any files older than a few days are strays and should be deleted.

Temporary setup files   Along with Windows setup files, these can be deleted, because a process long since finished created them.

Delete Windows 98 uninstall information   These are files you can obviously clear away once you have Windows 98 installed and running.

Put a checkmark next to the categories you want to delete. The zealousness with which you delete whole categories of files is largely dependent on the amount of hard drive space you can afford to squander. If your available free space consistently hovers at 50MB or less, use Disk Cleanup with as much ruthlessness as you can muster. If you have a more recent multi-gigabyte hard drive, and you have hundreds and hundreds of megabytes of free space, run Disk Cleanup every two or three months just to get rid of the totally useless stuff.

TIP   Click the Settings tab to set Disk Cleanup to run automatically if the drive runs low on space.

NOTE   The More Options tab in Disk Cleanup just offers you alternate paths to the Adding/Removing Programs program in the Control Panel (see Skill 10) and to FAT32 Drive Conversion (covered later in this skill).

Doing a System Tune-Up

We're all fallible. We promise ourselves to faithfully do our computer maintenance tasks, and yet in the press of events, they often don't get done. Fortunately, Windows 98 comes with a tune-up application called Maintenance Wizard that—run once—will set up Scan Disk, Disk Defragmenter, and Disk Cleanup to run automatically on a schedule you specify.

To start the Maintenance Wizard, follow these steps:

1. Click the Start button and select Programs ➢ Accessories ➢ System Tools ➢ Maintenance Wizard.

2. Select Express Setup and click Next. Choose one of three daily time slots for the tune-up process. The easiest, if you don't mind leaving your machine on all the time, is Nights. If it's an older machine that can't go to standby mode to conserve power, you may want to choose a different schedule.

3. Click Next, and the Wizard lists the three tasks to be performed, as shown in Figure 16.7.

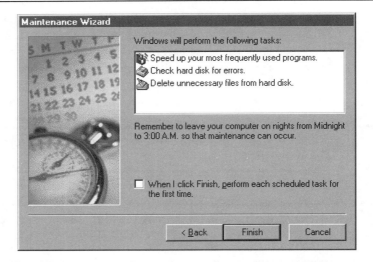

FIGURE 16.7: Here's what the Maintenance Wizard can do for you.

Speed up your most frequently used programs Disk Defragmenter will run weekly, processing all your hard drives with the option *Rearrange program files so my programs start faster.*

Check hard disk for errors ScanDisk will run weekly with its default settings, checking all your hard drives.

Delete unnecessary files from hard disk Disk Cleanup will run at the beginning of each month. It will remove temporary Internet files, downloaded program files, old ScanDisk files in the root directory, and temporary files.

4. Click the checkbox at the bottom of the dialog box if you want all the maintenance operations to run for the first time immediately after finishing the setup.

5. Click Finish. Now all you have to do is remember to leave the computer on at the appropriate times so that the programs can run.

You can also choose a custom setup which allows you to make very specific settings for when the programs will run and what their individual settings will be.

Using Task Scheduler

The Task Scheduler icon appears in the System Tray at the end of the Taskbar on your desktop.

Double-click the icon to open the Scheduled Tasks system folder. If you have already run the Windows Maintenance Wizard, you'll find a list of scheduled tasks already in the folder.

Click the Add Scheduled Task item to run the Scheduled Task Wizard, which will start any program on your computer according to a schedule you decide. The Wizard is simple and straightforward. You choose from a list of all the programs on your computer, then set the schedule. Schedule options include When My Computer Starts and When I Log On, so you can use Task Scheduler to start programs that you always want running when you work.

Windows Update

In years past, bugs or other problems in software were yours to live with until a new version of the software came out. If the maker of your printer or modem didn't produce satisfactory drivers for a particular operating system, you could even be forced to buy new hardware or do without. If you were very knowledgeable, you might be able to download bug fixes from the manufacturer's bulletin board system, or later, their site on the Internet. However, this was an avenue all but closed to the average user.

Windows Update is Microsoft's attempt to resolve this problem of keeping up-to-date by providing a single site for bug fixes, program patches, and hardware drivers.

Click the Start button and select Windows Update. This launches Internet Explorer and connects to the Windows Update Web site. To check for updated drivers or system files, click the Update Wizard link.

NOTE If you haven't previously registered your copy of Windows 98, you'll be asked to now. Read the registration screens carefully. You don't have to submit the systems and software information unless you want to.

The Update Wizard will start (see Figure 16.8).

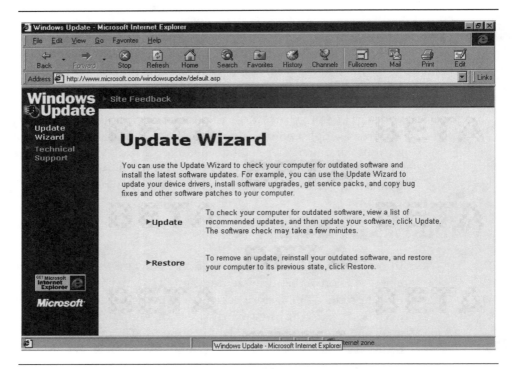

FIGURE 16.8: Running the system Update Wizard

The Update Wizard includes active components that must be downloaded and run by Internet Explorer on your system.

After the necessary components are downloaded, you will see a message that your system is being scanned to see what files need to be updated. When the scan is complete, the Update Wizard will present a list of available updates for your system. To install an update, click it and then click the Install button.

The Update Wizard also offers a restore function that allows you to return to your previous version of an updated file. You might need to do this if the update causes unexpected problems on your system.

TIP A system update requires that the update site communicate with your computer. This means you may have to bypass some security warnings. You are not going to receive any viruses or Trojan horses or other vermin from a Microsoft Web site. However, if you're at all squeamish about letting an automated program scan your system, don't use Windows Update.

Using Space Efficiently

Windows 98 takes hundreds of megabytes of hard disk space, and some applications nearly reach that scale. Space, on even a large hard drive, can soon be at a premium. Windows 98 includes two features that can effectively expand your hard drive by using the space on it more efficiently.

FAT32   Makes more efficient use of drives and partitions over 512MB by reducing wasted space

DriveSpace 3   Compresses files so they take up less space

The two systems are unrelated *and* mutually exclusive: You can't use DriveSpace on a FAT32 hard drive.

FAT32 is generally more useful on newer computers, which tend to have hard drives over one gigabyte (1,000MB), often in the two to three gigabyte range. DriveSpace is more useful on machines with hard drives of about a gigabyte or less. It is essentially the same in Windows 98 as it was in Windows 95, except that it includes features that were part of the Plus! Pack for Windows 95.

NOTE A *partition* is a section of a hard drive. When a hard drive is new, or if you are willing to wipe it clean, it can be divided into multiple partitions. Windows 98, like other operating systems, sees these partitions as separate drives, although they are located on the same physical hard drive. The drive sizes referred to in discussing FAT32 and DriveSpace actually refer to the size of individual partitions, not the whole physical drive. However, most computer manufacturers format hard drives as one giant partition, so it usually amounts to the same thing.

FAT32

FAT is an acronym for File Allocation Table. From their beginnings, MS-DOS and Windows have used the FAT system for keeping track of the contents of hard drives. Basically, the directory (or folder) tells the operating system where to look in the FAT, and the FAT stores the list of hard drive clusters, or allocation units, where the file is located.

The system used by DOS in the 1990s, and by the original version of Windows 95, is now called FAT16. It could divide a hard drive into, at most, 65,536 allocation units, which meant that as hard drives got bigger, allocation units also had to get bigger, and large allocation units waste space.

The FAT32 system allows for a much larger file allocation table, which means smaller allocation units and much less wasted space. On a drive in the one to two gigabyte size range, containing about 7,500 files (which is typical for a Windows 98 machine), the saved space amounts to about 100MB.

Conversion Facts

Microsoft introduced FAT32 in 1996 as an interim improvement to Windows 95, but made it available only to computer manufacturers to be installed on new machines. So although you couldn't buy the FAT32 version of Windows 95 in a store, the system has now been installed on millions of computers and is known to be reliable.

There are several limitations on the use of FAT32. The first is that it is not designed for use on hard drives smaller then 512MB, or about 537 million bytes, the units by which hard drive sizes are stated by the manufacturers.

The second important limitation has to do with the use of operating systems other than Windows 98. No other operating system (OS) can read a hard drive formatted with FAT32. If you run other operating systems on your computer (such as Windows NT, Windows 95, DOS, or UNIX), they will have no access to drives that you have converted to FAT32. It also means that you cannot dual-boot Windows 98 and any other OS if your C: drive is FAT32, nor will you be able to share removable hard drives unless all parties have FAT32.

About the only way to make effective use of FAT32 on a machine that needs to run multiple operating systems is to use a third-party utility, such as System

Commander, to choose the OS at start-up time. In that case, you can use FAT32 on the drive where Windows 98 is installed, as long as you don't store any files on that drive that you need to get to when running another OS.

 NOTE   If your computer is connected to a network, other machines on the network still have access to hard drives that you choose to share even if you're using FAT32 and they are not.

Another thing to think about before converting to FAT32 is third-party disk utilities. Most have now been upgraded to work with FAT32, but if you have older versions, you will not be able to use them.

Briefly put, if your hard drive is larger than 512MB, and you plan to run only Windows 98, you should convert to FAT32. Use only Windows 98's own disk utilities, or others that specify they are compatible with FAT32.

Converting to FAT32

If you install Windows 98 to a newly formatted (empty) hard drive, FAT32 can be part of the installation process. If you install Windows 98 over Windows 95 or Windows 3.1, FAT32 will not be used. After Windows 98 is installed and running, you can convert your hard drive to FAT32 by using the Drive Converter program.

 TIP   If your computer came from the manufacturer with Windows 95 installed, it may already be using FAT32. To find out, open My Computer and right-click on the drive. Choose Properties. On the General page, you will see File System; it will show either FAT (meaning FAT16) or FAT32.

To convert a partition to FAT32, just follow these steps:

1. Start Drive Converter by clicking the Start button, then selecting Programs ➢ Accessories ➢ System Tools ➢ Drive Converter.

2. Click Next to see the dialog box shown in Figure 16.9. On many machines, this dialog box will show only the C: drive. Make your choice and click Next.

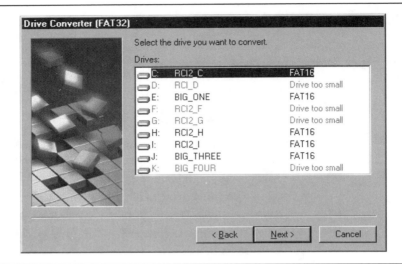

FIGURE 16.9: Choose the drive you want to convert to FAT32.

3. Windows 98 will then check your system for antivirus programs and disk utilities that are not compatible with FAT32. Once this is resolved, you can click Next.

4. The Wizard will now offer to start Backup so that you can back up your files before converting the drive.

 **WARNING** Although converting a drive to FAT32 is considered a safe operation, you should always back up important data before starting any task that tampers with your hard drive.

5. After creating the backup, click Next again to see the last dialog box before actual conversion of your drive. Be sure you have closed all running programs, then click Next.

6. Your machine will reboot to MS-DOS mode and run the conversion. If you use System Commander or another multiboot system, make sure the machine reboots to your Windows 98 partition.

TIP   Although the dialog box in step 5 says the process might take a few hours, the basic conversion to FAT32 actually takes only a few minutes. What *may* take several hours is running Disk Defragmenter, which starts automatically after your drive is converted to FAT32. You can interrupt the defragmentation process if you wish. However, performance of the FAT32 drive will probably be poor until you run Disk Defragmenter and allow it to completely defragment the drive.

Returning to FAT16

Windows 98 does not include a converter for going from FAT32 to FAT16. If you find you need to do this, you have two options:

- Back up all your data files on the FAT32 drive. Run FDISK on the partition and choose No to the option to enable large disk support. Then format the drive and reinstall Windows 98 and any applications that were on the drive. For more details, see the installation appendices.

- Get a program called Partition Magic, which can convert FAT32 to FAT16 without losing the content. There has to be enough unused space on the drive to allow for the extra space the files will occupy using FAT16. If not, you can first use Partition Magic to change the partition size.

TIP   Not only can Partition Magic do FAT32 to FAT16 conversion and resize partitions, it can also move programs from one partition to another without a reinstallation.

Compressing Hard Drives

Another way to make more efficient use of hard drive space is to use disk compression. Disk compression is helpful if you have a serious shortage of space—but in this era of super-cheap hard drives, it's a lot of trouble for a fairly modest return.

Windows 98 comes with DriveSpace 3. It will let you:

- Compress and uncompress a hard drive partition or a diskette

- Upgrade a DoubleSpace or DriveSpace compressed drive to DriveSpace 3
- Use your free space to create a new, empty, compressed partition

Compressing an Existing Drive

To compress a drive, you need only follow these steps:

1. Click the Start button, then select Programs ➤ Accessories ➤ System Tools ➤ DriveSpace.

2. Highlight the drive you want to compress and select Compress from the Drive menu.

3. The next screen (shown in Figure 16.10) will show before-and-after pie charts for the selected drive.

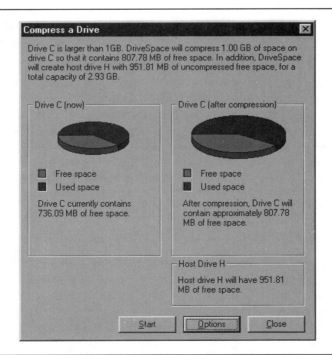

FIGURE 16.10: A drive before and after compression

4. Click Start. You'll be asked if you have an updated Windows 98 Startup disk. If you don't have a recent version of the Startup disk, make one now.

5. If you haven't backed up the files on the drive you want to compress, click the Back Up Files button and follow the instructions.

6. Click Compress Now.

7. The drive will be checked for errors, and then, if it's your C: drive that's being compressed, you'll be advised that your computer needs to restart. Once you click Yes here, there's no stopping, so be sure you've done all the preparatory steps correctly, and you have something else to do during the time the compression is going on. This process can't be run in the background.

 **WARNING**   If you're running more than one operating system, be sure the reboot is into Windows 98. This applies equally to reboots that are part of other DriveSpace conversion operations, such as uncompressing, creating a new partition, and adjusting free space.

The compression can take quite a while, especially on the older machines that are most likely to need it due to limited hard disk space. For example, on a 75MHz 486 laptop with 16MB RAM, compressing 230MB of files took about 90 minutes. At the end of the compression cycle (an on-screen progress bar is displayed), you get a before-and-after report showing the previous space on the disk and new statistics on free space and used space.

How Compression Works

When you compress a drive—let's say your C: drive—the whole thing ends up as one big file on a "new" drive called H (by default—though you can give it a later letter in the alphabet). The "new" drive H is called a host drive.

When you boot your machine, a DriveSpace command is loaded first. This tells the system to look for this big file and load it, so it looks to all the world like a regular boot into the C: drive. Any other compressed drives present when you boot your machine are also recognized and interpreted.

On the Properties sheet for the host drive, there's an option to hide this drive from view. This is a good option to take, because there's not a thing you can do in a host drive. There's a little bit of free space, but this big compressed file that you can't read and mustn't fool with takes up the rest.

DriveSpace 3 Settings

Choose Advanced ➤ Settings in DriveSpace to set the degree of compression to be used when saving new files or limit the circumstances where compression is used. For a more complete description of each option, click the ? button in the top-right corner, then click the item for which you want more information.

 TIP   To see the status of compression on a drive, right-click the drive in My Computer. Choose Properties, then look at the information on the Compression page.

Uncompressing a Drive

Providing you have room for the data once it's all uncompressed, you can get rid of the compression on a drive at any time. Just follow these steps:

1. Click Start ➤ Programs ➤ Accessories ➤ System Tools ➤ DriveSpace and highlight the drive you want to uncompress.

2. Select Uncompress from the Drive menu.

3. You'll see a window showing the drive as it is now and as it will be after uncompressing. Click Start to proceed.

4. You'll see a warning about backing up your files. If you haven't backed up the files on the compressed drive, click the Back Up Files button and follow the instructions.

5. Click Uncompress Now.

6. After a while, if this is the only compressed drive on your system, you'll be asked if you want to remove the compression driver at the end of the procedure. Choose:

   No   If you're still going to be reading compressed removable media (that is, floppies or removable hard drives)

   Yes   If you're through using any compressed drives for the foreseeable future

The drive will be checked for errors, and then the computer will restart. Uncompressing will be completed, and the computer will have to restart yet again (if drive C: is involved).

 NOTE   Uncompressing takes even longer than compressing. So it's not a task to undertake when you're in a hurry.

Creating a New Partition

DriveSpace can take the free space on your drive and make it into a new partition. This partition will be compressed and will provide more storage space than the amount of space it uses.

To make a new drive in this way, follow these steps:

1. Click Start ➤ Programs ➤ Accessories ➤ System Tools ➤ DriveSpace.

2. Highlight the drive that contains the free space you want to use, and select Create Empty from the Advanced menu.

3. Accept the suggested settings or make changes as you wish.

4. When you're finished, click Start.

Compression Agent

Compression Agent works with DriveSpace 3 to control and change the degree of compression used on your files. For example, you could improve performance on file save operations by telling DriveSpace to use No Compression (see Advanced ➤ Settings in DriveSpace). Then you can have Compression Agent compress these files when your computer is not in use.

Open Compression Agent from the System Tools menu. Click Settings to choose the compression options you want. The Overview button in Compression Agent takes you to the DriveSpace Help file, which explains all the options.

Changing the compression method used on files can take a substantial amount of time, so Compression Agent is best run on a regular basis by making use of the Task Scheduler, as described earlier in this skill.

Skill 16

Are You Experienced?

Now you can...

- ☑ **Use ScanDisk to fix hard drive errors**
- ☑ **Defragment hard drives**
- ☑ **Clean up unneeded files**
- ☑ **Perform a system tune-up**
- ☑ **Schedule regular maintenance**
- ☑ **Convert to the FAT32 file system**
- ☑ **Compress and uncompress a hard drive**

SKILL 17

SYSTEM TROUBLESHOOTING

- Using the System Information utility
- Checking system files
- Using System Monitor
- Using the Resource Meter
- Using Windows troubleshooters

In general, Windows 98 is pretty good at fixing itself. When a problem is detected, ScanDisk or some plug-and-play utility jumps into action, finds out the extent of the trouble, and notifies you what action needs to be taken. However, there are occasions when *you* must be the active party. Windows 98 includes enough system information and troubleshooting capability so that no fact about the system is hidden, if you're willing to look for it.

Using the System Information Utility

Support technicians require specific information about your computer when they are troubleshooting your configuration. You can use System Information to quickly find the data they need to resolve your system problem.

System Information collects your system configuration information and provides a menu for displaying the associated system topics. To access System Information, click the Start button and select Programs ➤ Accessories ➤ System Tools ➤ System Information. The display is organized into three sections: resources, components, and software environment.

> **Resources**   These are hardware-specific settings, namely DMA, IRQs, I/O addresses, and memory addresses. Click Conflicts/Sharing to see devices that are sharing resources or are in conflict (see Figure 17.1). This can help identify device problems.
>
> **Components**   Here you'll see information about the Windows configuration. You'll see the status of your device drivers, networking, and multimedia software. In addition, there is a comprehensive driver history, which shows changes made to your components over time.
>
> **Software Environment**   This is a view of the software loaded in computer memory. This information can be used to see if a process is still running or to check version information.

Depending on the individual topic, you may be presented with a choice of basic, advanced, or historical system data.

Check the Tools menu for quick access to other diagnostic tools that a technician may ask you to run, such as Dr. Watson, the System File Checker, and the System Configuration Utility.

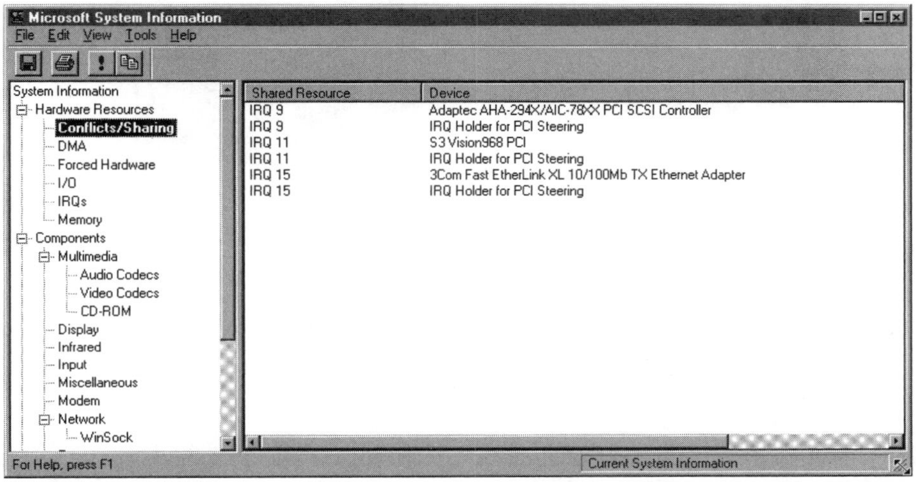

FIGURE 17.1: Checking for IRQ conflicts

Meet Dr. Watson

Dr. Watson is a utility that runs in the background and keeps a log of errors that occur. The output of the log may not make much sense to the average user, but it can speak volumes to a service technician.

To run Dr. Watson, follow these steps:

1. Click the Start button and select Programs ➤ Accessories ➤ System Tools ➤ System Information.

2. Select Dr. Watson from the Tools menu. The Dr. Watson icon will be placed in the System Tray at the end of your Taskbar.

3. Right-click on the icon to open this menu.

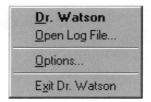

4. Choose Dr. Watson from the menu to get a snapshot of current conditions.

5. Choose Options to set how many error conditions Dr. Watson will record and to set the location of the log file (see Figure 17.2).

FIGURE 17.2: Settings for Dr. Watson, the system detective

6. Choose Open Log File to see the incidents recorded by Dr. Watson.

Checking System Files

System File Checker is a new utility that scans the system files on your machine, checking for file corruption or other errors. System File Checker maintains a data file with characteristics of your installed system files, so it can recognize unexpected changes.

Run System File Checker only if you're having otherwise inexplicable errors. If a system file turns out to be corrupted, you can also use System File Checker to extract a clean version from the Windows 98 installation CD.

To open System File Checker, click the Start button and select Programs ➤ Accessories ➤ System Tools ➤ System Information. Select File Checker from the Tools menu (see Figure 17.3).

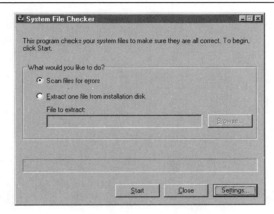

FIGURE 17.3: System File Checker

Click the Settings button to make configuration settings for System File Checker. If a system file is corrupted or missing, you can extract that file directly from the Windows 98 CD. Click *Extract one file from installation disk*. Type in the name of the file or click the Browse button to locate the file. (Make sure the Windows 98 disk is in the CD-ROM drive.)

Click Start when you're ready to extract the file.

Using System Monitor

The System Monitor gives you a graphical representation of a number of processes going on inside your computer. If you know what you're looking for, sometimes the information can be helpful.

To open System Monitor, click the Start button and select Programs ➤ Accessories ➤ System Tools ➤ System Monitor.

In the initial window (shown in Figure 17.4), System Monitor tracks the processor usage.

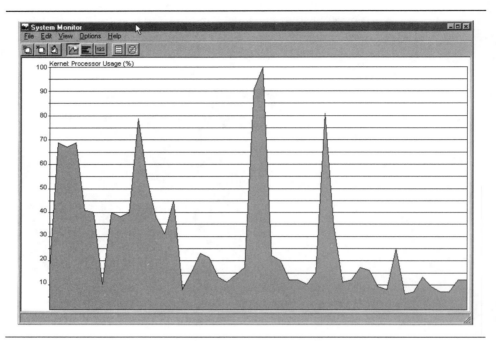

FIGURE 17.4: The System Monitor showing processor usage

To track other use, select Add Item from the Edit menu. Highlight a category (see Figure 17.5), and then select the item you want to view.

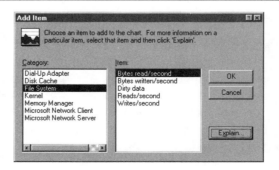

FIGURE 17.5: Choosing the items you want to monitor

On the toolbar, click the Bar Chart button:

to display the data as a bar chart (see Figure 17.6).

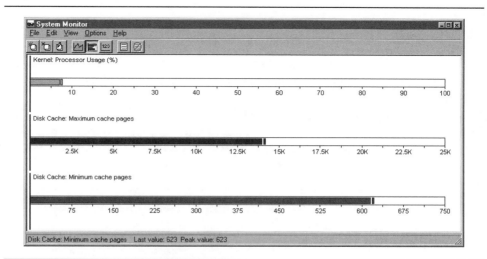

Skill 17

FIGURE 17.6: Viewing three kinds of data in a bar chart

 TIP   A numeric graph is also available. Click the Numeric Chart button next to the Bar Chart button to see one.

Using the Resource Meter

The Resource Meter offers visual feedback on the available Windows 98 resources. It's pretty hard to run out of resources in Windows 98, but you can get awfully low if you have enough windows open.

To put Resource Meter on the end of your Taskbar, take these steps:

1. Right-click on the Start button and select Open.

2. In the window that opens, double-click on Programs, then Accessories, and finally System Tools.

3. Right-click on Resource Meter and select Create Shortcut.

4. Right-click on the new shortcut and select Cut.

5. Next, go to the Windows Startup folder, using the Up icon on the toolbar at the top of the window. Click it twice to move up two levels to Programs.

6. Double-click on Startup. When the Startup window opens, right-click in an empty area and select Paste from the pop-up menu.

The next time you start up your computer, a small icon will be placed on your Taskbar. Place your pointer on the icon, and a flyover box will open showing available resources. Or right-click on the icon and select Details. A window like the one in Figure 17.7 will open.

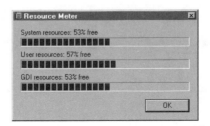

FIGURE 17.7: The Resource Meter in Details view

There's no point in trying to describe what the different resources mean, because the explanation would involve language like *memory heaps* and *device contexts*. Suffice it to say that if any of these numbers starts approaching zero, it's time to close some programs to give yourself more maneuvering room.

TIP   Sometimes, through no fault of your own, resources will dwindle dangerously, even though you have only one or two programs open. This is because one of those programs—or one you've had open recently—grabbed some resources and isn't letting them go. Blame it on bad programming practices, but the only practical solution is to reboot your computer (and then complain to the maker of the program).

Troubleshooting Tools

Windows 98 comes with its own set of relatively smart troubleshooting tools. If you run into a problem, try these troubleshooters first. They work very well, providing you observe some simple rules:

- Make sure that you can see the Help window that contains the troubleshooter text while you follow the instructions in the troubleshooter.

- Resize the Help window and move it to one side of the screen so you can use the rest of the screen to follow the instructions.

- Always follow the troubleshooter steps *exactly*. If you don't, the troubleshooter can't do its job.

- After you complete a step in a troubleshooter, review the information in the Help window, and verify that you've followed the instructions.

To use a troubleshooter, click the Start button and select Help. In the left pane, click Troubleshooting, then Windows 98 Troubleshooters. The list shown in Figure 17.8 will open.

Skill 17

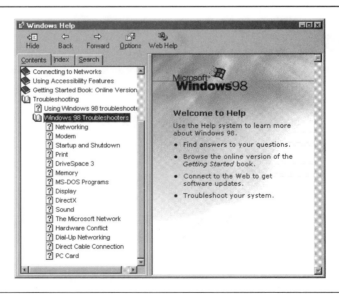

FIGURE 17.8: The list of built-in troubleshooting applications

Select one that seems most appropriate to your problem. You may have to run more than one troubleshooting application to solve the problem.

 TIP   After you start the troubleshooter, click the Hide icon at the top-left corner of the Windows Help window to close the left pane and make more room on the desktop.

Are You Experienced?

Now you can...

- ☑ **Use the System Information utility**
- ☑ **Run Dr. Watson to log errors**
- ☑ **Check your system files**
- ☑ **Use the System Monitor**
- ☑ **Track system resources**
- ☑ **Use the Windows 98 troubleshooters**

SKILL 18

USING THE REGISTRY

- Defining the registry
- The registry's structure
- Accessing the registry
- Backing up the registry
- Registry tips and tricks
- Searching the registry

Early versions of Windows stored hardware and user information in numerous files—autoexec.bat, config.sys, win.ini, system.ini, and more—which could be found all over the computer's hard drive. Windows NT first broke with this method; for a network-oriented operating system, it was clear that all these ASCII files would make it difficult (if not impossible) to manage even a single server. The goal of NT—to manage an environment with multiple servers—was quite impossible without a change in how configuration information was organized and stored.

When Windows 95 came along, it incorporated the *registry*, and Windows 98 continues the tradition.

What Is the Registry?

Try as you may, you won't learn anything of use about the registry from the Windows 98 help files. Even the Windows 95 Resource Kit, which topped out at over 1,300 pages, had only 20 pages on the registry.

First, let's define what the registry is. The registry is a binary hierarchical database that consolidates and simplifies the task of maintaining and configuring hardware and software information, as well as user options.

All clear?

I thought not. OK, let's try again. The registry is really the brains of Windows 98. It can be directly accessed only by using a program called regedit. It is accessed *indirectly* every time you make a hardware or software change, because all changes are reflected in the registry.

You'll encounter dire warnings about messing with the registry in a number of places. Fortunately, the registry is a good deal sturdier than those warnings would lead you to believe. However, a smart person always backs up the registry before starting to tinker.

Although the purpose of the registry is to get rid of the old text-based configuration files, you're sure to find many on your hard drive. A brief scan of my own computer yields desktop.ini, custom.ini, reg.ini, and several instances of setup.ini. These files are mostly retained for compatibility with older 16-bit programs that don't recognize the registry.

How the Registry Is Structured

The registry is organized in the hierarchical tree structure familiar to anyone who's dealt with the directory structure in DOS and Windows 3.x, or the folders, subfolders, and files in Windows 95 or Windows NT 4.

At the top level are five components called *hives*. Each hive contains numerous keys to divide the pieces of configuration information into different areas. The keys are divided into subkeys to further categorize the information. The subkeys can also be divided into lower-level subkeys, if required. Under the keys and subkeys, you will find values. Each value is assigned a name and can be set to store a specific piece of configuration information called the value's *data*.

The five top-level components are:

> HKEY_LOCAL_MACHINE
>
> HKEY_USERS
>
> HKEY_CLASSES_ROOT
>
> HKEY_CURRENT_USER
>
> HKEY_CURRENT_CONFIG

Of these five, only HKEY_LOCAL_MACHINE and HKEY_USERS are really hives. The other three are just pointers to information in the first two hives. They exist because the information they point to is accessed frequently by many different applications. Their sole reason for existence is to make it easier for the developers and applications to access that information. Since they just point to keys contained in HKEY_LOCAL_MACHINE and HKEY_USERS, you can change entries in the registry by directly modifying the entries in HKEY_LOCAL_MACHINE and HKEY_USERS, or you can use the pointer hives for quicker access to the configuration entries. The result is the same; either method will update the desired entries.

NOTE   A sixth hive called HKEY_DYN_DATA contains mostly hardware configuration data and can't be accessed directly.

Skill 18

The HKEY_LOCAL_MACHINE Registry Hive

HKEY_LOCAL_MACHINE is used to store information about the hardware, software, and users that are specific to the computer that the registry database is located on. There are seven keys located under it, listed below:

CONFIG key   This key contains the hardware configurations available to the machine.

ENUM key   Short for enumerator, the ENUM key contains a subkey for every hardware device installed since Windows 98 was installed.

HARDWARE key   The HARDWARE key contains information about all the hardware currently installed in the computer. This key is divided into two sub-keys called DESCRIPTION and DEVICEMAP, which contain all the options and configuration settings for the hardware installed on the computer.

NETWORK key   Present only on a networked computer, this key contains the current user's logon name and other configuration details.

SECURITY key   The SECURITY key is used to store information on a system configured for remote system administration.

SOFTWARE key   The SOFTWARE key contains information about installed software that applies to all users.

SYSTEM key   This key contains all system-specific data that's needed at startup and that may not be seen by detection software.

The HKEY_USERS Registry Hive

The HKEY_USERS registry hive contains information that is specific to the users who log onto the computer. Under the HKEY_USERS hive, you will find two keys. The first key is called .DEFAULT and contains the configuration information for a default user. When a new user logs onto the computer for the first time, that user's registry key is populated with the information contained in the .DEFAULT key. This makes it easy to set up common defaults for new users by modifying the .DEFAULT key's registry settings.

The second key found under HKEY_USERS will contain the configuration settings specific to the user currently logged onto the computer.

The HKEY_CLASSES_ROOT Registry Hive

As previously noted, the HKEY_CLASSES_ROOT registry hive is not a true hive, it's just a pointer to the SOFTWARE\Classes key located in the HKEY_LOCAL_ MACHINE hive. The SOFTWARE\Classes key stores the file associations that connect a file extension to an application (for example, .xls is associated with Excel). The primary purpose of this hive is to provide easy access to that information for developers and applications.

The HKEY_CURRENT_USER Registry Hive

Like the HKEY_CLASSES_ROOT hive, the HKEY_CURRENT_USER key is not a true hive, either. It's a pointer to the key under HKEY_USERS that represents the currently logged-on user. As you will recall, the HKEY_USERS hive has two keys located under it: .DEFAULT and a key for the currently logged-on user.

The HKEY_CURRENT_CONFIG Registry Hive

Like the previous two, the HKEY_CURRENT_CONFIG hive is also not a true hive. It's a pointer to the SYSTEM\CurrentControlSet\Hardware Profiles\Current subkey located under HKEY_LOCAL_MACHINE.

Accessing the Registry

Because the registry is in the form of a binary file, you must use a program to read it. The program is regedit.exe. To view and/or modify the registry, click the Start button and select Run. Type **regedit** in the Open text box and click OK. This will open the window shown in Figure 18.1.

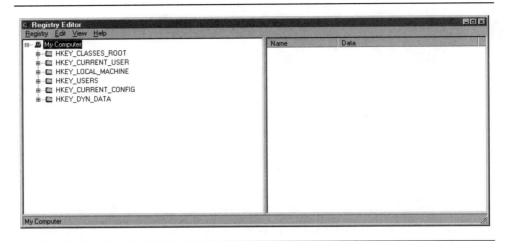

FIGURE 18.1 The Registry Editor window

Click a plus sign next to a key to open the next level of the hierarchy.

Backing Up the Registry

Always make a backup copy of the registry before making any changes. Making a backup copy of the registry is, fortunately, very easy to do. The easiest way presents itself just as you're about to poke around in the registry itself.

1.   Click the Start button and select Run.

2.   In the Open text box, type **regedit**.

3.   Click OK.

4.   Select Export Registry File from the Registry menu.

5.   Provide a name for the backup file. Today's date is usually a good choice.

6.   Under Export Range, make sure the All option is selected (see Figure 18.2). Click the Save button.

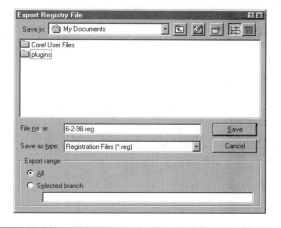

FIGURE 18.2: Saving a copy of the registry

Restoring a Backed-Up Registry

The easiest possible way to restore a registry is to reverse the procedure described in the previous section, "Backing Up the Registry."

Click the Start button, then select Run. In the Open text box, type **regedit** and click OK. Select Import Registry File from the Registry menu. Highlight the .reg file you want to restore and click the Open button.

But what if your adventures in the registry result in Windows 98 not booting?

From the DOS Command Line

From the DOS command line, you merely need to type in:

regedit /C filename.reg

Use this command only if you're restoring the entire registry, because the existing registry will be replaced by the contents of *filename*.reg.

If the restoration involves only a part of the registry, type in:

regedit filename.reg

without the /X parameter, and the contents of *filename*.reg will be restored without affecting other portions of the registry.

What the Registry Can Do

The registry, as mentioned, is the brain of the operating system, so it can be manipulated to do darn near anything. However, some changes are too dangerous and others too complicated for a modest result. In the next sections, you'll find some changes that you might find to your liking. All involve changing the registry, so making a backup of the registry is always recommended before beginning.

Adding a Cascading Control Panel to the Start Menu

If you'd like to have a cascading Control Panel menu like the one shown in Figure 18.3, just follow these steps (*after* backing up the registry):

1. Right-click the Start button and select Open from the pop-up menu.

2. Create a new folder in the Start Menu window and give it this name *exactly*:

   Control Panel.{21EC2020-3AEA-1069-A2DD-08002B30309D}

3. Click outside the name box, and the folder symbol will change to the Control Panel icon.

FIGURE 18.3: A cascading menu of the Control Panel

Control Panel is now an option on the Start menu, with each Control Panel icon available.

Denying Access to Display Properties

If the Display Properties are tampered with, your machine may not boot properly. So if you share your machine with an inquisitive child (of whatever age), you may want to turn off the ability to change Display Properties. To make sure that you aren't the instrument of your own downfall, do a backup of the registry first.

1. Click the Start button, then select Run. Type **regedit** in the Open text box and click OK.

2. In the Registry Editor window, open the following path by clicking the plus signs next to each entry:

   HKEY_CURRENT_USER\Software\Microsoft\Windows\
   CurrentVersion\Policies

3. Right-click the Policies folder and select New ➤ Key.

4. Type **System** as the new key name (see Figure 18.4).

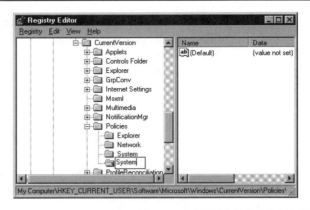

FIGURE 18.4: Creating a new registry key

5. In the right pane, right-click on a blank spot and select New ➤ String value. Provide one of the names shown in Table 18.1.

6. Right-click on the new string value name and select Modify. Provide a value shown in Table 18.1.

7. Close the Registry Editor window.

TABLE 18.1: Hiding part or all of the Display Properties

Name	Value	Description
NoDispCPL	1	Hides the entire Display Properties
NoDispSettingsPage	1	Hides the Settings, Web, and Effects pages on Display Properties
NoDispAppearancePage	1	Hides the Appearance page on Display Properties
NoDispBackgroundPage	1	Hides the Background page on Display Properties
NoDispScrSavPage	1	Hides the Screen Saver page on Display Properties

TIP   Changing the value to zero or deleting the value will enable access.

Denying Access to Password Properties

If display settings are important, the password settings are even more crucial. To prevent changes to passwords, make the following changes to the registry:

1. Click the Start button, then select Run. Type **regedit** in the Open text box and click OK.

2. In the Registry Editor window, open the following path by clicking the plus signs next to each entry:

   HKEY_CURRENT_USER\Software\Microsoft\Windows\CurrentVersion\Policies\System

3. If there isn't a System folder, make one by right-clicking Policies and selecting New ➢ Key. Type in the name **System**.

4. Open the System folder.

5. In the right pane, right-click on a blank spot and select New ➢ String Value. Provide one of the names shown in Table 18.2.

6. Right-click on the new string value name and select Modify. Provide a value shown in Table 18.2.

7. Close the Registry Editor window.

T A B L E 1 8 . 2 : Hiding Password Properties

Name	Value	Description
NoSecCPL	1	Completely hides the Password Properties sheet
NoPwdPage	1	Hides the Change Passwords page

TIP Changing the value to zero or deleting the value will enable access.

Removing Network Neighborhood

If networking is the last thing you're ever likely to do with your computer, you can tidy up your desktop by removing the Network Neighborhood icon. Just follow these steps:

1. Click the Start button and select Run.

2. In the Open text window, type **regedit** and click OK.

3. In the Registry Editor, open the following path by clicking on the plus signs next to each entry:

    HKEY_CURRENT_UDER\Software\Microsoft\Windows\CurrentVersion\ Policies\Explorer

4. In the right pane, right-click on a blank spot and select New ➢ String Value.

5. Name the new value **NoNetHood**.

6. Right-click NoNetHood and select Modify.

7. In the Edit String dialog box, enter **1** in the Value Data box (see Figure 18.5).

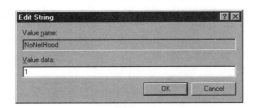

FIGURE 18.5: Setting this value to 1 will remove the Network Neighborhood icon.

8. Close the Registry Editor.

You will have to reboot your system before the change takes effect.

 TIP   Changing the value to zero or deleting the value will cause the Network Neighborhood icon to return.

Searching the Registry

If you know what key or value you're looking for, you can easily search for it in the registry. Just follow these steps:

1. Click the Start button and select Run.

2. In the Open text box, type **regedit** and click OK.

3. In the Registry Editor, click the Edit menu and select Find.

4. Type in the string of characters you're looking for. To speed up the search, check only the areas you want searched—if you know.

5. Click Find Next.

6. When the string is found, the Find window will disappear. To continue the search, click F3.

Are You Experienced?

Now you can...

- ☑ **Open the Registry Editor**
- ☑ **Edit the registry**
- ☑ **Back up the registry**
- ☑ **Search the registry**

SKILL 19

USING BACKUP

- Backing up your system
- Making partial backups
- Restoring backups

Backing up your computer or data files means making a copy that can be kept in a safe place and used to restore your computer or (at least) the important information you keep on your computer. It provides protection against everything from a hard drive failure to a fire in your office—if you keep the backup somewhere else. Windows 98 has a very good backup program.

Hard drives are very reliable these days. In fact, they very rarely fail. And if a complete, cataclysmic failure of your hard drive is something you can view with equanimity, then backups needn't be high on your list of priorities.

But for most people, the rule is: No matter how sure you are of your hardware, it's a good idea to back up your files regularly.

NOTE The Backup program is not included in the default installation of Windows 98. To install it, put the Windows 98 CD into the CD drive, then go to the Control panel and click Add/Remove Programs. On the Windows Setup page, highlight System Tools in the Components list. Click the Details button. Put a checkmark next to Backup. Click OK twice. The Add/Remove Programs utility will search the CD for the Backup program and install it on your computer.

Getting Started

To start Microsoft Backup, click the Start button and select Programs ➤ Accessories ➤ System Tools ➤ Backup. The Backup window will open with the dialog box shown in Figure 19.1 on top. For your first use of Backup, select *Create a new backup job*, then click OK.

NOTE The first time you run Backup, you may see a message saying that the program did not find any backup devices. It asks if you want to run the Add New Hardware Wizard. Click Yes if you have specific backup hardware, such as a tape drive, that may not have been properly installed in Windows 98. Otherwise, click No and continue. Backup can utilize lots of devices that aren't specifically recognized as "backup devices."

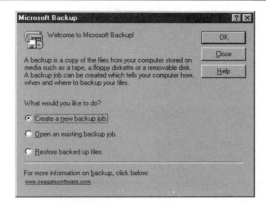

The Backup Wizard (see Figure 19.2) will start. Choose whether to back up everything on your computer or just certain drives, folders, or files.

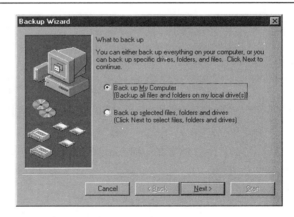

FIGURE 19.2: Back up completely or just partially?

Backing Up Everything

If you choose the first option—Back Up My Computer—the Backup program will prepare to back up your entire system. This will require considerable capacity on your backup device. For example, your Windows 98 installation alone is likely to exceed 250MB, without even considering your applications and data.

The most common devices that offer enough removable capacity for a full system backup are tape drives. Other likely candidates are Jaz or other removable hard-disk type devices with a capacity of at least several hundred megabytes. Before you buy a device to use for backup, be sure Microsoft Backup supports it.

TIP   When your hard disk suddenly sounds like an old gravel truck, there's nothing more comforting than having a full system backup on your shelf. If you have a tape drive or other suitable device, you should make a full system backup after you first install Windows 98, when you install new applications, and occasionally thereafter. Verify the backup by actually restoring part or all of it. While Backup automatically "verifies" files, nothing *truly* verifies a backup like a successful restore.

To make a complete backup of your system, follow these steps:

1. In the first Backup Wizard dialog box (shown in Figure 19.2), select Back Up My Computer, then click Next.

2. In the What to Back Up dialog box, choose All Selected Files, then click Next.

3. In the Where to Back Up dialog box, click this button:

   Navigate to the tape or disk drive that's receiving the backup and enter a brief, descriptive name for the backup location, then click Open. You'll be returned to the Where to Back Up dialog box with the backup location showing. Click Next.

4. In the How to Back Up dialog box, choose if you want the backup to be verified by the backup program. This is *always* a good idea. You must also

choose whether you want the backup program to use compression. This will save space on the backup media but will also slow the process.

5. Next you'll be asked to name the backup job. In Figure 19.3, I've named this job Complete_System; in the future I'll know to use this when I want to back up *everything*. This window also allows you to review all the choices you've made. Click the Back button to make any changes before proceeding.

FIGURE 19.3: Naming the backup job

6. Click Start and the backup begins. A Backup Progress window opens showing the details of the backup as it proceeds.

Microsoft Backup reports when the operation is completed. You can click the Report button in the Backup Progress window to see the details of the backup process just completed. Click OK to close the Backup Progress window.

NOTE Backup is based on the idea that you have a large hard disk with perhaps thousands of individual files in hundreds of folders. You don't often want to back up everything on the disk. Usually you will want to back up a select few folders—the folders containing your Photoshop pictures, your WordPerfect documents, your appointment book, contact list, and so on. Therefore, you need to tell Backup which folders need to be backed up every day or every week. A backup *job* specifies which directories to back up. In previous versions of Microsoft Windows Backup, backup jobs were called *file sets*.

Partial Backups

Partial backups involve less than your entire computer, and their size will probably depend on your perception of how valuable certain files are, how difficult they would be to recreate, and how often they change. This is the type of backup you should create on a regular basis, even if you never make a full system backup.

To begin making your first periodic backup, choose *Back up selected files, folders, and drives* in the Backup Wizard's first dialog box (shown in Figure 19.2). Click Next and you should see the window shown in Figure 19.4.

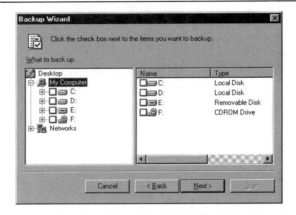

FIGURE 19.4: In this window, choose what you want to back up.

To select individual folders inside a drive, click the plus sign next to the drive letter in the left pane. Put checkmarks next to the folders you want to back up.

NOTE   Each of the drives shown in the Backup window has a checkbox next to it. If you want to back up the entire drive—every file and directory from the root to the farthest branch—check this box.

WARNING   Even if you use the My Documents folder created by Windows 98 to store your word processing and spreadsheet files, don't make the mistake of assuming that all your valuable information is in that folder. For example, if you use Outlook Express for your e-mail and newsgroups, those files are stored in folders within the Program Files\Outlook Express folder. Your Windows Address Book may be stored in the Windows\Application Data\Microsoft folder. For backup purposes, you need to think about the location of files created by every application in which you enter data.

To perform a partial backup, follow these steps:

1. Select the files and folders you want to save.

NOTE   If the folders and files are not in alphabetical order, you can click on the Name column header at the top of the list to sort them alphabetically. Or you can click on another column header to sort the list another way.

2. Click the Next button at the bottom of the Backup Wizard dialog box. Now you must tell the Wizard whether to back up all the files you have designated or only those that are new or changed since your last backup. If this is your first backup, choose All Selected Files.

3. Click Next again to bring up the dialog box shown in Figure 19.5. Here you tell Backup where to create the backup file. Generally, this will be your tape drive (if you have one) or some other removable storage device, such as a Zip drive or even your diskette drive.

4. Click the folder button to the right of the lower text box to open a standard browse window. Navigate to the device you want to use for backup and enter a filename that will identify this backup for you. I called this one *June*. Click Next.

5. Tell the Wizard whether you want your backup verified, and whether it should be compressed. Both will slow the process somewhat. Verification is particularly important, however.

Skill 19

FIGURE 19.5: Tell the Wizard where to create your backup.

6. .Click Next and verify all the choices you have made (see Figure 19.6). If necessary, click Back to change an option. Also, choose a job name under which this set of options will be saved for future use. Label the tape or disk with the same name, along with the date.

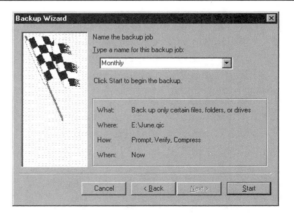

FIGURE 19.6: Check this dialog box to verify your selections.

7. Click Start and the backup will be created. As the backup proceeds, you will see the dialog box shown in Figure 19.7.

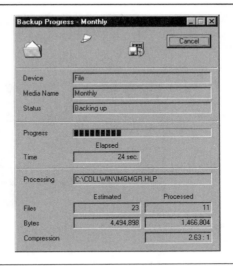

FIGURE 19.7: Viewing the progress of the backup

8. Microsoft Backup reports when the operation is completed. You can click the Report button in the Backup Progress window to see the details of the backup process just completed. Click OK to close the Backup Progress window.

 TIP Not sure if you have room on the tape or disk to complete the backup? Go to the View menu and click Selection Information. The backup program will check the files you've selected and tell you just how many bytes they add up to.

Backing Up an Existing Job

Once you've created a job—a set of files and folders that you want to back up regularly—it's a simple matter to do a repeat backup. Just follow these steps:

1. Click the Start button, then select Programs ➢ Accessories ➢ System Tools ➢ Backup.

2. In the Welcome to Microsoft Backup dialog box, select *Open an existing backup job* and click OK.

Skill 19

3. In the Open Backup Job dialog box, highlight the name of the backup job you want to use, then click Open. The Microsoft Backup window will open with the backup job selected (see Figure 19.8).

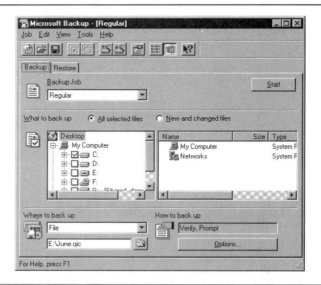

FIGURE 19.8: The backup job is ready to start.

4. Make sure there's a new disk or tape in the drive. Click Start and your backup will be created on the disk or tape, under the same name.

If you want to create the backup on the *same* disk or tape as before, you can change the filename in the lower left corner of the Backup window to create a separate backup file (assuming you have room on the disk or tape). Or you can click Start and then choose to overwrite the old backup.

You can also modify the backup options before clicking Start. For example, with the same disk or tape in place, you might choose to back up only New and Changed Files and change the name in the Where to Back Up dialog box. The two backups taken together would then be up to date.

NOTE   A combination of backup jobs works the best. Back up really important directories once a day (or once a week) and less important ones at the end of major projects. How often you back up is strictly a question of what makes you comfortable. Rotate backups among multiple tapes or disks. For complete safety, keep a recent backup in a separate location. Multiple backups are of little use if they were all side by side on the same shelf when the building burned.

Choosing Backup Options

Specific options are available for backups. Choose Options from the Job menu in the main Microsoft Backup window to open the Backup Job Options dialog box (shown in Figure 19.9).

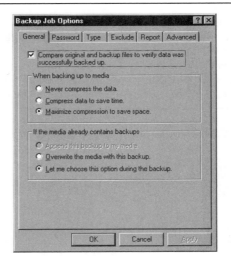

FIGURE 19.9: The options available for backup jobs

These options allow you to customize each backup job to suit your needs. Additional options include:

- Degree of compression to use

- Whether to automatically overwrite a backup of the same name on the same media (disk or tape)

- Password encryption

- Whether to use differential or incremental backup when you choose to back up new and changed files only

- File types you want to exclude from backups

- What details to include in backup reports

- Whether to back up the Windows registry. (This is on by default and should remain so unless you have a specific reason to exclude it.)

 NOTE   A *differential* backup backs up all selected files that have changed since your last All Selected Files backup. To restore, you need the All Selected Files backup plus your most recent differential backup. An *incremental* backup backs up only selected files that have changed since the last backup of any kind. To restore, you need your last All Selected Files backup plus *all* backups made since then.

Any time you make changes to backup options, those changes relate only to the current backup job named in the box at the upper left of the Backup window. When you exit Backup, you will be asked whether you want your changes to be made a permanent part of that backup job.

Restoring a Backup

Restore is useful for more than recovering from disaster. If you've backed up a large file that isn't needed immediately, you can use restore to return it to active duty on your hard drive.

To restore a backup, follow these steps:

1. Click the Start button, then select Programs ➤ Accessories ➤ System Tools ➤ Backup.

2. In the Welcome to Microsoft Backup dialog box, choose Restore Backed Up Files and click OK.

3. The Restore Wizard starts, asking you to choose the location from which to restore files, as shown in Figure 19.10. Click the folder icon to open a browse window and select the drive and backup location. If the location is correct, simply click Next, and a window opens allowing you to select the backup jobs available in that location.

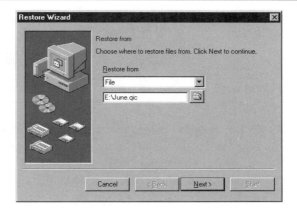

FIGURE 19.10: Choosing the location from which to restore files

4. Next you'll be asked what to restore. Navigate through the folder structure as necessary and put a check beside the folders or specific files you want restored. Checking the top-level box will restore all backed-up files in the backup job you selected. In Figure 19.11, I've chosen to restore only the My Documents folder.

5. Next you choose where to restore the files. Generally this would be the original location. Choose Alternate Location if you are using Backup and Restore to move files from one machine to another, or if you want to compare the backed-up versions to current versions of the same files. If you choose Alternate Location, a folder icon will appear. Click it to browse for the location where you want the files restored. Click Next.

Skill 19

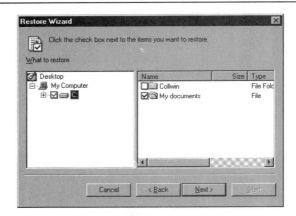

FIGURE 19.11: Restoring just some of the files that were backed up

6. In the How to Restore dialog box (see Figure 19.12), you must tell Restore what to do with files of the same name in the same place as those you are restoring. The recommended option is to leave the files on your computer undisturbed. The second option is to keep whichever version of the file is more recent. If the files on your computer are corrupted, you would want to choose the last option, to restore from the backup regardless of file dates. When you are ready, click Start.

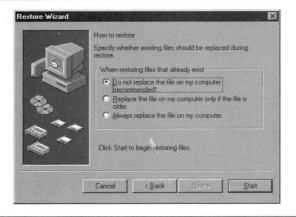

FIGURE 19.12: Consider what you want done if Restore encounters files of the same name.

7. The Restore program shows the name of the backup media required to complete your restore. Be sure the tape or disk containing that file is in the appropriate drive and click OK.

The files will be restored as you have specified. When the operation is complete, you can examine a report if you wish.

Restoring Options

Like Backup, the Restore procedure has its own set of options. Select the Restore tab in the main Backup window, and then choose Options from the Job menu. A few of the available options haven't been covered here:

- On the Report tab (shown in Figure 19.13), you can specify the details you want included in a report on a restore job.

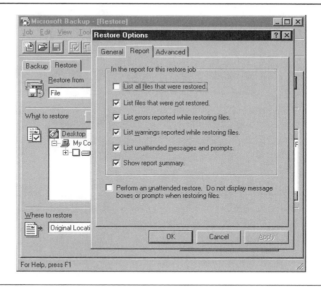

FIGURE 19.13: Options for restoring backed up files

- Also on the Report tab, you can check that you want an *unattended* restore. This is a good idea if you're restoring a large amount of data and don't want the process paused for messages or prompts.

- On the Advanced tab, specify if you want the registry restored. This is set to Off by default. Only check this box if you are *specifically* restoring a good registry over an existing bad one.

You can run the Backup or Restore Wizards any time by choosing them from the Tools menu. Once you are comfortable using Backup, you can bypass the Wizards, if you wish. Just click Close in the Welcome dialog box when you start Backup. If you don't want to see the Welcome dialog box any more, choose Tools ➤ Preferences to set this and a couple of other options.

Are You Experienced?

Now you can...

- ☑ **Back up your entire system**
- ☑ **Make partial backups of files and folders**
- ☑ **Restore backed-up files**

SKILL 20

HARDWARE MASTERY

- Installing and removing modems
- Configuring modems
- Troubleshooting a scanner or camera
- Installing and removing printers
- Configuring infrared settings
- Installing a new mouse
- Configuring a game controller
- Changing video cards and drivers
- Configuring video settings

Imagine that you've bought a new kitchen appliance from Blenders 'R Us, and it turns out that different manufacturers are the sources for the glass container, push buttons, blade, and motor. Each piece comes with an instruction booklet and its own warranty card. After assembling all the pieces, you go to make yourself a milkshake, and a message pops out: "Sorry, the Framjit 34ExY894 blade isn't sharp enough to cut frozen products. You need to upgrade to the Framjit 34ExY894 Plus." (And incidentally, the new blade exerts additional torque, requiring a new shaft—but you don't find that out until after you've bought the blade upgrade and spent several fruitless hours trying to install it.)

Welcome to the world of computers! Except to actually resemble computers, the blender's new blade must not fit on the new shaft, and the manufacturers blame each other. But don't worry—a new blade-shaft adapter will be available by spring at the latest.

OK, so I exaggerate for effect. But not by much.

Fortunately, starting with Windows 95, sanity has begun to triumph in the world of computer hardware. The sanity goes by the name of the *Plug and Play* standard. Forget that the standard used to be called Plug and Pray—these days, "PnP" in Windows 98 really works. Nevertheless, there are so many manufacturers and so much new hardware, not everything will go perfectly. This skill addresses the possible problems and their solutions.

Modems

Installing and configuring a modem in Windows 98 is fairly simple (almost as simple as it should be). When you first install Windows 98, the modem should be detected automatically. You'll only need to deal with the following steps if the modem wasn't detected or if you later change modems.

Installing a Modem

Before starting any modem procedure, make sure the modem is plugged in and turned on (if it's an external modem) and that the telephone wire is plugged into the modem and into the wall receptacle (internal and external modems). To install a modem (where none has been before) follow these steps:

1. Click the Start button, then select Settings ➤ Control Panel.

2. Click the Modems icon in the Control Panel. This will start the Install New Modem Wizard (see Figure 20.1).

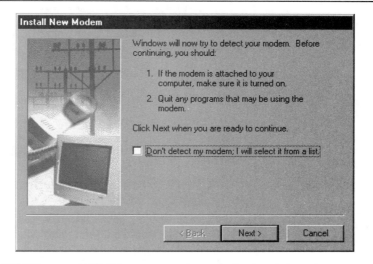

Install New Modem

Windows will now try to detect your modem. Before continuing, you should:

1. If the modem is attached to your computer, make sure it is turned on.

2. Quit any programs that may be using the modem.

Click Next when you are ready to continue.

☐ Don't detect my modem; I will select it from a list.

< Back   Next >   Cancel

FIGURE 20.1: A Windows 98 Wizard steps you through the process of installing a modem.

3. You can let Windows 98 search for the modem, or you can select your modem directly. As a rule, let Windows try first—it's the easiest way. If Windows 98 has difficulty, you can always specify your particular modem on a second go-round. Windows will search around your communications ports and try to find a modem. When it finds one, you'll see a Verify Modem page. If the modem isn't correct, or the designation seems too generic, click on the Change button and continue with the next step.

4. If Windows 98 fails to find the modem (or if you click Change in the Verify Modem page), you'll be asked to get specific. Figure 20.2 shows the window where you select a manufacturer in the left box and the particular model in the right box. If your modem isn't listed, but you have an installation disk that came with it, click Have Disk.

5. Keep clicking OK, Next, or Finish until the installation is complete.

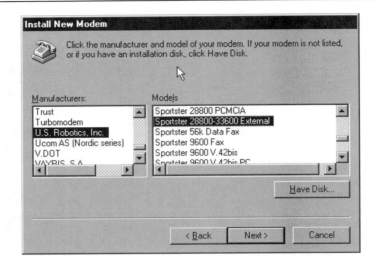

FIGURE 20.2: If Windows 98 doesn't find your modem, you can install a modem by selecting a particular manufacturer and model.

Deleting a Modem

If you change modems (or install the wrong one), it's easy to correct the situation:

1. Click Start ➤ Settings ➤ Control Panel.

2. Open the Modems icon in the Control Panel.

3. On the General page, highlight the modem name.

4. Click the Remove button, and it's gone!

INSTALLING A REPLACEMENT MODEM

When the time comes to replace your modem with something faster, the process is easy. Just delete the old modem using the procedure described above. Unplug the old modem and plug in the new one at the same location. Make sure the modem is turned on and that all connections—including the one to the phone line—are made, then follow the steps described under "Installing a Modem."

Modem Settings

To find the hardware-type settings for your modem, click Start ➤ Settings ➤ Control Panel and click the Modems icon. Highlight your modem (if it isn't highlighted already) and select Properties. The modem's Properties sheet opens (see Figure 20.3).

The General Page

On the General page are:

- The full name of the modem
- The port it's connected to
- A slider for setting the volume of the modem speaker
- A drop-down box for setting the maximum speed

Skill 20

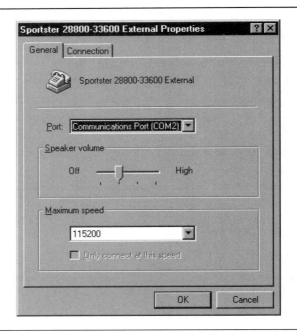

FIGURE 20.3: This is the place to check up on the settings for your modem.

These settings (except for volume, which is strictly a matter of preference) rarely need to be fooled with. That's because they come from what Windows 98 knows about your specific modem. Only change the settings when you've had some difficulty with your modem being recognized and you're sure a particular setting is wrong.

The Connection Page

More of the hardware settings are on the Connection page (see Figure 20.4). Again, unless you have a good reason for changing the Connection preferences, leave them alone. The Call Preferences can be changed if you find the default ones unsuitable. In particular, you may want to set a time to disconnect a call if the line is idle for an extended time. Although many online services will disconnect an inactive line, they may take quite a long time to do it.

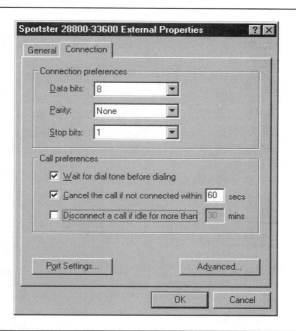

FIGURE 20.4: The properties for the modem's connection

Advanced Settings

If you click the Advanced button on the Connection page, you'll see the page in Figure 20.5. These settings are rarely anything to be concerned about. They're just here for those odd and infrequent times when it might be necessary to force error correction or use software for error control. The one thing on this page that you might use more often is the log file. If you're troubleshooting a bad connection, click View Log to open a text file containing a log of the last connection (or attempt). Normally, this file is overwritten with the new log each time you connect. If you want to keep an ongoing log, check the Append to Log box.

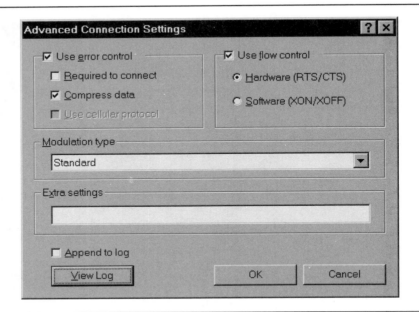

FIGURE 20.5: You might try these advanced settings with a connection that's otherwise difficult.

Dialing Properties

In addition to centralizing the modem's hardware and software settings, you also want to enter information about how you're dialing and where you're dialing from. Windows 98 allows for the configuring of multiple dialing locations, so if you travel with your computer, you can make calls from your branch office (or the condo in Maui where you take your vacations) without making complex changes every time you change locations.

Click the Modems icon in the Control Panel. Click Dialing Properties on the General page of the Modem Properties sheet and fill out the information for your location. Click the Add button to supply additional locations. When you change physical locations, you need only tell Windows 98 where you are (see Figure 20.6), and all your necessary dialing information will be loaded.

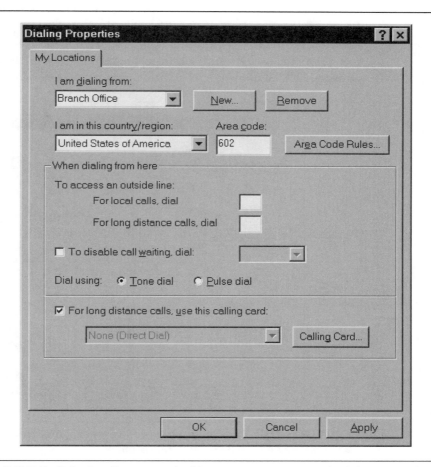

FIGURE 20.6: If you travel with your computer, you don't have to redo your communications settings when you change locations.

Troubleshooting

As a rule, when your modem is uncooperative, it's for obvious reasons:

- It's not plugged into a phone line.

- The modem is turned off or it's not plugged into an active electrical socket (external modems).

- One or more programs have confused the settings.

After you check the first two items, click on the Modems icon in the Control Panel. On the Diagnostics page, highlight the port your modem is connected to and click More Info. The resulting page (see Figure 20.7) tells you that the system recognizes the modem and describes it in terms of speed, interrupt, memory address, and the modem's response to various internal commands.

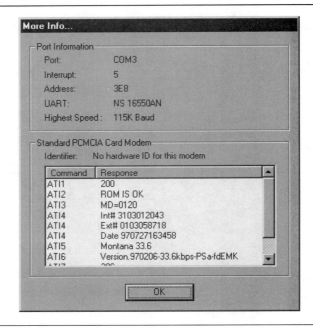

FIGURE 20.7: Here's where you verify that the system can find the modem and that the modem is responding correctly.

If you receive a message that the system can't communicate with the modem, then the modem is either not plugged into a usable port, not turned on, or defective.

 NOTE   ATI2 is a check of the modem's read-only memory (ROM); if the response isn't "OK," the modem may be defective. The other information in the window is of little interest except to someone with an advanced degree in modemology. Depending on your modem, however, some actual information may filter through.

If your modem isn't recognized, go back to the main Modem Properties sheet and click the Remove button. After the modem is removed, close everything and reboot your system. Then go back to the Modems icon in the Control Panel and add your modem back.

Scanners and Cameras

Most scanners and digital cameras come with their own installation programs. Windows 98 has added a Scanners and Cameras icon to the Control Panel to supply additional information and configuration options for these devices.

Click this icon to troubleshoot a problem with either a scanner or camera or to set logging options. Color profiles can also be added or removed. Color profiles are issues best addressed to the manufacturer or a photography expert.

Adding and Configuring Printers

Printing is generally a lot easier in Windows 98 than in any previous system. As in earlier versions of Windows, printers are set up to use a common set of drivers so you don't have to configure each program independently for printing. Adding or removing a printer is as easy as point and click, and sharing printers over a network is painless.

You can access your printers in several ways:

- Click My Computer and select the Printers folder.

- Click Start ➢ Settings ➢ Printers.

- Click Start ➢ Settings ➢ Control Panel and select the Printers folder.

And of course, you can drag a shortcut to the folder (or any of the printers in it) to your desktop or any folder where you'd like it.

Adding a Printer

You probably installed a printer when you installed Windows 98, but if you didn't or you want to add another or a network printer, it's very easy to do.

Adding a Local Printer

To add a printer that's connected directly to your computer, open the Printers folder as described above and follow these steps (clicking the Next button after each entry):

1. Select Add Printer.

2. When the Add Printer Wizard starts, click Next and check the Local Printer entry.

3. Highlight the printer's manufacturer and the model name.

4. Select the port you want to use. Unless you know of some special circumstances, choose LPT1, the standard connection point for printers.

5. Type in the name you want the printer to be known by and indicate whether this is the default printer for all your Windows programs. If this is the printer you plan to use practically all the time, select Yes. Otherwise say no—you'll still be able to select the printer when you want to use it. In the Printers folder, the default printer will have a checkmark by it.

6. Print a test page to verify all is well. Then click Finish.

Adding a Network Printer

A network printer is plugged into someone else's computer—a computer to which you have access via a network. A networked printer shows up in the Printers window with a drawing of a network cable attached.

To tell your computer about a network printer that you want to use, open the Printers folder as described above and follow these steps (clicking Next after each entry).

1. Open Add Printer. When the Add Printer Wizard starts, click Next and select Network Printer.

2. You'll need to tell the system the address of the printer. Click on the Browse button to look for available printers. Highlight the printer (as shown in Figure 20.8) and click OK.

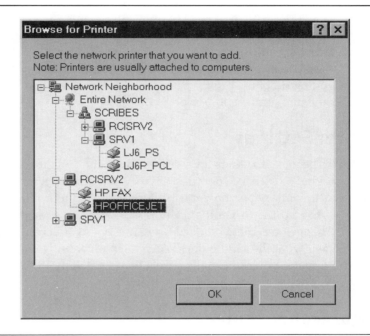

FIGURE 20.8: Here's where you select a printer on the network.

3. If you expect to print from DOS programs, click on Yes so the system can add the necessary information to the printer setup.

4. Enter the name you want to call the printer and check whether you want this printer to be the default printer. Only check Yes if you expect to be using the network printer for the majority of your printing.

5. Print a test page to make sure everything is running properly, then click Finish.

NOTE To use a printer set up this way, the printer and the computer it's connected to must both be switched on.

Uninstalling a Printer

Sometimes you may need to uninstall a printer, which is quite easily done. Just right-click on the printer's icon in the Printers folder and select Delete. You'll be asked to confirm the deletion. You may also be asked if you want to delete files associated with this printer that won't be necessary if the printer is gone. If you're getting rid of the printer permanently, select Yes. If you're planning on reinstalling the same printer soon, select No.

Printer Settings

To get at the settings for a printer, right-click on the printer's icon in the Printers folder and select Properties. On the Properties sheet that opens, you can set details as to fonts, paper, how the printer treats graphics, and so on.

The printer driver that installs with Windows 98 makes most of these settings. Change ones that you need to change but avoid changing settings if you're not clear what the setting does. You can inadvertently disable your printer. If this happens, you can usually cure it by uninstalling the printer (see the previous section) and then installing it again.

Troubleshooting

If you're not having any success getting your printer to print, or there appears to be something wrong with the printer, Windows 98 comes with excellent tools for troubleshooting the problem.

Select Help from the Start menu. On the Contents page, open Troubleshooting. Then open Windows 98 Troubleshooters and select Print. The guide is interactive: You select the problem you're having, and then you're stepped through the process of finding a solution.

Changing a Mouse

Usually, you can change the pointing device on your computer by simply turning the computer off, unplugging the old mouse, plugging in the new mouse, and then rebooting your computer.

Sometimes you'll see a window informing you that Windows 98 has found new hardware and is installing it, but more often than not, the new mouse will simply *work*. However, if your mouse needs a new (or different) driver, you can install it manually by following these steps (described in terms of keyboard commands because you can hardly use your mouse if the mouse isn't functional):

1. Use the Tab and arrow keys to move the highlight to the My Computer icon. Press Alt+Enter to open the System Properties dialog box. (The Tab key cycles from Start through any open program buttons and the last icon used, back to Start again. Once the focus is on an icon, the arrow keys can be used to move around the desktop icons.)

2. Use the Tab and arrow keys to move the focus to the Device Manager page.

3. Press the Tab key twice to move the focus to the list of devices, then use the down arrow to highlight Mouse.

4. Press the right arrow to display the devices under Mouse. Then press the down arrow to highlight the device (see Figure 20.9).

5. Press the Tab key once to move the focus to the Properties button, then press Enter. This will open the mouse's Properties sheet.

Skill 20

FIGURE 20.9: Selecting the pointer device (that's *mouse* to you, pal)

6. Press Tab again to move to the Driver page. On the Driver page, keep tabbing until the Update Driver button is selected, then press Enter. The Update Device Driver Wizard will start.

From here on you can let the Wizard do the work. Use the default settings except when you get to the window shown in Figure 20.10. This window is where you specify the location for the new driver. You can check more than one box if you want to search in multiple locations.

FIGURE 20.10: Specify the location for the new driver.

Game Controllers

Game controllers are what used to be called joysticks. It's possible that the name changed because not all game controllers are sticks, but I think it's because joystick sounds too much like fun.

Click on the Game Controller icon in the Control Panel to open a Properties sheet for adding a controller to the setup. Click Add to see a list of more than two dozen types that are ready to go (shown in Figure 20.11) or highlight Custom to specify another type altogether.

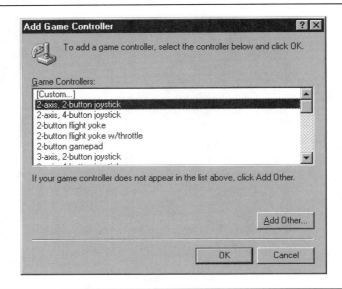

FIGURE 20.11: Game devices for all occasions

Using Infrared Devices

Many new computers—particularly laptops—have infrared ports that allow for wireless communication. To communicate with a printer, for example, your computer needs an infrared port, and the printer must have a corresponding infrared port and be within range. "Within range" means that the two ports must have an unobstructed "view" of each other. (Think of a television or VCR remote control.)
To set up the device, click the Infrared icon in the Control Panel.

On the Status page, you'll see what (if any) devices are in range (see Figure 20.12).

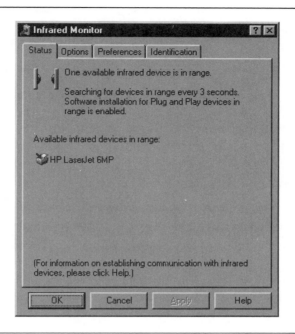

FIGURE 20.12: Infrared devices are reported on this page of the Infrared Monitor dialog box.

On the Options page, specify the port on which you wish to enable communications. It's important to understand that infrared communications are, shall we say, still developing. Depending on the devices involved, you may be able to communicate easily, or you may have to experiment with settings—at length—before you get results. Be prepared to call the manufacturer of the devices involved.

Setting the Display Adapter

The performance of the video system is absolutely critical to all versions of Windows. A slow video system makes your whole computer seem painfully slow—regardless of the processor or amount of RAM on your motherboard. Windows 95 increased the pressure on your video card and monitor and Windows 98 continues to up the ante.

Skill 20

TIP   If your video card has 1MB of memory or less, you'll want to upgrade. You'll also have to consider whether your monitor can handle the increase in resolution and colors that the video card promises.

There are three video-related chores that you may have to deal with at some point in your Windows career. You may have to change a video card, change a video driver, or most commonly, optimize the appearance of the video system that you already have. All three are addressed in the next sections.

Changing a Video Card

Installing a new video card is one of the easiest computer chores—provided you're not completely averse to opening your computer box. Here are the steps:

1. Open the box with the new video card, make sure all the pieces are there, and read the instructions. Handle the card only by its edges. Don't handle the edge with the gold contacts.

2. With the computer turned off, unplug the monitor cable from the main computer box and then open the case.

3. Remove the screw holding in the video card (the one the monitor was plugged into). Save the screw.

4. Using a gentle rocking motion, remove the video card from the slot.

5. Put the new video card in the same slot—again, using the same gentle rocking motion. Make sure the card is firmly seated into the slot.

6. Replace the screw holding the card in place. Replace the monitor cable.

7. Close the computer case and restart the computer.

8. After the initial boot process, Windows 98 will start. The system will detect the new hardware and install it.

Video cards that are in production at the time Windows 98 is released will have drivers included with Windows 98. If you are installing a new card a year or more after the release of Windows 98, you may need to supply the floppy disk or CD that came with the new card to get the best driver.

Changing a Video Driver

Often the manufacturer of a video card will release new drivers sometime after the card has been in production. This may be to take advantage of a feature in a new operating system (like Windows 98) or to fix a bug that wasn't apparent at the time the card was manufactured.

To install a new video driver, just follow these steps:

1. Select Start ➢ Settings ➢ Control Panel and click the Display icon.

2. Click the Settings tab and then the Advanced button. This opens even more settings. Click the Adapter tab here.

3. The Adapter page (shown in Figure 20.13) shows the name of the video card and something about its features. Click the Change button.

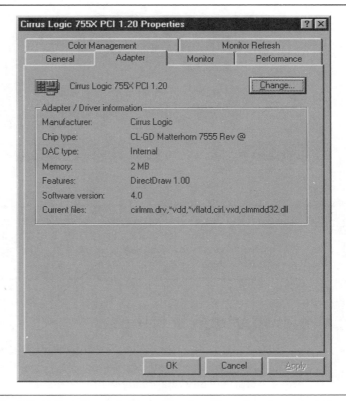

FIGURE 20.13: The Adapter page describes the characteristics of the video card.

4. The Update Device Driver Wizard will launch and search for updated drivers.

Use the default settings except as shown in Figure 20.14, where you can be specific about the location of the new driver. If you want, you can let the Wizard search all the locations.

FIGURE 20.14: Places the system should search for the new video driver

NOTE Deselect the floppy disk drive option if you don't have a floppy disk. Likewise, if you want the system to search the CD-ROM drive, make sure there's actually a CD in the drive. It won't do any harm, but you'll receive error messages that will slow the process.

Optimizing Video Settings

The video settings you can make are limited only by the capacity of your video card and monitor. Also, some settings—such as very high resolutions on small monitors—are aesthetically unappealing, not to mention rendering icons practically invisible. Feel free to experiment; you can't do any harm (except as noted on the following pages).

To modify your video settings, you need to open Display Properties. You can do this by clicking the Display icon in the Control Panel. Or you can right-click on a blank spot on the desktop and select Properties from the pop-up menu. Then click the Settings tab.

Changing Resolutions

Displays are described in terms of their resolution—the number of dots on the screen and the number of colors that can be displayed at the same time. The resolutions you can choose using the slider under Screen Area are determined by the hardware you have (see Figure 20.15).

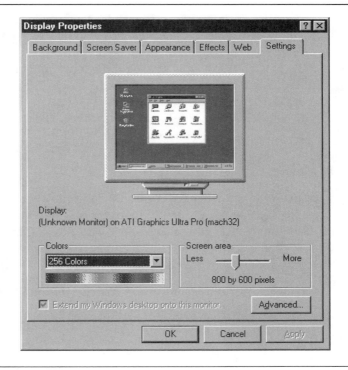

FIGURE 20.15: Colors and resolution are configured on the Settings page.

You can't make your monitor and video card display more than is built into them. Here are the most likely possibilities:

640×480   A standard VGA display that's 640 pixels wide by 480 pixels high

800×600   A typical SVGA display (super VGA)

1024×768   This is the upper limit of SVGA and the beginning of more advanced systems such as 8514/A and XGA. This is a very fine (that is, nongrainy) resolution, but if your monitor is 15 inches or smaller, you'd better have very good eyes.

1280×1024   A very fine resolution, but it requires a large monitor. Even with a 17-inch screen, you'll need good eyes.

You'll notice as you move the slider toward higher resolutions that the number of colors displayed in the Colors box changes. As resolution numbers go up, color numbers have to go down because they're both competing for the same video memory. That's why, if you want the most realistic color represented on your screen, you'll need a video card (also called a display adapter) with two or four or more megabytes of its own memory.

Resolution choices are based on what you like to look at—constrained by the capabilities of your monitor and video card.

Making Advanced Changes

Also on the Settings page is a button labeled Advanced. Click this button to get to additional pages for video configuration. Different types of video cards will have different effects on these pages. You may have other pages in addition to the ones described below. Consult the documentation for your video card and monitor for information on how these additional pages are to be used.

General   If you're using a very high resolution, the desktop elements can be very small. Try Large Fonts under Display to see if that works better for you. (Under the Display Properties' Effects page, you can also choose to use Large Icons.) This way you can preserve the higher resolution *and* have objects on the desktop that are legible.

Under Compatibility, the default is to prompt you whenever you make new color settings. While it's true that some programs require a reboot after colors and resolution have changed, most do not. If you don't have a problem program and you change color settings frequently, choose *Apply the new color settings without restarting*.

Likewise, if you change display settings often, put a checkmark next to *Show setting icon on task bar*. This will place a miniature Display icon on the Taskbar. Click the icon and you can change your display on the spot.

Monitor   If you change your monitor, you usually only need to plug it in and start Windows 98. The monitor will be detected and correctly installed. If the monitor isn't correctly detected, you'll have to provide the right information. Click the Change button and then supply the name of the manufacturer and the model.

 NOTE   There's no reason to change settings if everything is functioning. Sometimes Windows will report "Unknown Monitor," and yet the monitor appears to work perfectly well.

Also on the Monitor page are several options relating to power management and Plug and Play. These are probably set correctly. However, if you have display problems such as a flashing screen after the monitor returns from Suspend mode, right-click on each option and read the description. Try checking or unchecking these options to see if your problem is solved. If you don't *have* a problem, leave the settings in their default state.

Skill 20

TIP   If weird things are happening to your screen—particularly a laptop screen—sometimes merely disabling the screen saver will set everything right. Screen savers often conflict with Power Management settings on laptops and computers with EnergyStar monitors.

Performance   The Performance page lets you adjust graphics acceleration. Again, if your display is working fine, leave the Hardware Acceleration set to Full. If your mouse pointer disappears frequently, try moving the slider down one notch.

Color Management   Many color profiles are included with Windows 98 and you can choose one or many. Click Add and select a profile. Add as many as you like. Highlight one and click Set As Default.

NOTE   See the previous section "Changing a Video Driver" for information on the Adapter page.

Are You Experienced?

Now you can...

- ☑ **Install and configure a modem**
- ☑ **Install and remove a printer**
- ☑ **Configure an infrared device**
- ☑ **Install a new mouse**
- ☑ **Configure a game controller**
- ☑ **Change video settings**

SKILL 21

THE SOUND AND LIGHT SHOW

- Configuring sounds
- Playing audio CDs
- Using Media Player
- Viewing WebTV

Only a few years ago, multimedia computers were exotic, expensive machines used by professional musicians, animators, and a few others. But today, just about every new computer can be described as multimedia-capable. After all, it's a rare machine that doesn't come equipped with a sound card, CD-ROM drive, and speakers—and many include a microphone and a high-end video card.

In this skill, we'll go over the special sound and video capabilities built into Windows 98.

Utilizing Sound

Computers can do lots of things with sound. You can associate sounds with various actions that take place. For example, you might want to play a particular bit of music when you start your computer. Or have a voice announce when you receive mail or when an appointment is due. In this first section, I'll cover how to associate sound files with events, and then I'll describe how to acquire sound files and make your own.

A Sheet Full of Sounds

To make basic sound settings, select Start ➢ Settings ➢ Control Panel and click the Sounds icon.

Sounds

This will open the Sounds Properties sheet shown in Figure 21.1. The Events window lists everything on your system that can be associated with a sound. Most are Windows events. For example, opening a program can cause a sound, as can maximizing or minimizing a window. As you add programs to your system, some of them will add sound files and events that are associated with the sounds.

FIGURE 21.1: Use the Sounds Properties sheet to associate a sound with an event.

If there's a Speaker icon next to the event, a sound is associated with it. Highlight the event—the name of the sound file will appear in the Name window—and click the button next to the Preview window to hear it. (If your speakers have an On/Off switch, make sure they're turned On.)

Several sound schemes are included with Windows 98, and you can choose one of them from the drop-down list.

NOTE   If sound schemes don't appear in the Schemes drop-down list, you'll need to install them. Go to the Add/Remove Programs icon in the Control Panel. Under Windows Setup, click Multimedia and select the sound schemes you want. Select OK, and then follow the instructions.

Customizing a Sound Scheme

All the sound schemes that come with Windows are nice enough, but none of them is perfect. There are either too many sounds, not enough, the wrong sounds attached to various events, or whatever. Fortunately, you can make as many customized sound schemes as you like. Here's how:

1. Select Start ➢ Settings ➢ Control Panel and click the Sounds icon.

2. Starting at the top of the Events list, select an item that you want a sound associated with.

3. Select a file from the Name drop-down list. To make sure it's the one you want, click the Preview button to hear it.

4. Select (none) in the Name list for events that you want to keep silent.

5. Repeat steps 2 through 4 until you've completed the list.

6. Select Save As to save this particular assortment of sounds under a specific name. (The new scheme will appear in the Schemes drop-down list.)

Acquiring New Sound Files

Thousands of sound files are available from the World Wide Web. A central index for .wav files is at http://www.jukeboxcentral.com/entry.html. A search for "sound files" using any of the WWW search tools will turn up many, many entries. Bear in mind that .wav files tend to be large and that your search may find many that are rude and crude. But there are many more that are amusing and entertaining.

Making Your Own Sound Files

With a microphone or a CD-ROM player, you can use the Sound Recorder to make a .wav file that can then be associated with a Windows event.
   Here's how to make a .wav file with the Sound Recorder:

1. Click the Start button, then select Programs ➢ Accessories ➢ Entertainment ➢ Sound Recorder.

2. Select New from the Sound Recorder's File menu.

3. To begin recording, click the button with the dark red dot.

4. Start the CD or start speaking into the microphone.

5. To stop recording, click the button with the black square.

6. Select Save from the File menu to save the sound clip.

Figure 21.2 shows the Sound Recorder recording from a CD being played in the Media Player.

FIGURE 21.2: You can record a .wav file from a CD-ROM with the Sound Recorder.

You can also play other types of sound clips in the Media Player and record them as .wav files. The .wav files you make can be played back with the Sound Recorder or the Media Player.

 NOTE   Windows 98 stores sound files in the Windows\Media folder. You'll probably want to move any additional sound files you acquire to that folder, because a single location makes setting up and changing sound schemes much easier.

Special Effects and Editing

Use the Effects menu in the Sound Recorder dialog box to change some of the sound's qualities—to add an echo or decrease the speed. The sound can also be edited, using the menu controls.

TIP   You can only edit an *uncompressed* sound file. If you don't see the green line in the Sound Recorder, the file is compressed, and you can't edit it unless you change the sound quality. You can change the sound quality when you save the file by clicking the Change button at the bottom of the Save As window.

Playing Audio CDs

In addition to running data CDs, your CD-ROM drive can also play music. To start the CD Player, click the Start button, then select Programs ➢ Accessories ➢ Entertainment ➢ CD Player.

All you have to do is supply a music CD. The player will play it through your sound card, through the headphone jack in the front of your CD-ROM drive, or through audio jacks on the back of your CD-ROM controller card. Plug speakers into the sound card or your headphones into any of the jacks.

TIP   By default, the CD Player will start playing as soon as you put a music CD in the drive. To overrule this automatic play feature for a particular CD, hold down the Shift key while you insert the CD. To turn the automatic play feature off completely (or back on), right-click on the My Computer icon and select Properties. On the Device Manager page, double-click on CD-ROM, highlight your CD-ROM drive's name, and click Properties. On the Settings page, click Auto Insert Notification. With a check in the box, music CDs will play automatically.

How It Works

To illustrate, I popped some Bach in the drive and clicked on the large triangle next to the digital read-out (the Play button). The playing CD Player can be seen in Figure 21.3.

FIGURE 21.3: The CD Player in action

Use the buttons on the CD Player as follows:

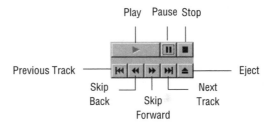

Play   At the top, the Play button is gray because the CD is playing. (Why would you want to click the Play button when the CD is playing? On the other hand, you'll do no harm. Go ahead and click it if you want to.)

Pause   Click the Pause button to hold your playback while you run to answer the door or the phone.

Stop   Click the Stop button when you're tired of listening to the music or when the boss walks into your office.

Previous Track   The Previous Track button will move you to a previous track on the CD.

Skip Back   Each time you click the Skip Back button, you will move back one second in the music.

Skip Forward Each time you click the Skip Forward button, you will move one second forward in the music.

Next Track This button will take you instantly to the next song.

Eject The Eject button will pop out your CD.

Setting Time and Play Options

Is that all there is? Certainly not. Click on the digital readout. The first time you click, the readout will tell you the current track number and the time remaining on the track. The second time you click, you will see the time remaining for the CD. The third time you click, you'll see the track number and the elapsed time for that track.

If you want to set these without clicking on the digital display, pull down the View menu and select one of the following options:

- Track time elapsed

- Track time remaining

- Disc time remaining

The Options menu lets you opt for continuous play, random play, or intro play (each track plays for 10 seconds and then CD Player moves to the next track). Select the Preferences option. It allows you to set the font size for the digital readout as well as the length of intro play (10 seconds is the default).

Editing the Play List

It takes some data entry, but you can edit each of your music CD's play lists. Play only the tracks you want to hear and in the order you want to hear them. To edit a CD play list, put the CD in the drive, open the CD Player, then follow these steps:

1. Pull down the Disc menu and select Edit Play List. You'll see the dialog box shown in Figure 21.4. Let's set up the CD-ROM to play Tracks 5, 12, and 3, in that order.

2. Click the Clear All button to clear all the entries on the Play List.

3. In the Available Tracks list box, double-click on Tracks 5, 12, and 3 in turn. They'll appear in the Play List (see Figure 21.5). This is a good start, but how will you remember what tracks these are? You need to identify them by name.

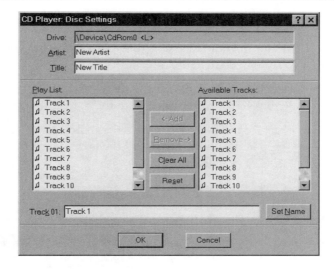

FIGURE 21.4: The Disc Settings dialog box lets you program a play list.

FIGURE 21.5: We've chosen the tracks we want to hear.

4.   Click on Track 5 in the Available Tracks list.

5.   Click the text box next to the Set Name button.

6.   Refer to your CD packaging to get the name of the third track. Type the name in the text box.

7.   Click the Set Name button. In the Available Tracks list and in the Play List, Track 5 will be replaced with the name. Repeat for the other tracks.

8.   Just for the sake of completeness, click on the text box marked Artist and type in the name. Highlight the text box marked Title and enter the title of the CD (see Figure 21.6).

9.   Click on the OK button.

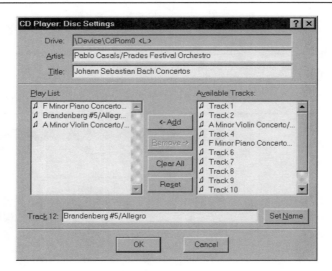

FIGURE 21.6:   This CD is programmed to play these tracks only.

Once you've supplied your CD Player with this information, the program will remember it, recognize the CD, and follow your programmed instructions every time you play it.

NOTE   If you have a CD-ROM player capable of playing multiple disks, Multidisc Play will be an option on the Option menu. Select it, and when you click on the downward-pointing arrow at the right end of the Artist box, you will see each of the CDs available to you. Select the CD you want to play.

WHEN YOU CAN'T FIND THE PROGRAM

If one of the applications in this skill doesn't appear on the Entertainment menu, you'll need to install it. Just follow these steps:

1. Select Start ➢ Settings ➢ Control Panel and click on Add/Remove Programs.

2. Insert your Windows 98 install disk into the CD-ROM drive.

3. Click on the Windows Setup tab at the top of the Add/Remove Programs Properties dialog box.

4. Scroll through the list of options in the dialog box until you locate the program either under Multimedia or, in the case of WebTV, listed by itself.

5. Click on the checkboxes next to as many programs as you want to install, then click OK.

Using the Media Player

The Media Player can also be used to play CDs—because it lacks programming capability, however, it's usually used in that capacity only in conjunction with the Sound Recorder. The Media Player will play Video for Windows animated files (.avi), sound files (.wav), MIDI files (.mid and .rmi), or your audio CDs. To open the Media Player, click on the Start button, then select Programs ➤ Accessories ➤ Entertainment ➤ Media Player. This will open a window like the one shown in Figure 21.7.

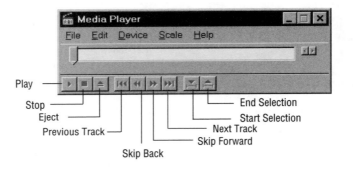

FIGURE 21.7: The Media Player looks like this.

Playing Files

Windows 98 comes with a variety of multimedia files. To play a file, follow these steps:

1. In the Media Player dialog box, pull down the Device menu and select the type of file you want to play.

2. Locate the file you want to play and double-click (or highlight it and select Open). Make sure the Files of Type box shows All files.

3. Click on the right-pointing arrow (the Play button).

You can select sections of animation or movies just like you select recorded music tracks (see "Playing Audio CDs" earlier this chapter). Although the buttons are in different places than the ones on the CD Player, you should be able to identify them by their icons.

Copying and Pasting Files

You can copy and paste sound, animation, or movie files using the Select buttons, shown in Figure 21.7.

Selecting a Section

To select a section of a media file:

1. Listen until you reach the point where the section begins, then click on the Start Selection button.

2. Continue until you reach the end of the section, then click the End Selection button.

3. Pull down the Edit menu and select Copy. (The file portion you have selected will be placed on the Clipboard for pasting into any document that supports sound files.)

After a file portion is pasted into a document, you can play it from within the document by double-clicking its icon or frame.

Getting Looped

If you want a piece of music, film, or animation to repeat continuously, pull down the Edit menu and select Options. Click on the option marked Auto Repeat. Your media file will play repeatedly until:

- The end of time.
- You turn off the media player.
- You lose your mind and destroy your computer with a fire ax.

Watching WebTV

Perhaps there are millions of people who have been waiting around for the ability to watch television on their computers. If you're among those folk, WebTV is for you. And if you're old enough to remember Pong, the primitive computer game that was played on your TV screen, you'll realize that we've come full circle.

To view WebTV, you'll need a video card with a built-in TV tuner. The initial release of Microsoft Windows 98 supports the ATI Technologies All-in-Wonder and All-in-Wonder Pro display adapters, which include TV tuners.

Other TV tuner cards may offer their own WDM (Windows Driver Model) drivers that are compatible with WebTV for Windows after the initial release of Windows 98. WebTV for Windows should work with any WDM driver that supports video capture and tuning. Check with the manufacturer of your TV tuner card for more information about installing your card and drivers.

In addition to the TV tuner, you'll need a cable television connection or an amplified antenna. A passive antenna—like the classic rabbit ears—won't do. The signal needs to be amplified.

Installing WebTV

WebTV isn't part of the default installation of Windows 98. To install it, follow these steps:

1. Click the Start button, then select Settings ➤ Control Panel.

2. Click the Add/Remove Programs icon.

3. Click the Windows Setup tab.

4. Scroll to the bottom of the Components window and put a checkmark in the box next to WebTV for Windows. Click OK.

Setting Up WebTV

To configure WebTV, you can start by selecting Start ➤ Programs ➤ Accessories ➤ Entertainment ➤ WebTV or, more simply, by clicking the icon that WebTV adds to the Quick Start toolbar:

This will open the window shown in Figure 21.8.

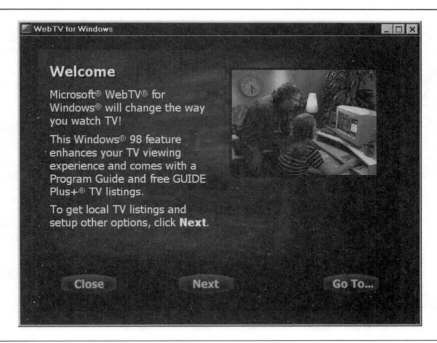

FIGURE 21.8: The beginning window for WebTV setup

Here are the steps you'll go through:

- Read the information in the window (shown in Figure 21.8) and then click Next. You're asked how you plan to view the TV programs. Answer, then click Next.

- On the following screen, you have the option of starting the process of scanning for channels. Make sure you have the TV cable or antenna plugged in, then click Start Scan. WebTV will scan for channels that it can receive. It will accept all such channels, but you can later weed out the ones you don't want.

No Scanning Option?

If Configuration does not offer this option, it's possible your display settings for Color and Screen Area are not set correctly for video reception. To change your Color and Screen Area settings:

1. Click the Windows 98 Start button, and then select Settings ➤ Control Panel.

2. On the Control Panel, click the Display icon. Click the Settings tab.

3. Under Colors, click High Color (16 bit) in the drop-down box.

4. Under Screen Area, move the slider until you see 800x600 pixels. Click OK.

Start WebTV for Windows again, switch to the Configuration channel, and complete the configuration process.

 TIP   You might want to turn the computer speaker volume down during the scanning because the channels that can't be received come through as a lot of loud static.

- After the scanning is complete, turn the sound back up and verify that you're receiving sound OK. If not, try the alternative sound inputs.

No Sound?

Use the Windows 98 Control Panel to check your system sounds:

1. Click the Start button, then select Settings ➣ Control Panel.

2. In the Control Panel, click the Sounds icon.

3. In the Sounds Properties dialog box, click a sound with a Speaker icon next to it.

4. Click the right arrow next to the Preview window to play the sound. If you can't hear the sound, click the Speaker icon in the Windows 98 Taskbar.

5. In the Volume Control panel under Wave Balance, look to see if the Mute checkbox has a checkmark. If it does, click the checkbox to remove the checkmark. Try to preview the sound in the Control Panel again.

If you can't hear your system sounds, use the Sound topic under Windows 98 Troubleshooters in the Windows 98 Help system to locate the solution to your problem.

If you can hear your system sounds, Start WebTV for Windows, tune to a channel that should have sound, and reduce the TV window. Then, click the Speaker icon on the Windows 98 Taskbar to check the Volume Control settings.

Make sure the TV tuner is physically connected to the sound card via an external or internal cable. (See the documentation accompanying the card for specific instructions.)

If these steps fail, your sound card is probably not hooked up correctly. If you installed the card yourself, check the documentation accompanying the card. If you need additional assistance, contact the card manufacturer. If your computer came with the sound card already installed, contact your computer manufacturer.

Skill 21

- Provide your zip code. This is used to retrieve the programming information for the channels.

- On the next screen, you decide how to collect the programming data. Click Get Now, and the programming information will be downloaded through the cable (or over the antenna) using Star Sight. However, this will take some time—and in the meantime, WebTV will be unavailable. The best solution is to use the Guide Plus+ Web site. If that's not convenient, click Next and schedule a time for download when the computer will be on but you won't be using it (see Figure 21.9).

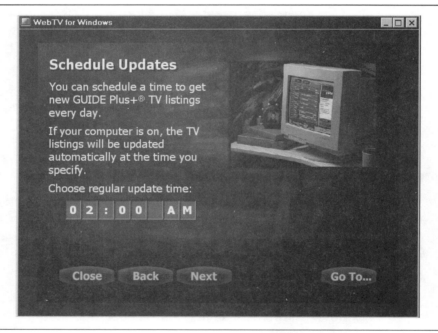

FIGURE 21.9: Selecting a time for program information to be downloaded to your computer

 NOTE   Even if you download the information from the Web site, it can be slow. Count on being connected for at least five minutes.

- Next, you can assign a channel to a VCR or to a game player.

- A little Guide to the Program Guide follows. Click Finish at the end.

Your first view of WebTV will be the Program Guide, which displays next (see Figure 21.10). On the left are the channels. You can scroll either vertically or horizontally to see more listings. Click on a program in the listings, and a small screen will display on the right. Click the Watch button, and the channel will display full-screen.

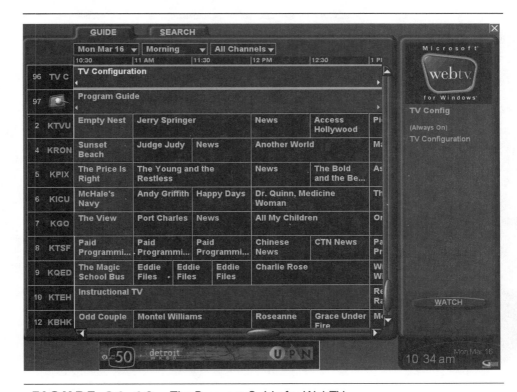

FIGURE 21.10: The Program Guide for WebTV

 TIP   Click the Other Times button for a list of alternate viewing times for the show you've selected. Of course, only the times downloaded will be available.

Viewing WebTV

When you want to watch television, click the WebTV icon on the Quick Start toolbar. WebTV will start up at the channel last viewed. Move the mouse pointer to the top of the screen and click to open the toolbar (see Figure 21.11).

FIGURE 21.11: The toolbar for WebTV

Click the Guide button to return to the program guide.

Choosing Channels to View

Click Settings to choose among the available channels. For example, in my case, the scan for channels included a bunch of premium channels that I don't subscribe to. There's no point in including them in the display if I can't actually view them. In the Settings window (see Figure 21.12), I removed the checkmarks for these channels. When I click OK, only the channels with checkmarks will be included in the Program Guide.

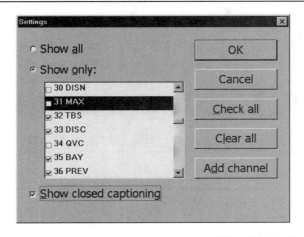

FIGURE 21.12: Use the Settings Window to determine which channels appear in your Program Guide.

Adding and Removing Favorites

You can place four of your favorite channels on the TV toolbar where you can easily choose them. You can change your favorites as often as you like. Tune to a channel and click the Add button. A button for that channel will appear on the toolbar.

To remove a channel from the toolbar, just reverse the process. Tune to the channel and click the Remove button.

Resizing the Viewing Window

To resize the viewing window, just click the Restore button on the TV toolbar.

The Close button will end the TV session.

You can click and drag the edges of the window to resize it further.

Viewing Interactive TV

Using WebTV for Windows, you can watch TV programming that includes interactive TV. Interactive TV is additional content that supplements the traditional program. It can take many forms, such as background information about the stars of a show, statistics about players in a ball game, chat rooms, and so on.

Channels, series, and individual programs can include interactive TV. Icons in the Program Guide and on the TV toolbar indicate whether interactive TV is available.

If you see this icon, interactive TV is available.

The red icon means that interactive TV is not available.

Keyboard Shortcuts

Just about every WebTV function can be handled from the computer keyboard. Table 21.1 shows the keys and the functions they perform. The key described as "Windows logo" is available on keyboards designed specifically for Windows operating systems.

TABLE 21.1: Keyboard functions in WebTV

Key	Function
F10	Display the WebTV menu
F6	Switch between a full screen and a window
Up and down arrows	Scroll up or down through channels
Windows logo	Open Windows 98 Start menu
Windows logo+Ctrl+Shift+Z	View the Program Guide (grid view)
Windows logo+Ctrl+Z	Start WebTV or, if WebTV is already started, switch between a full screen and a window
Windows logo+Ctrl+V	Turn volume up
Windows logo+Shift+V	Turn volume down
Windows logo+V	Toggle mute on or off
Windows logo+Ctrl+Alt+Z	Increase the TV channel by one
Windows logo+Ctrl+Alt+Shift+Z	Decrease the TV channel by one

Are You Experienced?

Now you can...

- ☑ **Set up sound schemes**
- ☑ **Make your own sounds**
- ☑ **Use the CD Player**
- ☑ **View WebTV**

SKILL 22

RUNNING DOS PROGRAMS

- Installing a DOS program
- Configuring DOS properties
- Troubleshooting DOS programs

Anyone who's been fooling around with computers for a while usually has an old, favorite DOS program or two hanging around. No need to get rid of a program that does what you want it to do, just because it's DOS-based and not Windows. Most DOS programs can be run in a window on the desktop or full screen. Only the most aggressive programs (games, for the most part) require any fiddling with settings. In this skill, we'll talk about the simple way to run DOS programs and how you can persuade even poorly behaved DOS programs to run without complaint.

Installing a DOS Program

Most programs come with installation instructions—if yours did, follow those instructions. If you don't have instructions, put the first floppy disk in the appropriate disk drive, then click the Start button and select Run. Click the Browse button.

In the Browse window, double-click My Computer and then the floppy drive. Look for an installation file. It'll be named Install or Setup (see Figure 22.1).

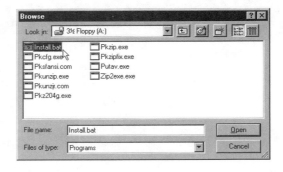

FIGURE 22.1: Looking for the installation file

Once you find the file, click it and then click the Open button. DOS installations require direct input from you, so you usually have to tell the computer where to install *from* as well as where to install *to*. You supply this information in the Run dialog box. Figure 22.2 shows the command Install with the necessary directions—in this case, the program is in drive a: (that's the *from*) and the installation is to be done on drive c: (that's the *to*).

FIGURE 22.2: Installing from the floppy disk in drive a: to drive c:

Click OK. A DOS window will open with further instructions if they're needed. You can follow the progress of the installation in the window (see Figure 22.3).

FIGURE 22.3: The installation as shown in the DOS window

The title bar of the DOS window will indicate when it's finished. Close the DOS window when the installation is complete.

When you install a DOS program, it isn't automatically placed on your Programs menu the way Windows programs are. You can create a shortcut to a DOS program and put the shortcut either on your desktop or in one of the folders that make up the Programs menu.

Open Windows Explorer and find the folder with your program in it. Right-click on the program name and drag it to the desktop to make a shortcut. You can handle DOS programs like Windows programs. The vast majority of DOS programs will open with a simple click. But what about one that won't? Or a program that opens in a window and you'd like it to run full screen? Fortunately, every DOS program has an extensive collection of Properties sheets that you can tweak to improve performance.

DOS Properties Sheets

When you run a DOS program, whether from the desktop or off the Start menu, you can set a variety of properties for the program. As elsewhere in Windows 98, you get to those properties by right-clicking on the icon for the program or its shortcut in any of three different places:

- Highlight the program's executable file in Windows Explorer or My Computer and right-click on it.

- Right-click on a shortcut to the program.

- Open a DOS window and click once on the little icon in the upper left corner.

In all cases, you'll select Properties from the menu that appears. This will open up a Properties sheet for the DOS program like the one in Figure 22.4.

There are six pages on the Properties sheet—five if you got to Properties by right-clicking in the upper left corner of a DOS window.

General   Shows information about the file and file attributes. You won't see this one if you examine the properties of a running program or DOS window.

Program   Sets command line options and sets the program's icon.

Font   Sets the font to be used when the program is run in a window.

Memory   Sets how much and what kind of memory is made available to the DOS program.

Screen   Changes whether the program runs full screen or in a window and the characteristics of the window.

Misc   Like miscellaneous files everywhere, gets stuff that doesn't fit in any other category.

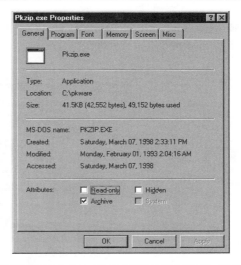

FIGURE 22.4: The first page of a DOS program's six pages of Properties sheets

The default settings are usually adequate for most programs, but if you need to fuss with one or more of these pages, the following sections contain some guidance.

General Properties

The General tab shows information about the program and lets you set the attributes of the underlying file. As you can see in Figure 22.4, this tab shows you the type of program or file, its location and size, the DOS filename associated with it, and when the file was created, modified, and last accessed.

If you're looking at a shortcut, the information about the file size, location, and type will refer to the shortcut and not to the original object (the file itself). If you are looking at an open DOS window or program, you won't see this page.

On this tab, you can change the MS-DOS attributes of the program, including whether the archive bit is set, whether the file can be modified or not (read-only bit), and whether the file is a hidden or system file. Generally you won't want to change these bits except in very special circumstances. And then only if you're sure you know why you're making the change.

Program Properties

The Program tab of the Properties window (see Figure 22.5) lets you change the running parameters of the program as well as the name and icon associated with it.

FIGURE 22.5: Control the command options of a DOS program from the Program tab.

Here's what those settings mean:

Cmd line   This box shows the actual command line executed. Here you can add any command line parameters that you need. (If you want to be able to add parameters each time you run the program, add a question mark as the only command line option, and Windows 98 will prompt you for parameters.)

Working   If your program has a favorite working directory, set that here. This isn't common any more, but some older programs need to be told this information. If there's already an entry in this box, Windows 98 and the program have figured out that it's necessary. Don't change this setting unless you're sure you know why.

Batch file   If you want to run a batch file either before or as part of the program, place the name (and full path, if necessary) for that batch file in this box.

Shortcut key   This box lets you add a shortcut key. (Some DOS programs may not work well with this option, but there's no harm in trying.)

Run   You can decide whether the program will run in a normal window, maximized, or minimized. Some DOS programs may pay no attention to this setting.

Close on exit   When this box is checked, the DOS window will close when you close the program.

Advanced Settings

Use the Advanced button only if you have an extremely ill-behaved or aggressive application—such as a game or other very specialized, hardware-dependent program. Click on Advanced to open the Advanced Program Settings dialog box shown in Figure 22.6.

FIGURE 22.6: A program will run in DOS mode if it needs its own config.sys and autoexec.bat to run correctly.

Skill 22

Here is where you can keep the program from knowing it's even running in Windows. If really drastic measures are required, you can set the program to run in MS-DOS mode. This closes all your applications, restarts your computer in DOS mode, and may reboot your computer.

NOTE It's not necessary for you to guess whether your game needs DOS mode to run. Go ahead and run the game. By default, the system will suggest DOS mode if the program requires it.

In MS-DOS mode, you can only run a single program, and when you exit from it, the system starts Windows 98. Again, this may well mean a reboot, so don't be startled. If you need to set up a specialized configuration for the program, you can type in new config.sys and autoexec.bat files. And you'll need to load your older 16-bit (pre-Windows 95) drivers in order to have access to your mouse, CD-ROM, and sound card in MS-DOS mode.

The Last Resort

Running programs in MS-DOS mode is really a last resort. Almost everything should run fine in a full-screen DOS session or a DOS window. It is unlikely you will want or need to run anything in MS-DOS mode—even when running Flight Simulator or DOOM.

NOTE IA primary reason for avoiding DOS mode is that you lose multitasking for the duration of the session. Plus, since a reboot may be required, the whole process takes a substantial amount of time.

Change the Icon

Click the Change Icon button on the Program page to change the way the program displays in icon form. You can accept one of the icons offered or use the Browse button to look elsewhere.

Font Properties

The Font tab of the Properties sheet (see Figure 22.7) lets you set which fonts will be available when the program is running in a window on the desktop. You can select from either bitmapped or TrueType fonts or have both available.

In general, bitmap fonts look better on high-resolution displays and are easier to read. If you want to be able to scale the window when it's open on your desktop, set Font Size to Auto, and the fonts will change as you resize the open window.

FIGURE 22.7: The Font tab gives you control over which fonts are used for the DOS program when it's running in a window.

Resizing the DOS Window

To change the size of a DOS window, go to the program's Properties sheet and try setting Font Size to Auto, running the DOS program, and then clicking on and dragging the edge of the DOS window. Sometimes setting the font to a fixed size and then dragging the edge of the DOS window will also work. Different programs have different abilities to shrink and expand.

Memory Properties

The Memory tab of the Properties sheet (see Figure 22.8) lets you control how much and what kind of memory DOS programs have available when they run.

On this tab, you can make sure your program has a specific amount of conventional, expanded, and extended memory. You can also let Windows 98 automatically determine how much to make available. Generally, you'll want to leave the settings here on Auto, but if you know you have a program that requires a specific amount of expanded memory to run well, you can set that here.

FIGURE 22.8: Special memory settings for some DOS programs

And Memory Problems

If you have a program that has a habit of crashing occasionally, and you want to be sure it doesn't cause problems for the rest of the system, check the Protected box in the Conventional Memory section. This may slow the program a little but will provide an additional layer of protection.

Some programs can actually have a problem with too much memory. Older versions of Paradox, for example, have difficulty coping with unlimited extended memory. If you leave the Expanded and Extended sections set to Auto, programs like this may not run reliably. Try setting Expanded and Extended Memory to some reasonable maximum number, such as 8192, which should be enough for most programs.

Screen Properties

The Screen tab of the Properties sheet (shown in Figure 22.9) lets you set your program's display. If you're running a graphical program, set it for full screen. Most text-based programs run better in a window. Windows 98 handles windowed DOS programs extremely well, and there's no real gain to running them full screen unless you need the extra space for the program to look good.

Except for the choice of full screen versus window, the options on this page are best left alone unless you know why you're changing them. If you're sure you need to make a change but don't know exactly what to change, right-click on an item and select What's This? If you understand what's in the box, you're hereby authorized to make the change.

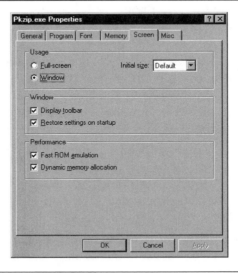

FIGURE 22.9: Display options for a DOS program

Switching from a Window to Full Screen (and Back Again)

To switch a DOS program window to full screen, just press Alt+↵. Press Alt+↵ a second time to return to the window.

To switch from a DOS program running full screen to the Windows 98 desktop, press Alt+Tab.

Miscellaneous Properties

The Misc tab of the Properties sheet (shown in Figure 22.10) lets you tweak several characteristics that don't fit in any of the other categories.

The properties you can set here include the following areas:

Allow screen saver When this box is checked, the Windows screen saver is allowed to come on when this program is in the foreground. If this box isn't checked, an active DOS program will keep your screen saver from kicking in.

QuickEdit Allows you to use your mouse to select text for cut-and-copy operations. If this box is cleared, you must use Mark on the Edit menu of the program to mark text.

Exclusive mode Lets the mouse work exclusively with this program. This means that when this program is open, the mouse won't be available outside the program's window.

Always suspend When this box is checked, no system resources are allocated to this program while it's in the background (open but not the active window). If this is a communications or other type of program that you want churning away in the background while you do something else, don't check this box.

Warn if still active Some DOS programs are very fussy about being closed properly (like WordPerfect for DOS). When this box is checked, you'll get a warning message if you try to close the window without closing the program first.

Idle sensitivity When this slider is set to high, the DOS program will release resources and processing time more quickly to other foreground tasks. For communications programs, however, you set this to the low side.

Fast pasting This allows a faster method of pasting, but if you have troubles with pasting correctly in this application, clear the box.

Windows shortcut keys Generally you will want to leave these alone unless your DOS program absolutely needs to use one of these keystrokes.

Clear the appropriate box or boxes if there are special keystrokes normally used by Windows 98 that you want passed on to your DOS program instead.

FIGURE 22.10: Setting other behavior characteristics for a DOS program

Making Stubborn DOS Programs Run

If your favorite DOS application is having trouble running in Windows 98, there are a variety of ways to get it going. They are presented here in approximately the order you should try them—from the relatively mild to the seriously serious.

 NOTE The default settings in Windows 98 are excellent for the vast majority of DOS-based programs and should only be messed with if you're having problems.

- Run the program full screen. You can do this by pressing Alt+↵ when the program is active, or from the program's Properties sheet. Select Full-Screen from the Screen page. This should be all that most graphical programs need, and this step can usually be skipped with text-only programs.

Skill 22

- Give the program only the kind of memory it absolutely needs. From the Memory page of the Properties sheet, select None for any memory types that you know the program doesn't need. Most DOS programs will not use Extended (XMS) memory or DPMI memory, so those are good choices to try turning off first. Check the program's documentation for hints on what it needs.

- Give the program the exact amount of memory it needs. If there's a minimum amount of memory that you know the program requires, set the conventional memory setting of the Memory page to some figure slightly above that. This will ensure that the program will only attempt to run when there is sufficient memory available.

- Protect the memory that the program uses. On the Memory sheet, check the Protected box in the Conventional Memory section.

- Turn off Dynamic Memory Allocation on the Screen page. If the program uses both text mode and graphics mode (an example would be the DOS version of Symantec's TimeLine), this will prevent Windows 98 from trying to change the amount of memory allocated when there's a mode change.

- Turn off Fast ROM Emulation on the Screen page. This may make the program run a bit more slowly, especially in text mode, but if the program is having problems with writing text to the screen, this may help.

- Turn off the Windows 98 screen saver by clearing the Allow Screen Saver checkbox on the Misc page.

- Turn Idle Sensitivity down to the minimum by moving the slider on the Misc page all the way to the left.

- If your program refuses to run from within Windows, try lying to it. Click the Advanced button on the Program page, and check the box labeled *Prevent MS-DOS-based programs from detecting Windows*. Only do this as a last resort before trying DOS mode.

- OK, everything else failed, so it's time to get serious. Run the program in MS-DOS mode. This is the last resort for reasons I have already gone into. If nothing else works, this will. Click the Advanced button on the Program page and check the MS-DOS Mode box. If the program needs special config.sys and autoexec.bat files, type them into the appropriate boxes, or use the current versions by checking the Use Current MS-DOS Configuration box.

 **WARNING**   This list of troubleshooting tips should help you get that recalcitrant DOS pro-gram to behave. But a word of warning: Never change more than one thing at a time!

If you try something and it doesn't work, return to the default settings and try the next one on the list. If you try to change too many things at once, you're likely to make the situation worse. And even if you do manage to improve the situation, you won't be able to tell which setting was the crucial one.

MS-DOS Prompt

As you've probably noticed by now, there's an MS-DOS Prompt listing on your Start ➤ Programs menu. Select it and you get a DOS window on your desktop. You can use this window to run most DOS commands.

If you're the sort of person who frequently uses a DOS window, you can put a shortcut to the DOS prompt on your desktop or in the Startup folder. Then it'll be ready and waiting on the Taskbar each time you start the computer. To make a shortcut to the DOS prompt window, follow these steps:

1. Right-click the Start button and select Open.

2. Double-click the Programs folder.

3. Scroll down until you see the MS-DOS icon.

4. Right-click on the icon and either select Create Shortcut to make a shortcut on the spot or drag and drop to another location and select Create Shortcut(s) when you get there.

DOS Commands

The DOS commands that come with Windows 98 are fairly few in number compared to DOS 6.22 or earlier. All the external DOS commands are in the Command folder inside your Windows folder.

Table 22.1 lists the DOS commands and a brief description of what each one does.

TABLE 22.1: DOS commands with Windows 98

Command Name	What It Does
attrib.exe	Displays or changes file attributes
chkdsk.exe	Reports on disk status and any errors found; has been superseded by scandisk.exe
choice.com	Allows for user input in a batch file
debug.exe	Hexadecimal editor and viewer
diskcopy.com	Makes a full copy of a diskette; same function available in Windows Explorer
doskey.com	Beloved of all DOS-geeks, edits command lines, makes macros
edit.com	New version of older file editor
extract.exe	Extracts files from a cabinet (.cab) file
fc.exe	File compare
fdisk.exe	Makes and removes hard drive partitions
find.exe	Locates text in a file
format.com	Formats disks
keyb.com	Configures a keyboard for a specific language
label.exe	Adds, removes, or changes a disk label
mem.exe	Displays total memory, amount in use, and amount available
mode.com	Configures system devices
more.com	Displays output one screen at a time
move.exe	Moves one or more files
nlsfunc.exe	Loads country-specific information
scandisk.exe	Checks a disk for errors and makes corrections
scanreg.exe	Scans registry for errors
sort.exe	Sorts input
start.exe	Runs a program
subst.exe	Associates a drive letter with a particular path
sys.com	Copies system files to a disk, making the disk bootable
xcopy.exe	Copies whole directories, including subdirectories
xcopy32.exe	A juiced-up version of xcopy with more functions, plus the ability to copy long filenames

There isn't a lot of help available in Windows 98 for DOS commands, but you can get basic information if you go to a DOS prompt, type in the name of the command followed by / ?, and then press Enter.

Are You Experienced?

Now you can...

- ☑ Install a DOS program
- ☑ Configure DOS properties
- ☑ Troubleshoot a troublesome DOS program

SKILL 23

PUTTING ADDITIONAL PROGRAMS TO WORK

- Making calculations
- Using Imaging
- Painting a picture
- Taking note of Notepad
- Using WordPad

Windows 98 comes with a number of small programs, sometimes called *applets*. Some, like Calculator and Notepad, are absolutely sufficient for what they're designed to do. Others, like WordPad, are OK for simple use but aren't really a substitute for a *real* application. (More on that under the specific entries.)

Using the Calculator

You actually have two calculators in Windows 98: a standard calculator, the likes of which you could buy for $2.95 at any drugstore, and a scientific calculator that does advanced mathematical functions.

Basic Math

To start the standard calculator, click the Start button in the Taskbar, then select Programs ➤ Accessories ➤ Calculator to display the calculator shown in Figure 23.1.

Using the mouse, click on the numbers and functions just as if you were pressing the keys on a hand-held calculator. If you have a numerical keypad on your keyboard, press NumLock to use the keypad keys to enter numbers and basic math functions.

FIGURE 23.1: The basic calculator

TIP   My calculation is that I number among the mathematically impaired, so I keep a shortcut to the calculator on my desktop. To do this, right-click the Start button and select Open. Click Programs ➢ Accessories. Click the Calculator icon, then drag and drop it on your desktop.

Getting More Advanced

To access the scientific calculator, pull down the View menu on the Calculator and select Scientific. That displays the version shown in Figure 23.2.

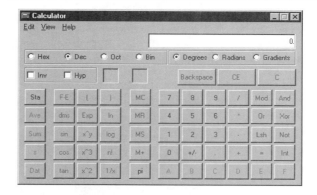

FIGURE 23.2: The scientific calculator

TIP   If you're unsure of the use for a function, right-click on its button. You'll see a rectangle containing the words "What's This?" Click on the text to see a short explanation of the function.

A Statistical Inquiry

As a sample of what the scientific calculator can do, let's enter a list of data for deriving statistical results:

1. Click the Sta button. The Statistics Box will open.

2. Enter the first value and click Dat. (The value will display in the Statistics Box.)

3. Enter the next value in the series.

4. Click Dat.

5. Repeat steps 3 and 4 until you have entered the last value in the series.

6. Click the function key that corresponds to the statistical command you want to enter.

Figure 23.3 lists four numbers in the Statistics Box, and the Calculator window shows the result of pressing the Ave key, the mean of the values displayed.

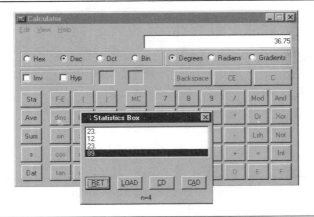

FIGURE 23.3: Using the scientific calculator to calculate the mean

Translating Number Systems

The scientific calculator easily translates numbers from one number system to another. By default, the calculator uses decimal numbers. To translate a decimal number, enter the number, then click the number system (*Hex*adecimal, *Oct*al, or *Bin*ary) you want it translated to.

To translate a hexadecimal number, click the Hex button and enter the number (the A, B, C, D, E, and F keys are for hex numbers), and then click on the number system into which you want to translate the value.

Imaging

The Imaging applet is a scaled-down version of some of the full-fledged imaging applications that ship with scanners. You can use it to scan and then manipulate images of various kinds, or you can import an image in one of a variety of common formats, including GIF, TIF, BMP, and JPG.

Only images in the BMP (Windows Bitmap) and TIF (Tagged Image File) formats can be modified; other formats are read-only. However, you can open a file in another format, save it as a BMP or TIF file, and then operate on it at will.

The Annotation menu is where you'll find the most fun. To get there, select Start ➤ Programs ➤ Accessories ➤ Imaging. Open a BMP or TIF file and add a note (see Figure 23.4), draw on it, or mark it with a rubber stamp.

FIGURE 23.4: A TIF file with a note attached

Scanning an Image

Scanning an image is very simple. You can either click the Scan New button on the Imaging toolbar (it's the leftmost button, the one with the picture of a scanner on it), or you can pull down the File menu and select Scan New (see Figure 23.5). Before scanning anything, you may want to look at the Select Scanner and Scan Preferences options on the File menu to make sure your scanner's all set up to go.

FIGURE 23.5: A scanned photo in Imaging

Painting Pictures

Paint is another graphics-oriented program. Unlike Imaging, it includes an assortment of drawing and painting tools to make your own images and modify existing ones. When you click on a BMP (bitmap) image, it's automatically loaded into the Paint program.

Committing Original Art

To open Paint, click the Start button, then select Programs ➤ Accessories ➤ Paint. Use the tools down the left side of the window to make a drawing. When you're done, you can:

- Select File ➤ Save and give the picture a name. You can save it as one of several different kinds of bitmaps (see the Save As Type list).

- Select File ➤ Send, which will open Exchange and let you select an e-mail recipient worthy of receiving your work.

- Select File ➤ Save As Wallpaper. This will let you tile or center your work of art as the wallpaper on your screen.

Modifying the Work of Others

Any file with the extension .bmp, .pcx, or .dib can be opened in Paint. Use the tools to make any modifications you want and then do any of the things listed in the section above.

Modified files are all saved as bitmaps (.bmp).

TIP   For a really good drawing, paint, and graphics program at a very reasonable price, check out the excellent PaintShop Pro. It's available for download on the major online services as well as from the manufacturer's Web site at www.jasc.com.

Working with Notepad

Notepad is a bare-bones text editor that's easy to use, although it includes few of the features found in a word-processing program. Unlike word-processing programs like WordPerfect or Word for Windows, Notepad adds no formatting that might modify a configuration file. So it's the perfect tool for viewing and editing text files such as those with extensions like .ini, .bat, or .sys.

Click on a text file (a file with the .txt extension), and the file will immediately load into Notepad. (An exception would be any file larger than 64KB, in which case you'll be asked if you want to load it into WordPad instead.)

To open Notepad, click the Start button and select Programs ➤ Accessories ➤ Notepad.

Notepad has the bare minimum of features on its menus. You can:

- Search for characters or words
- Use Page Setup to set margins, select a printer, and customize page headers and footers
- Cut, copy, and paste text
- Insert the time and date into a document

 TIP For some inexplicable reason, word wrap is not on by default. You have to select it from the Edit menu or all your text will be on one very long line.

Creating an Activity Log

Notepad does have the handy ability to keep an activity log. To set one up, follow these steps:

1. Click Start ➤ Programs ➤ Accessories ➤ Notepad. On the first line, type in **.LOG** exactly. Make sure there's a period before *LOG* and all the letters are capitals.

2. Save the document under any name you choose, then close it.

3. Open the document again, and the time and date from your computer's clock will be entered automatically (see Figure 23.6).

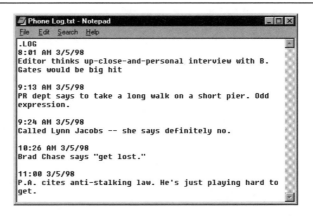

FIGURE 23.6: Keeping a phone record with Notepad

Save the log to your desktop or to the Start menu. Every time you open it, the time and date will be entered.

Using WordPad

WordPad is a very simple word-processing program. It's a good deal more elaborate than Notepad but still falls in the category of "pretty basic."

To open WordPad, click the Start button and select Programs ➢ Accessories ➢ WordPad.

When you open WordPad (see Figure 23.7), it looks like most other editors, and on the menus you'll find the usual things one associates with text editors. Pull down the menus to see the various options.

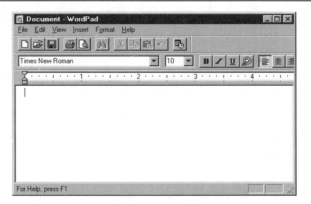

FIGURE 23.7: The opening window for WordPad

WordPad is completely integrated into Windows 98. You can write messages in color and post them to the Microsoft Network so recipients see your messages just as you wrote them—fonts, colors, embedded objects, and all. WordPad also has the distinct advantage of being able to load really big files.

Making and Formatting Documents

You can click on several types of documents and drag them into WordPad. Documents made by Microsoft Word (.doc) and Windows Write (.wri), as well as text (.txt) and Rich Text format (.rtf) documents, are all instantly recognized by WordPad. You can also just start typing.

Skill 23

Formatting Tools

The toolbar (shown in Figure 23.8) and format bar (see Figure 23.9) are displayed by default. You can turn either of them off by deselecting it from the list under the View menu.

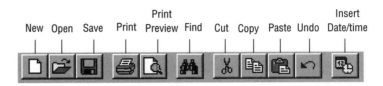

FIGURE 23.8: Functions of the WordPad toolbar

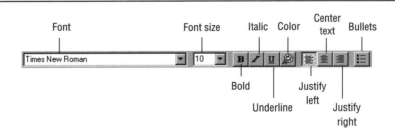

FIGURE 23.9: Functions of the WordPad format bar

Tabs are set using the ruler. Click on the ruler at the spot where you want a tab. To remove a tab, just click on it and drag it off the ruler.

Other Options

Other formatting tools are under Options on the View menu. Here you can set measurement units as well as word wrap and toolbars for each of the different file types that WordPad recognizes.

Page Setup and Printing

The File menu has the usual Print command, but there's also a Page Setup option for setting margins, paper size, and orientation. Unlike its predecessor, WordPad can print envelopes as well as varying sizes of paper.

It may take some fooling around to get envelopes lined up correctly, but fortunately there's a Print Preview choice (also on the File menu). There you can see how the envelope or paper is lining up with your text. Adjust the margin in the Page Setup dialog box until you get it the way you want.

 TIP To change printers, select Page Setup from the File menu. Click on the Printer button and select any printer currently available to you.

Are You Experienced?

Now you can...

- ☑ **Use the calculator**
- ☑ **Manipulate graphics files**
- ☑ **Create paintings and drawings**
- ☑ **Use Notepad and WordPad to create documents**

APPENDIX A

INSTALLING FOR WINDOWS 95 USERS

The designers of Windows 98 have worked hard to make the installation process as simple and trouble-free as possible. If you use only Windows 95, and you are satisfied with the way it's working for you, the preliminaries are minimal, and the upgrade will probably proceed without problems.

On the other hand, if the performance of Windows 95 on your machine has you twiddling your thumbs, you may want to consider hardware improvements.

Hardware

On the same machine, Windows 98 starts a bit faster than Windows 95, and application start-up is somewhat quicker. However, Windows 98 can't do much to reduce the demands made on hardware by ever more complex applications. In fact, new applications and technologies have raised hardware requirements substantially since the introduction of Windows 95.

Officially, Microsoft says that the minimum hardware required to run Windows 98 is a 486DX4-75 and 16MB of RAM. This is the real minimum, not a suggested one. Attempting to install Windows 98 on a lesser machine is futile. But *any* 486 machine is going to be very slow, and the newer technologies, such as streaming audio or video from the Internet, will test your patience sorely.

If you are happy with the way your applications run under Windows 95, you should be just as satisfied with their performance under Windows 98. If you intend to take advantage of Windows 98's support for advanced technologies that place heavy demands on the processor, your hardware decisions should be based on those uses, rather than on Windows 98.

Multiple Operating Systems

If you currently run multiple operating systems and simply want to upgrade your Windows 95 installation to Windows 98, you can just run the Windows 98 installation from Windows 95. To be on the safe side, set your boot menu to default to Windows 95 before you begin. When you are done, you will probably find that the installation process has disabled your boot manager or System Commander. You will need to reinstall or reactivate it by following the instructions that came with it.

Appendix A

If you want to keep your current Windows 95 installation in working order, things are a bit more complex. You need a separate primary partition on your hard drive for your Windows 98 installation. If the partition doesn't already exist, you will need to create it. Since doing so with Fdisk would delete everything on your hard drive, you'll probably want to invest in a program such as Partition Magic, which can repartition a hard disk without losing its contents. Set the partition where you will install Windows 98 to be active, then proceed through the instructions in the rest of this appendix. You will be doing a fresh (or clean) installation of Windows 98, not an upgrade installation.

Preliminaries

Before installing Windows 98, there are several tasks you need to undertake to ensure a smooth—and safe—installation. Some depend on whether you want to install as an upgrade over Windows 95 or as a fresh installation. Let's begin with the things everyone should do.

Back Up Your Data

We've all heard how important it is to do backups, and we've all ignored those warnings (at times). That doesn't change my obligation to warn you yet again! Please, make a backup of your system before you start this upgrade. I cannot stress this enough. While the installation program of Windows 98 is remarkably good, and the number of systems that fail is small, you should never, never make changes to your operating system without doing a backup.

Choosing a Backup Program

If you haven't invested in a third-party program, the backup program included with Windows 95 is adequate. It's safe, easy to use, and reasonably fast. If you have another backup program you prefer and are more comfortable with, by all means use it.

What to Back Up

If you have a tape drive or other high-capacity backup system, you can do a full system backup and be secure in the knowledge that everything is safe. You could even use it to return to your current Windows 95 setup, if necessary. If your backup device has a more limited capacity, you will probably only want to back up your data files. Even though it would take time, everything else could be recreated from the original disks.

Take your time and review all the directories and even subdirectories on your hard drive. Besides all the places that you have knowingly created files, check the directories of programs that save data without a specific command from you. These would include personal information managers, e-mail programs, and navigation programs for online services, among others. If you have any doubts about whether you should back up a particular file or group of files, it's best to err on the side of caution.

Upgrade or Make a Fresh Start?

One of the most important decisions you need to make is whether to install Windows 98 as an upgrade over Windows 95 or to do a clean installation from scratch. An upgrade installation is satisfactory if Windows 95 and your applications are running well. If most of the programs you've ever installed are ones you still use, or if you can remove unused programs with Windows 95's Add/Remove Programs, upgrading should be fine. The same is true if you can remove unused programs using the uninstall routines that came with them, or if you use a good third-party uninstaller. The advantages of installing Windows 98 as an upgrade are that it's faster and you won't have to reinstall your applications.

If Windows 95 or your application programs have not been running smoothly, you may be well advised to get a fresh start by doing a clean installation of Windows 98. The same is true if you suspect your hard drive of carrying a heavy load of application-related files you no longer use. Another reason to do a clean install is if you have already done an upgrade installation of Windows 98 and are experiencing problems. The advantage of a clean installation is that you get rid of anything old that might be causing trouble. The main disadvantages are the additional preparation required and the fact that you will have to reinstall all of your Windows 95 applications. Also, you will lose Windows 95's built-in fax capability, because Windows 98 has no fax feature.

If you decide on an upgrade installation, you should read the following three sections on faxing, additional housecleaning, and defragmenting your hard drive. Then skip ahead to "Step-by-Step Installation." If you will be doing a clean install, you should work through everything.

Fax

Windows 95 has a faxing capability built into Exchange. Windows 98 does not include Exchange, nor is there any other fax software built in. If you do a clean install of Windows 98, the fax capability will be gone. Do an upgrade and you'll retain Exchange and faxing.

If Exchange is installed on your machine but you don't use it, you should remove it before upgrading Windows 95 to Windows 98.

1. Click Start ➤ Settings ➤ Control Panel.

2. Open Add/Remove Programs.

3. Click the Windows Setup tab.

4. Remove the checkmark in front of Microsoft Exchange.

5. Click OK.

More Housecleaning

Now's the perfect time to ponder which programs on your system are really needed and to clean up some of the clutter and detritus that build up on your hard drive. Windows 98 is going to need substantially more hard disk space than Windows 95, so this is an even better reason to clean house.

The first step is to look at installed programs you haven't used in the last year or two—time to get rid of them! If they're DOS programs, just delete them. If they're Windows programs, you have to delete them and find all the files they've stuck in your Windows directories without telling you.

Your best bet here is to get one of the ingenious programs designed to remove all traces of ill-behaved Windows applications. Two of the better ones are Uninstaller and CleanSweep.

 TIP   If you have any doubts about removing a program from your hard drive, just save any data files off to a floppy. You can always reinstall the program from the original disks if you suddenly need it.

Defragmenting Your Hard Drive

Once you have all the extraneous files cleaned off your hard drive, you should do a complete disk defragmentation. This will consolidate your existing files on the disk, creating the maximum possible room for Windows 98 Setup.

1. On the Windows 95 Start menu, go to Programs ➤ Accessories ➤ System Tools ➤ Disk Defragmenter.

2. The default drive to defragment is C:, so just click OK and let the program proceed.

If you're installing Windows 98 as an upgrade over your existing Windows 95, skip ahead to "Step-by-Step Installation."

Create a Boot Disk

A boot disk is necessary only if you'll be doing a clean installation of Windows 98. In Windows 95, click Start ➤ Settings ➤ Control Panel ➤ Add/Remove Programs. Click the Startup Disk tab and follow the instructions. After you have created the disk, put it in the floppy drive and restart your machine. After your machine boots to an A: prompt, do this:

1. Type **c:** and press Enter.

2. When you see the C: prompt, type **dir** and press Enter.

You should see a listing of the contents of the root directory on your C: drive. If neither of these steps produces an error message, your boot disk is giving proper access to your hard drive.

Now for the more demanding part: Depending on how you plan to install Windows 98, you may need the boot disk to provide access either to your CD-ROM drive or to your local area network. Neither capability is part of the Windows 95 boot disk you just created; you will have to add the one you need.

Get out the instructions and driver disk that came with your CD-ROM drive or network card. Follow the instructions that tell you how to set up the device under DOS. This will generally involve creating config.sys and autoexec.bat files on your boot disk. You will also have to copy any required files to the boot disk. Driver files can be copied from the disk supplied by the device manufacturer. DOS files can be found in the \Command subdirectory of your current Windows directory.

When you have finished, be sure to test the boot disk. Restart your machine with the disk in the floppy drive, and be sure you have access to the Windows 98 CD-ROM, whether it's in a drive on your machine or connected via the network.

TIP   If you currently have CD-ROM or network access in a DOS window under Windows 95, the lines that load the necessary drivers should be present in your current config.sys and autoexec.bat files. You can copy them from there. If you have a DOS boot disk that provides access to the necessary resource, you can use it rather than create a Windows 95 boot disk. Finally, if you have plenty of hard drive space, you can just copy the entire contents of the Win98 folder on the CD to a folder or partition on your hard drive before proceeding any further. When the time comes, you can install from there. This is probably the simplest option, if you can spare the nearly 200MB of hard drive space required.

WARNING   The upgrade version of Windows 98 will expect to find an older version of Windows already installed on the computer. To do a clean install, you will either need to buy the full version of Windows 98, or be prepared to insert disk 1 from Windows 3.1 or the Windows 95 CD-ROM when requested by Setup.

WHAT ABOUT FAT32?

While it's theoretically possible to create a FAT32 partition and install Windows 98 to it, the hazards are many. Not least is that you must first create a FAT32-aware boot disk, including FAT32 versions of Fdisk and Format, something that can only be done with Windows 98 itself (or some later versions of Windows 95). My recommendation: Even if you're doing a clean install of Windows 98, ignore FAT32 until after you've run Setup. Then convert to FAT32 by following the instructions in Skill 16.

Network Identification and Configuration

To do a clean install on a machine connected to a local area network, you should gather the information you will need to identify and configure your machine for the network. Right-click on Network Neighborhood and choose Properties. Go through each of the tabs in the dialog box and copy down all the information and selected options.

The information from the Identification page will be entered during setup. The options on the other two pages can be set after you finish installing Windows 98.

Step-by-Step Installation

As operating systems go, Windows 98 is very clever. For many configurations, you can just boot up, put the CD in the drive, and start running Setup. The system will install without a hiccup.

While I have included nearly every step of the setup procedure in the following sections, I have skipped a few that require no comment. I'm confident you can enter your name when requested, with no help from me.

Starting

After you've done the prep work in the previous sections of this appendix, reboot your system to Windows 95. Insert the Windows 98 CD in your CD-ROM drive. If Windows 95 is set up to automatically run a CD when it is inserted, a screen will open with an option to start the installation. Otherwise, open My Computer and double-click your CD-ROM drive to get to the same screen. Either way, click Yes to begin.

 NOTE   If you're doing a clean install of Windows 98, start your computer with the boot disk you created earlier. Switch to your CD-ROM drive by typing **d:** and pressing Enter, where *d* is the letter of the drive. Then type **setup.exe** and press Enter. Alternatively, switch to the appropriate drive on your network connection, or to the directory or hard drive where you copied the Win98 folder from the CD. When Setup starts, it will run Scandisk to check your hard drives. When Scandisk finishes, press **x** to exit.

You'll see the Windows 98 Setup screen shown in Figure A.1. The left side of the screen, including the estimated time required to complete the installation, will be visible throughout the setup process. Total time estimates vary from 30 to 60 minutes or more, depending on how much you install and the speed of your system.

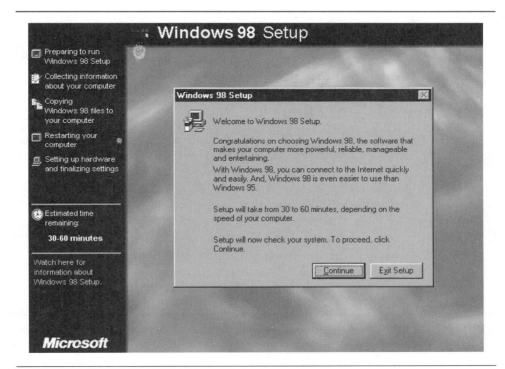

FIGURE A.1: This Setup screen will keep you informed of the progress of your installation.

Read the information presented in the dialog box, then click Continue. Windows 98 will perform a quick survey of your system, prepare the Setup Wizard, and ask you to read and consent to the license agreement. Click Next to move on.

TIP

If you are doing a clean install, your mouse may not be functional at this time. Use the Tab key to move the highlight among dialog box choices, and press Enter to OK the dialog box.

NOTE   When doing a clean install, you'll be asked at this point to choose a directory for installation—the default is \Windows on your C: drive, but you can choose another location or a different name for the directory.

Setup will then perform a more thorough check of your system, including looking for installed components of Windows and making sure you have enough hard drive space to complete the installation.

Save System Files

A dialog box will ask if you want the install program to save your Windows 95 system files. These files make it possible to uninstall Windows 98 should you run into trouble, so it's a good idea to select Yes.

You can then skip down to the section on choosing an Internet channel set. You won't see the Setup Options dialog box because Windows 98 will set up the same options and components as you have in Windows 95. Remember that after installation, you can use the Add/Remove Programs function in the Control Panel to easily add or remove any components.

If you're doing a clean install, you won't be offered the option to save system files because you're not overwriting anything.

TIP   To uninstall Windows 98 successfully, you must do so very soon after installation. Even then, you should plan on doing a reinstallation of your previous operating system.

Setup Options

The next choice you have to make, for a clean install only, is about how much of the operating system you want to install. You can select:

Typical   The major components (as defined by the setup program) are installed.

Portable   Includes options appropriate for laptops. You can choose the components you want to install or let the system install the major components (as in the Typical install).

Compact   Selects a minimum configuration—for situations where space is tight.

Custom   Lets you make selections at every step. Don't be put off by the designation of this choice as for "experts." This doesn't require any special expertise, and it does let you choose which accessories, communication applets, and other components you want right at the beginning.

Selecting Components

If you select Custom install, you choose the components you want. For a Typical, Compact, or Portable installation, you can choose the components you want or let Windows 98 choose what to install based on the type of installation selected.

The main categories of components are listed in the window. Click Details to see the total items that make up the category. Check the ones you want installed. A click of the mouse will also remove checkmarks in front of items you don't want.

Identify Your Computer

This dialog box asks you to give your computer a name that will identify it on your local area network. You are also asked to enter the name of your workgroup and a description of your computer. This is the information you gathered from the Identification tab of the Network dialog box before you eliminated Windows 95.

Choose an Internet Channel Set

Channels are designed to offer easy access to selected parts of the Internet. Windows 98 Setup comes with default channel sets based on country and language. Choose the set that you want installed. Skill 11 describes how to use and change channels, so your selection here is only a starting point.

Making a Startup Disk

The setup program asks if you want to create a startup disk so you can boot your computer in case of trouble. The answer is definitely, positively YES.

The startup disk contains several programs that will enable you to boot your system and edit important files in case something gets mangled. It also contains the invaluable uninstal.exe, which enables you to get rid of all of Windows 98 and start over in case things are severe enough to require reinstallation. You'll need a floppy disk.

NOTE   Not only should you make a startup disk here, in the future you should update it after every hardware change. Go to the Control Panel ➤ Add/Remove Programs and select Startup Disk.

After the startup disk is made, there's a long period while Setup copies files. Go get a cup of tea. Come back every 10 or 15 minutes to check the estimated time remaining (on the left side of the screen).

The Finishing Touches

After all the copying, the Setup Wizard needs to restart your computer and finish up. Your system might not restart by itself. Wait five minutes or so, and if nothing appears to be happening, hit the Reset button on your computer. This won't harm your installation and is not a sign of installation failure.

After the restart, Windows 98 still has a few chores. It will detect and set up plug-and-play devices and possibly other hardware whose settings couldn't be taken over from Windows 95. This may involve restarting again.

If you did a clean install, Setup will ask you to set your time zone. Use the right and left arrow keys on the keyboard to move east and west. This is important for network connections and so that daylight time is properly scheduled. Then Setup will run through a series of other tasks, including setting up the Control Panel and putting your programs on the Start menu. The last one, updating system settings, may take quite a while. Finally, there will be another restart, and you will see the Welcome to Windows screen, which offers online registration and an introduction to Windows 98 features.

Installing Additional Hardware

If a piece of your hardware wasn't detected during the install, use the Add New Hardware function in the Control Panel to tell Windows 98 about it. See Skill 20 if you need help with this. You may have to restart yet again after installing your hardware.

Deleting Unnecessary Files

After Windows 98 is installed, and you feel safe and secure with the new system, you can free up the hard drive space occupied when you chose Save System Files early in the installation. Go to Add/Remove Programs in the Control Panel. On the Install/Uninstall page, choose the *Delete Windows 98 uninstall information* option and click OK.

Super Safe Clean Installation

For users who've already experienced problems with upgrading, or who just *expect* problems because they are well-acquainted with Murphy's Law, I present the following method for doing a clean install. It is even more careful and more conservative than any method already described.

You will need 450 to 500MB of free hard drive space. Note in the instructions that follow, I use the term *folder* and capitalized folder names when you are working in Windows. I use *directory*, with all lower-case names, when working at the DOS prompt.

1. Do all of the things discussed in the "Preliminaries" section of this appendix.

2. Run an up-to-date virus scanning program.

3. Copy the entire Win98 folder from the CD-ROM to a folder on your hard drive. Call the folder something like **Win98src**, for Windows 98 source.

4. Restart your machine using the Windows 95 boot disk you created.

5. At the DOS prompt, rename the existing Windows directory. For example, if Windows is installed in a directory called C:\Windows, type **ren c:\ windows oldwin** and press Enter.

6. Change to your source directory. For example, type **cd c:\win98src** and press Enter.

7. Type **setup** and press Enter.

8. When Setup asks you to choose a directory to install Windows 98, give the directory name of your previous Windows installation (before you changed it)—probably C:\Windows.

9. Work through the setup procedure as detailed in the section "Step-by-Step Installation."

10. When you're done, any DOS or Windows 3.1 programs you have can be easily migrated by copying their parts of the Start Menu folder in the Oldwin folder to the new Start Menu folder. If the programs keep .ini files in the Windows folder, these will need to be copied as well.

11. Try running these older programs. A Windows 3.1 program may complain it can't find a .dll file. Copy the file from the Oldwin folder or its System subfolder to the same location in the new Windows folder.

12. Reinstall only those Windows 95 programs you really need.

When you've gotten everything back to where you expect it to be, and you're sure you don't need anything more from the Oldwin folder, delete it.

This may be a good option for some people, and makes a *ton* of sense in a corporate environment, where all the sources for supported programs are readily available on the network.

If your attempts at an upgrade installation have failed, this method will work. It gives you a clean installation without having to reformat your hard drive and start from zero—a discouraging prospect. In addition, a clean installation means you get rid of any niggling problems with Windows 95. Any problems that remain, you can blame with some confidence on Windows 98.

APPENDIX B

INSTALLING FOR WINDOWS 3.1 USERS

The recommended-by-Microsoft approach is to install Windows 98 right on top of your existing Windows 3.x. Advantages to this approach include:

- You'll keep all your programs and their settings.

- If you have problems, you can use the uninstall program to automatically remove Windows 98 and get your original DOS and Windows 3.x back intact.

You won't be able to boot into your previous version of DOS, but you will have the DOS mode of Windows 98, which works just as well, if not better.

 TIP A "clean install" on a freshly formatted hard drive is more trouble—you have to reinstall all your programs—but no traces of previous versions of Windows will hang around to cause difficulty. Appendix A includes instructions for a clean install.

FROM PLAIN DOS TO GLORIOUS WINDOWS

If you've been true to your DOS all this time and now want to add the benefits of Windows 98 to your computing life, the installation is fairly straightforward. You'll need to make sure you have the full version of Windows 98 (not the one designed to be installed on a system with some version of Windows already present).

You'll still need to review the check list later in this chapter and do all of the tasks that apply to your setup.

Minimum Hardware

Microsoft has upped the hardware ante with Windows 98 just as they did with Windows 95. This time, you must have:

- A 486DX4/75 or better microprocessor

- 16MB RAM
- 200MB of free hard drive space

Some 50MB of that space is used to save your Windows 3.1 system files so you can uninstall Windows 98. You can reclaim that space once you feel safe and secure with Windows 98.

The installation will fail on a lesser processor, a machine with less than 16MB of RAM, or if you have insufficient hard drive space.

Before You Install

The Windows 98 installation program works very well, although sometimes it acts dumber than necessary. And since there's no way to tell in advance how smart Windows 98 is going to be about your particular system, I recommend a fail-safe approach to installation. Do yourself a favor and read all the items in this section carefully. Some may not apply to you, but most will.

Do Some Housecleaning

Now's the perfect time to ponder which programs on your system are really needed and to clean up some of the clutter and detritus that's built up on your hard drive. Windows 98 is going to use much more hard disk space than the combination of DOS and Windows you now have, so this is an even better reason to clean house.

The first step is to take a look at installed programs you haven't used in the last year or two—time to get rid of them. If they're DOS programs, just delete them. If they're Windows programs, you have to delete them and find all the files they've stuck in your Windows directories without telling you.

Your best bet here is to get one of the ingenious programs designed to remove all traces of ill-behaved Windows applications. Two good ones are Uninstaller2 and Remove-It. Both do a good job of finding all the pieces of the programs they know about and removing them.

 TIP

If you have any doubts about removing a program from your hard drive, just save any data files off to a floppy. You can always reinstall the program from the original disks if you suddenly need it.

Defragment Your Hard Drive

Once you have all the extraneous files cleaned off your hard drive, you should do a complete disk defragmentation. This will consolidate your existing files on the disk, creating the maximum possible room for Windows 98 to do its thing.

 TIP   If you have a permanent swap file in your current Windows configuration, change it to a temporary one before you defragment. Otherwise, Windows 98 will detect and use the same swap file—a waste of resources, because Windows 98 can make its own fast and dynamic swap file on a regular or compressed disk. In other words, it can grow and shrink according to the demands of your programs. This is much more efficient and convenient.

Any defragmentation program will do. I use SpeedDisk in Norton Utilities, but DEFRAG, provided in MS-DOS 6.x, is perfectly adequate for the job. If you're using Stacker or another third-party disk compression utility, make sure you also run their disk defragmentation utility. If you're using SpeedDisk from version 7 or later of the Norton Utilities, you won't need to run the Stac defrag utility separately, since Norton understands Stacker.

Make an Emergency Rescue Disk

If you have a utility package like Norton Utilities, it includes a program to create a "rescue" or "emergency" disk that contains an image of your BIOS, boot sector, and hard drive partition table, as well as enough files to boot from and recover in case of serious problems. By all means, do this before beginning your upgrade process. The best time to do it is right after you've finished the defragmentation step.

If you don't have a way to automatically make such a disk, here's how to do it yourself:

1. Format a new disk in the floppy drive you can boot from (the A: drive), and use the SYS command from DOS or File Manager's Make System Disk command to make the floppy bootable.

2. Copy to the floppy all the DOS files you need to boot and get at all the drives in your system plus whatever tools you need to revive the system after a problem (including compression software if you use it). Include:

   - scandisk.exe or chkdsk.exe

- mem.exe (to check memory usage)

- msd.exe (to check the system's view of itself)

- attrib.exe (to gain access to hidden, read-only, or system files, if needed)

- edit.com (or your favorite text editor)

- fdisk.exe, format.com, sys.com (for the worst-case scenario, where you have to repartition and reformat your drive)

- Copies of your current autoexec.bat and config.sys files

- Any other special drivers you need

After you've made the disk, make sure it works by booting with it in the floppy drive.

Clean Out autoexec.bat and config.sys

In the process of installation, Windows 98 will go over your autoexec.bat and config.sys files and remove drivers and settings that aren't needed. It places a REM at the beginning of every line loading something that Windows 98 knows. But however clever the install routine is, it still can miss some items and end up trying to execute commands that cause difficulties. You're much better off doing a preemptive strike of your own.

Here's how to make it simple:

- Disable any third-party memory managers like QEMM. Type **REM** at the beginning of every line that loads a memory manager. Replace these lines with DEVICE= lines that point to himem.sys and emm386.exe.

- Disable any virus protection programs that run at start up. Check your BIOS to see if you have boot sector virus protection, and disable that too. Windows 98 is going to make changes to your boot sector that will cause the installation to fail.

- REM out any fancy footwork in your autoexec.bat such as calls, branches, or conditional executions.

- Disable hardware drivers except those for hardware you need to boot up and start Windows 3.x. If you're installing from a CD, leave the drivers for your CD-ROM drive, otherwise disable it. If you have an SCSI hard drive, leave those drivers too. Other candidates for REMing out include drivers for your:

- Sound card
- Scanner
- Mouse (both versions of Windows provide their own)
- Tape backup

NOTE   The idea is to let Windows 98 recognize and supply its own drivers for as much of the hardware as possible. If it happens that Windows 98 doesn't have a driver for a piece of hardware, you can always reinstate your 16-bit drivers until such time as a 32-bit driver is available.

ALL ABOUT MEMORY MANAGERS

A good memory manager, such as QEMM and NetRoom, can use areas of memory that would not normally be available. It does this by tricking DOS and Windows into believing that certain addresses are not being used when they are.

Such stealth features are essential in DOS if you're to circumvent the problem of inadequate available room to load everything you need into DOS's limited memory space. It's unnecessary in Windows 98, however, and can interfere with Windows 98's ability to correctly sense what hardware is on your machine.

Do a Backup

We've all heard how important it is to do backups, and we've all ignored those warnings (at times). That doesn't change my obligation to warn you yet again!

Please, make a backup of your system before you start this upgrade. I cannot stress this enough. While the installation program of Windows 98 is remarkably good, and the number of systems that fail is small, you should never, never do changes to your operating system without doing a backup. Going from any version of DOS to Windows 98 is about as significant a change as can be imagined.

Choosing a Backup Program

If you haven't invested in a third-party program, the backup program included with MS-DOS versions 6 and above is excellent. It's based on the Norton Backup program and is safe, easy to use, and reasonably fast. If you have another backup program you prefer and are more comfortable with, by all means use it.

What to Back Up

Back up at least the root directory of your boot drive (usually C:) and your DOS and Windows directories, along with any files you simply could not live without or easily recreate. What this includes is really a personal decision, but obviously, if you're a business, the answer is different than if you use your computer primarily to run DOOM.

Take your time and review all the directories and even subdirectories on your hard drive. If you have any doubts about whether you should back up a particular file or group of files, it's best to err on the side of caution. What you don't need to back up are program files, because you can, in the worst case, reinstall them from the original disks.

Installing

Once you've done all the preparatory work described, put the Windows 98
CD in the CD-ROM drive and start Windows 3.x. Open File Manager and
double-click the icon for your CD-ROM drive (see Figure B.1). In the right
pane, double-click setup.exe to start the installation.

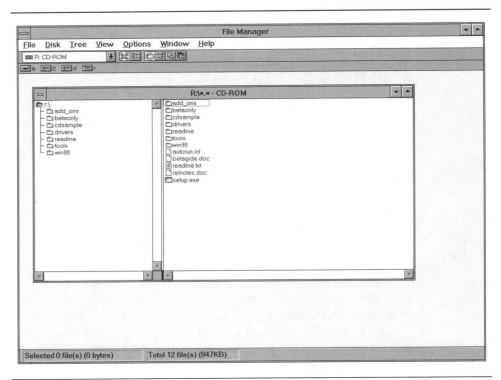

FIGURE B.1: Use File Manager to view the files on the Windows 98 CD-ROM.

Welcome Screen

The first screen "welcomes" you to Windows 98 (as if it were a hotel) and gives
an estimate of the time it will take to install. On most machines, this will be 30 to
60 minutes. Click the Continue button.

Next, a setup window will open, announcing that the Setup Wizard is starting. Look at the list of installation steps on the left side of your screen. The step being performed will be highlighted.

License Agreement

A window will open like the one in Figure B.2, showing the license agreement. Click the button next to *I accept the Agreement* and then click the Next button. (If you don't accept the agreement, the installation stops right here.)

FIGURE B.2: The license agreement

Select the Directory

In the next dialog box, you're asked to specify the directory for the installation of Windows 98. The default is C:\Windows. Unless you have a good reason to install elsewhere, accept the default.

If you select Other Directory, you'll be prompted for the directory name and location.

Checking Your System

The next procedure looks at your system to first determine what Windows components are installed and then to see if you have enough hard drive space to install Windows 98 (see Figure B.3).

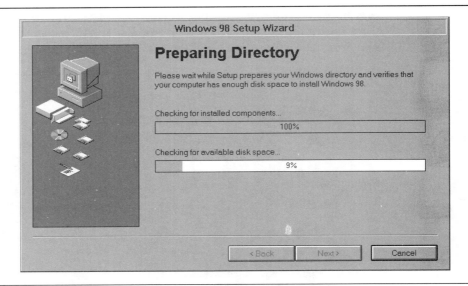

FIGURE B.3: Setup checks for installed components and for available hard drive space.

Save System Files

The Save System Files dialog box gives you a chance at an additional bit of security. If you select Yes, the Setup Wizard will save enough of your existing Windows 3.x files so that (should worse come to worst), you can uninstall Windows 98.

This is highly unlikely to be necessary, but as you can tell from the earlier parts of this appendix, "Better safe than sorry" is my motto. So, the strong recommendation is to select Yes.

This step will require additional hard drive space, but once you're up and running with Windows 98, you can delete the old system files and free up the space.

After you click Yes, another dialog box (shown in Figure B.4) will show the progress of the system files being located and then saved.

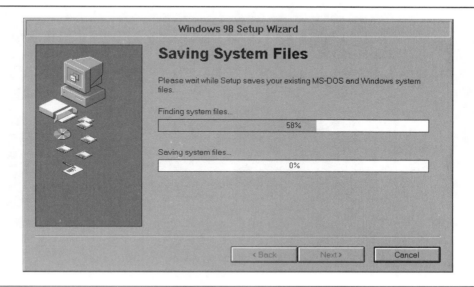

FIGURE B.4: Saving the Windows 3.x system files

 NOTE   If you have more than one hard drive, you'll be prompted for the preferred location for the system files. You can pick any drive where you have enough open space.

Setup Options

The Setup Wizard presents you with four possible setup options (shown in Figure B.5). For the majority of people, Typical is the best option. It requires the least input from you, and anything you later decide you want to install is easily available.

If you're an experienced Windows user and a bit of a control freak, Custom is also a perfectly good option. You have to provide more information and make more choices as you go, so installation is a little slower. In exchange, however, you get the opportunity to customize as you go.

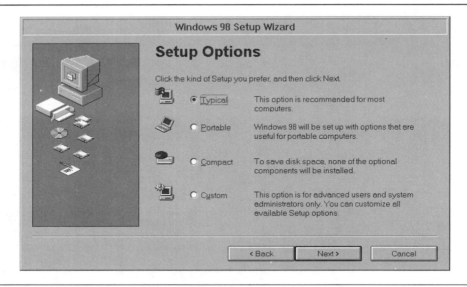

FIGURE B.5: Choosing a setup option

The Portable option is useful for laptop computers, but not necessary. The Typical installation can detect PC Cards and built-in pointers without being told that a portable computer is involved.

Compact is recommended only when hard drive space is limited and cannot be enlarged. You'll get the basic functionality, but most applets and many system tools will not be installed.

After you choose the option you want, click Next.

Windows Components

The next dialog box for the Typical installation asks if you want to view the components and decide which to install. Select Yes and you'll see the window shown in Figure B.6. The Custom install choice takes you directly to the Select Components window.

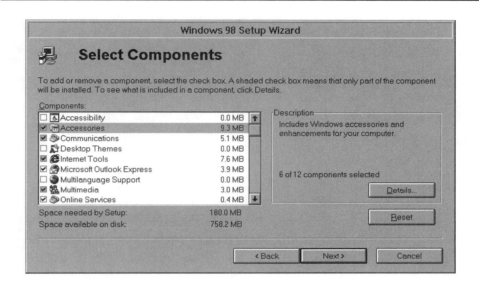

FIGURE B.6: Windows components

To decide what to install, view each option in turn. For example, as shown in the figure, when you highlight Accessories, a description appears to the right. Directly under the description, you'll see how many of the components have already been selected (by the Setup Wizard) to be installed. For the Accessories option, it's 6 of the 12 available.

Click the Details button for a list of the 12 accessories (see Figure B.7). As you highlight each item, a description appears to the right. Items with checkmarks next to them will be installed. Remove the checkmarks next to items you *don't* want installed.

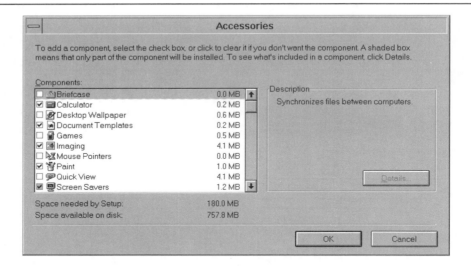

FIGURE B.7: Selecting the accessories to install

When you've made your choices—bearing in mind that any you miss can be installed later—click the Next button.

Identification

The next dialog box, Identification, asks for the name of your computer, the workgroup name, and a description of the computer. If you're on a network, provide the correct information. If you're not connected, leave the default information and click Next.

Computer Settings

In the Computer Settings dialog box, you'll see a list of the keyboard and language settings that will be installed. If any are incorrect, highlight the setting and click the Change button. For example, Figure B.8 shows different types of keyboards that can be installed.

FIGURE B.8: Some of the keyboards that Windows 98 can recognize

Internet Channels

Windows 98 starts with a default listing of channels that are tailored to specific countries. In the Internet Channels window, choose the country whose channel set you'd like to see.

Emergency Startup Disk

The next step is to create an emergency startup disk. In case of a complete freeze, you can use this disk to start your computer. You'll need a single high-density floppy disk. It doesn't have to be new, but anything already on the disk will be deleted in the process of making the emergency startup disk. Click Next.

Put the floppy disk in the drive when the setup program requests it.

When the process of creating the disk is completed, you'll be notified to remove the floppy disk and then click OK.

Start Copying Files

The process of copying files is the longest stage of the installation. It'll go faster if you have a high-speed CD-ROM drive, slower if you don't. But expect to wait a half-hour or so before you have to do anything more.

Identifying Hardware

After all the copying, the Setup Wizard needs to restart your computer and finish up. Your system might not be able to restart by itself. Wait five minutes or so, and if nothing appears to be happening, hit the Reset button. This won't harm your installation and is not a sign of installation failure.

Windows 98 then builds a driver database and attempts to identify all the hardware attached to the computer. That includes the video card, monitor, sound card, modem, and printer. In general, plug-and-play technology does a very good job of figuring everything out. If it doesn't, you can later manually install a modem, printer, or other device.

 TIP

You'll be asked at some point for a Windows password. If you're not on a network, don't provide one. Just press Enter. You can always add a password later, but *once you provide one*, you won't be able to get rid of that password window at boot up again. To stop being *asked* for a password after installation (because even if you don't supply one, Windows will keep *asking* for it), right-click the Network Neighborhood icon on the desktop and select Properties. On the Configuration page, under Primary Network Logon, select Windows Logon. Click OK. When you reboot, the password window will not appear.

Welcome to Windows 98

After a restart or two, Windows 98 will begin, and you'll see a "Welcome to Windows 98" dialog box, as shown in Figure B.9. Click a subject to register the product or to take a lesson in how Windows 98 works.

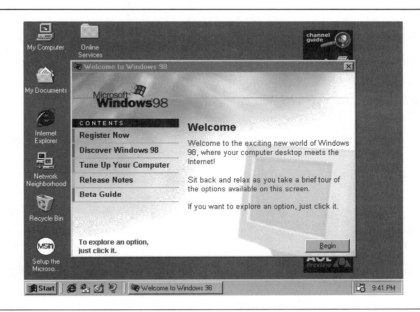

FIGURE B.9: The Windows 98 welcome window

Index

Note to the Reader: Throughout this index **boldface** page numbers indicate primary discussions of a topic. *Italic* page numbers indicate illustrations.

j

W

X

y

z

Master Your
WINDOWS® 98
Destiny

WITH THESE BESTSELLING SYBEX TITLES

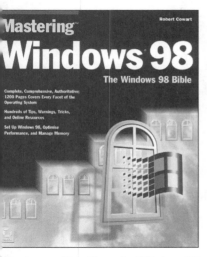

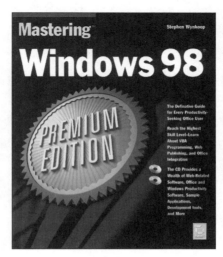

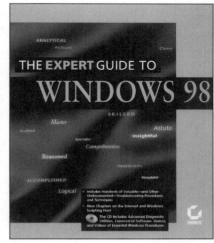

The best-selling *Mastering Windows 95* just got better in its latest edition. It not only covers Microsoft's new 32-bit operating system from beginning to end, but also includes new additions and enhancements. The new Explorer, installation, built-in applications, networking, optimization—it's all here in this absolutely essential guide to the newest version of the Windows operating system.

ISBN: 0-7821-1961-1
1,184pp; 7½" x 9"; Softcover; $34.99

This special Premium Edition is the complete solution for Windows users. It covers all of the essential topics, including an overview of the operating system, installation concerns, settings, and the file management system. Secrets of scripting, the Registry and other powerful features are explained. Also included are more than 400 pages of advanced customization and internet coverage for power users, as well as two CDs.

ISBN: 0-7821-2186-1
1,584pp; 7½" x 9"; Hardcover; $59.99

Based on Mark Minasi's seminar, this book is the Windows 98 troubleshooting bible for MIS professionals, consultants and power users. It's the most accessible guide to networking, installing, and supporting Windows 98. The companion CD includes animations of the book's procedures, and several commercial Windows antivirus, diagnostic, and troubleshooting utilities.

ISBN: 0-7821-1974-3
1,008pp; 7½" x 9"; Softcover; $49.99

SYBEX®
www.sybex.com

MAKE THE TRANSITION TO
WINDOWS® 98
QUICKLY, PAINLESSLY, AND SUCCESSFULLY

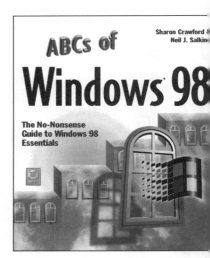

This easy-to-use guide gives Windows 95 and 3.1 users all the information they need to upgrade to Windows 98. It gives users the tips and tricks they need to get the most out of Windows 98—easy networking, troubleshooting, hardware upgrading, Internet tips, and invaluable connectivity advice.

ISBN: 0-7821-2190-X
432pp; 7½" x 9"; Softcover; $19.99

This no-nonsense guide teaches the essential skills necessary for using Windows 98 effectively at home or at the office. Each chapter presents scores of real-world examples that let readers learn the practical skills they need to succeed in today's workplace.

ISBN: 0-7821-2128-4
576pp; 7½" x 9"; Softcover; $24.99

Learn about the Windows 98 features you need—ignore the ones you don't. This straightforward, easy-to-read guide is designed for users familiar with computers, but new to Windows 98. The book also includes a comprehensive index and a useful glossary of the latest Windows terminology.

ISBN: 0-7821-1953-0
384pp; 7½" x 9"; Softcover; $19.99

SYBEX®
www.sybex.com

START USING NEW
WINDOWS® 98
FEATURES IMMEDIATELY

This convenient, almanac-sized book has over 1,000 pages of Windows 98 and essential PC information. It includes coverage on the Windows 98 operating system and command reference, PC upgrading and maintenance advice, guides to Microsoft and Netscape browsers, an Internet/Hardware/Software resource directory and a PC/Internet dictionary.

ISBN: 0-7821-2219-1
1,008pp; $5^7/_8$" x $8^1/_4$"; Softcover; $19.99

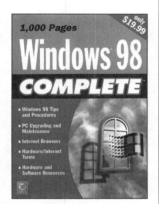

This easy-to-use guide gives Windows 95 and 3.1 users all the information they need to upgrade to Windows 98. It gives users the tips and tricks they need to get the most out of Windows 98—easy networking, troubleshooting, hardware upgrading, Internet tips, and invaluable connectivity advice.

ISBN: 0-7821-2190-X
432pp; $7^1/_2$" x 9"; Softcover; $19.99

Easy to use and alphabetically organized, this guide is your key to every command, feature, menu, toolbar, and function of Windows 98. This book also provides fast answers about Internet Explorer, WebView, and all of the Internet features and functions of Windows 98.

ISBN: 0-7821-2191-8
304pp; $4^3/_4$" x 8"; Softcover; $14.99

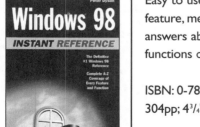

SYBEX®
www.sybex.com

SYBEX BOOKS ON THE WEB!

Presenting a truly dynamic environment
that is both fun and informative.

- access special book content
- view our complete online catalog
- preview a book you might want to own
- find out about job opportunities at Sybex
- order books online at special discount prices
- learn about Sybex
- what's new in the computer industry

http://www.sybex.com

SYBEX Inc. • 1151 Marina Village Parkway • Alameda, CA 94501 • 510-523-8233